Italian American Writers on New Jersey

Italian American Writers on New Jersey

AN ANTHOLOGY OF POETRY AND PROSE

Edited by
Jennifer Gillan,
Maria Mazziotti Gillan,
and
Edvige Giunta

Rutgers University Press
NEW BRUNSWICK, NEW JERSEY
AND LONDON

Library of Congress Cataloging-in-Publication Data

Italian American writers on New Jersey : an anthology of poetry and prose / edited by
Jennifer Gillan, Maria Mazziotti Gillan, and Edvige Giunta.
p. cm.
ISBN 0-8135-3316-3 (hardcover : alk. paper) —
ISBN 0-8135-3317-1 (pbk. : alk. paper)
1. American literature—New Jersey. 2. American literature—Italian
American authors. 3. Italian Americans—Literary collections. 4. New
Jersey—Literary collections. I. Gillan, Jennifer. II. Gillan, Maria M.
III. Giunta, Edvige.
PS548 .N5I83 2002
810.8'08510749—dc21 2003005943

British Cataloging-in-Publication data for this book is available
from the British Library.

This publication is supported in part by
The Institute of Italian and Italian American Heritage Studies,
State of New Jersey.

The publication program of Rutgers University Press is supported by the
Board of Governors of Rutgers, The State University of New Jersey.

Manufactured in the United States of America

This book is dedicated to
Angelina Schiavo Mazziotti and Arturo Mazziotti,
Cettina Minasola Giunta and Vincenzo Giunta,
and to all the Italians of Riverside.

CONTENTS

Contents

PART TWO

Blending In

PART THREE

Crossing Bridges

Contents

IN DEPTH

Interstate Commerce, New York & New Jersey Bound

PART FOUR

Changing Direction

FOREWORD

Immigrants have always shaped America just as America has shaped them: our culture is strengthened and invigorated by the introduction of new ideas, traditions, and practices from around the world and in turn America changes immigrant lives into American lives. With its multilayered history, formed by successive waves of immigrants, New Jersey derives deep benefits from the ever-refreshed diversity of its citizenry. The Italians have long been among the most vital of these groups in New Jersey, where, according to the 2000 U.S. census, 18 percent of the population claims Italian heritage, the single largest ethnic group in our state.

The New Jersey Italian American Heritage Commission, which was created by the New Jersey Legislature in January 2002 "to survey, design, encourage, and promote the implementation of Italian and Italian American programs . . . culture, history, heritage, and language . . . on a regular basis throughout the state," welcomes this rich anthology. This volume presents the works of an extraordinarily talented group of writers, whose moving essays, memoirs, stories, and poems provide poignant insights into the lives of Italians in America, of Italian Americans, and, indeed, of all Americans. The experiences of the Italians in New Jersey shed light on the complex experiences of all immigrants–the challenges, hopes, compromises, fears, losses, misunderstandings, loneliness, successes, courage, stamina–that finally result in the creation of a cohesive community and the emergence of a coherent identity in the new country. Also revealed in these words of first-, second-, third-, even fourth-generation Italians is America itself, which has sometimes greeted newcomers with a wary welcome and a challenge to prove themselves. The editors, Jennifer Gillan, Maria Mazziotti Gillan, and Edvige Giunta, have assembled a superb collection that reveals an honest and moving portrait of life in America.

Joseph J. Seneca
University Vice President for
    Academic Affairs
Rutgers University

N. Larry Paragano
Chair, New Jersey Italian American
Heritage Commission

ACKNOWLEDGMENTS

We thank Rutgers University Press, and especially our editor, Marlie Wasserman, who embraced this project with enthusiasm from its onset. We would also like to express our gratitude to Michele Gisbert, Nicole L. Manganaro, and Jessica Pellien at Rutgers University Press for their invaluable assistance. Special thanks to the staff at the Botto House, the National Labor Museum in Haledon, Nunzio Pericone at the Drexel Institute in Philadelphia, and Jennifer Guglielmo, for their help locating the writings of early Italian immigrants. We thank the Poetry Center at Passaic County Community College and the members of the Collective of Italian American Women for their help in the organization of the symposium "Speaking of Jersey: Italian American Women Writers on the Garden State."

Maria Mazziotti Gillan would like to thank her husband for his infinite patience while she was working on this book. She wishes to acknowledge the generous support of Passaic County Community College and Binghamton University, SUNY, especially Dr. Steven Rose, President of Passaic County Community College, the Poetry Center and its staff, Dr. Peter Mileur, Dean of Harpur College of Arts and Sciences, and Dr. David Bartine, Chairperson of the Department of English at Binghamton University, SUNY. She gratefully acknowledges Eleanor English, T. J. Naik, Aline Papazian, Jane Haw, Susan Amsterdam, Angela Helenek, and John Ming.

Jennifer Gillan wishes to thank Bentley College for its continuing, generous support of her work, especially Dr. Bruce Herzberg, Chair of the Department of English, Dr. H. Lee Schlorff, Vice President for Academic Affairs and Dean of Faculty, President Joseph Morone, and the Faculty Affairs Committee. She is grateful to Gregory Carlson and the Academic Technology Center for their much needed technical assistance.

Edvige Giunta gratefully acknowledges the continuous support she has received from New Jersey City University, and particularly from Dr. Larry G. Carter, Vice President for Academic Affairs, Barbara Hildner and Laura Wadenpfuhl, former and current chairs of the Department of English, and Jo Bruno,

Associate Vice President for Academic Affairs. The Separately Budgeted Research Fund at New Jersey City University granted her release time that was precious while working on this volume. She wishes to express her deep appreciation for Peter Covino and Louise DeSalvo for their support. Finally, she thanks her family, and especially her husband, Joshua Fausty, and her children, Emily Giunta-Cutts and Matteo Giunta Fausty, who make her work possible in so many ways.

The editors would like to acknowledge the pieces which are reprinted in this volume with permission. "Nevertheless, It Moves" and "Elizabeth" from *Body Toxic* by Susanne Paola Antonetta, © 2002. Reprinted with permission of Counterpoint Press, a member of Perseus Books, L.L.C. "Suburban Backyards" originally appeared in *The Mill Street Forward* Fall/Winter 1987, a progressive Paterson-based publication edited by June Avignone. Reprinted with permission of June Avignone. Tom DeBlasio Carroll's "Downtown Paterson" from *Downtown Paterson* (Arcadia Publishers), edited by June Avignone, ©1999 June Avignone. "Trenton": Grateful acknowledgement to Belle Mead Press, NJ, which first published *Trenton* (1990). "Miracle Baby" from *A Boy Named Phyllis* by Frank DeCaro, © 1996 by Frank DeCaro. Used by permission of Viking Penguin, a division of Penguin Putnam Inc. "A Trip Home" by David Della Fera originally appeared in *VIA: Voices in Italian Americana*. "Combat Zones" reprinted from Vertigo, © 1996 Louise DeSalvo, by permission of the Feminist Press at the City University of New York, *www.feminist press.org*. "The Tangerine Plymouth and the Gilded Cage" originally appeared in the anthology *My Father's Daughter: Stories by Women* (Crossing Press, 1990), edited by Irene Zahava. Reprinted by permission of Rachel Guido deVries. "Hoboken" reprinted from Chapter One of *Three Circles of Light* (Julian Messner, 1960) by permission of the Estate of Pietro di Donato. "Letter from New Jersey," © 1999 Diane di Prima. All rights reserved by author. "Greenwood Lake" reprinted from "Chapter 15" from *Recollections of My Life as a Woman*, Diane di Prima, © 1999 by Diane di Prima. Used by permission of Viking Penguin, a division of Penguin Putnam Inc. "Summer Job" reprinted from *To the Shore Once More* (Bay Head: Jersey Shore Publications, 1999, 2000). "Third-Generation Hawthorne" by Jennifer Gillan reprinted by permission of the author, © 2002 Jennifer Gillan, originally appeared in *Paterson Literary Review*. "Public School No. 18, Paterson, New Jersey" by Maria Mazziotti Gillan appeared in *Winter Light* and *Where I Come From: Selected and New Poems* (Guernica, 1995, 1998) by Maria Mazziotti Gillan. Reprinted with permission of the author. "In the Stacks at the Paterson Public Library" by Maria Mazziotti Gillan from *Italian Women in Black Dresses* (Guernica, 2002); "Growing Up Italian in Paterson, New Jersey" by Maria Mazz-

Acknowledgments

iotti Gillan appeared in *Where I Come From: Selected and New Poems* (Guernica, 1995, 1998) by Maria Mazziotti Gillan. Reprinted with permission of the author. "Daddy, We Called You" by Maria Mazziotti Gillan appeared in *Things My Mother Told Me* (Guernica, 1998) by Maria Mazziotti Gillan. Reprinted with permission of the author. "Carlton Fredricks and My Mother" by Maria Mazziotti Gillan appeared in *Growing Up Ethnic in America* (NY: Penguin/Putnam, 1997), © 1997 Maria Mazziotti Gillan. Used by permission of the author. "Dorissa" is part five of the novel *Americans: One Minute to Midnight* by Daniela Gioseffi. Reprinted by permission of the author, © 1994 by Daniela Gioseffi. It originally appeared in *The Voices We Carry: Recent Italian/American Women's Fiction* (Guernica, 1994), edited by Mary Jo Bona. "*Litania* for My Mother's Hands" reprinted by permission of the author, Edvige Giunta. Originally appeared in *Barrow Street* and was reprinted in the *Penguin Anthology of Italian American Writing*. "Gardener," "St. Therese," and "Quench a Plant's Thirst" reprinted by permission of the author, © 2002 Edvige Giunta. Originally appeared in *Paterson Literary Review*. "I Check Other" is reprinted by permission of the author, Carla Guerriero. Originally appeared in *Paterson Literary Review*. "Rebel Girls" reprinted by permission of the author, © 2002 Jennifer Guglielmo. "1915" reprinted from *Mill Song* by William Harry Harding. © 1985 by William Harry Harding, reprinted by permission of the author. "Scents" from *Were You Always an Italian? Ancestors and Other Icons of Life in Italian America* by Maria Laurino, © 2000 by Maria Laurino. Used by permission of W. W. Norton & Company, Inc. "Circolo" by Michele Linfante reprinted by permission of the author, © 1991 Michele Linfante. *Pizza* reprinted by permission of the author, appeared in *The Dream Book*, revised edition (Syracuse University Press, 2000), edited by Helen Barolini. All rights strictly reserved by author. Professionals and amateurs are hereby warned that *Pizza* is subject to a royalty. It is protected under the copyright laws of all countries covered by the International Copyright Convention. Permission in writing must be secured before any kind of performance is given. All inquiries should be addressed to Michele Linfante, 7777 Bodega Avenue #A4, Sebastopol, CA 95472. "June Wednesdays" and "On the Beaches of Wildwood, New Jersey" by Mary Ann Mannino, © 2001 Mary Ann Mannino. Used by permission of the author. "Paterson, New Jersey" from *Break Every Rule* by Carole Maso, © 2000 by Carole Maso. Reprinted by permission of Counterpoint Press, a member of Perseus Books, L.L.C. "Today Your Name Is Mary" from *Ghost Dance* by Carole Maso, © 1986 by Carole Maso. Reprinted by permission of Georges Borchardt, Inc., Literary Agency. "Dye House Strike, 1933" by Arturto Mazziotti reprinted by permission of Maria Mazziotti Gillan, originally appeared in *Downtown Paterson* (Arcadia), edited by June Avignone.

Acknowledgments

"Race Riot" from *Bad Haircut* by Tom Perrotta, reprinted by permission of BridgeWorks Publishing, Bridgehampton, NY. "Hungry Dog" from *The Quick,* ©1992 by Agnes Rossi, reprinted with permission of the Wylie Agency, Inc. "Paterson: 1913" printed from an interview of Josephine Stifano by journalist June Avignone. Reprinted from *Downtown Paterson* (Arcadia Publishers), edited by June Avignone. Reprinted by permission of June Avignone. "Ocean City" by Gay Talese from *Unto the Sons* by Gay Talese, © 1992 by Gay Talese. Used by permission of Alfred A. Knopf, a division of Random House. "Class Quartet" by Janet Zandy originally appeared in *Calling Home: Working Class Writings* (Rutgers University Press). "Liberating Memory" by Janet Zandy originally appeared in *Liberating Memory: Our Work and Our Working Class Consiousness* (Rutgers University Press). Both reprinted by permission of Janet Zandy and Rutgers University Press.

Italian American Writers on New Jersey

INTRODUCTION

Jennifer Gillan, Maria Mazziotti Gillan, and Edvige Giunta

The smells of New Jersey . . . to outsiders, they range from the chemical smells of the turnpike that bombard drivers as they pass the state's chemical plants to the saltwater smells of the shore that come wafting into the mini-vans of day-trippers as they turn off the highway onto local shore roads. To insiders, the smells of New Jersey exist on a more complicated scale, a range of topographically and culturally diverse scents, from the saltwater scent that permeates Ocean Boulevard in Long Branch to the espresso scent that wafts onto Cianci Street from the Roma Club in Paterson. Some of the most pleasing smells emanate from the gardens, kitchens, grocery stores, restaurants, and bakeries of New Jersey's Italians. New Jersey triumphs as a full sensory experience, a place that seeps into one's body, into one's memory with its sights—the Great Falls, the Great Gorge, Cape May, the Meadowlands, the Palisades, and the Pine Barrens; its sounds—the crash of waves at Wildwood, the pulse of the cicadas chirping at Greenwood Lake, the bustle of its myriad small towns and neighborhoods, the multicultural choruses in the streets of Paterson, Newark, Union City, and Jersey City; but perhaps most of all, with its tastes and aromas—prosciutto, pecorino, salami, provolone, bread, pizza, lasagna, calamari, meatballs, tomatoes, rosemary, garlic, and basil.

Smells trigger sensory memories, conjure our pasts, make our families, our gatherings, our homes materialize before us, no matter whether we are still in those New Jersey neighborhoods or are living or traveling in some other part of the world. The sensory memory of food still brings Italian Americans of every generation together—it is the memory of pastchille, of strufoli, and of twisted Easter egg bread. It is the memory of figs, freshly picked from backyard trees. It is a smell associated with early fall. Before the first frost, the trees are wrapped in burlap to protect them, a ritual early Italian immigrants passed on to their descendants.

Not surprisingly, the sensory memory of food became the topic of discussion at a table of writers at a recent symposium on the literature of Italian American women called *Speaking of Jersey: Italian American Women on*

1

the Garden State. During the symposium we discovered that pastina had been a source of comfort for so many of us. Even though we had grown up in different Italian American communities and were of different generations, we all associated this simple, characteristically Italian dish with the memory of being soothed. During the symposium, around the suddenly quiet table, each woman had returned momentarily to her childhood home and was looking down at the steam rising off the bowl of pastina her mother or grandmother had placed in front of her.

It was at this symposium, organized to celebrate Women's History Month, that the seeds of this anthology were planted. Held at the Poetry Center at Passaic County Community College on March 31, 2001, and coordinated by Maria Mazziotti Gillan and Edvige Giunta, this event was co-sponsored by the Poetry Center and the Collective of Italian American Women (reborn in 2001 as Malìa: A Collective of Italian American Women), which is a New York– and New Jersey–based group that promotes multicultural relations; since 1998 it has organized gender-focused events on the Italian American cultural experience. *Speaking of Jersey* was one of the many cultural gatherings that has occurred in the last decade across the United States, and one of the many that testifies to the growth of this literature, one that in the last few years has begun to receive due recognition as an important segment of American literary and cultural history. This symposium was perhaps the first to focus specifically on New Jersey as the subject matter chosen by so many Italian American writers. Here we challenged many of the cultural expectations and stereotypes that have thwarted the authenticity and diversity of Italian American experiences. We found it especially productive to hold this event in the context of a critical discussion of the stereotyping to which New Jersey has been subjected. The women authors who gathered in Paterson had different stories to tell, stories that pointed to a complexity and richness of experiences not yet widely depicted by American popular culture and media.

In the intimate atmosphere of the conversation that followed the writers' presentations, authors and audience shared stories that revealed that indeed New Jersey has been and still is a fertile site for Italian Americans and their creative work. *Speaking of Jersey* captured the warm feeling of sitting around a table with other Italian Americans and marveling at the commonalities we shared despite our differences in origins, in ages, in life choices, and experiences. It became clear that these stories, while specific to the histories of Italian American communities, also spoke to a large and diverse constituency— across gender, racial, and ethnic borders. Like other anthologies of its kind,

Jennifer Gillan, Maria Mazziotti Gillan, and Edvige Giunta

Italian American Writers on New Jersey: An Anthology of Poetry and Prose bespeaks the achievement of cultural consciousness and claims the relevance of the stories and histories of the writers included in this volume to Italian American as well as American literary and cultural history.

As the three of us sat down to revisit and reconceptualize the ideas that had shaped the symposium, we began to envision a project broader in scope and subject. While the symposium had focused on the contributions of contemporary women writers, primarily from northern New Jersey—many of which appear here—the anthology that it inspired includes male and female Italian American writers from the late nineteenth century to the present from diverse geographical areas of New Jersey. Gender and ethnicity were the focus of the symposium, but this anthology also draws from our commitment to the study of the culture produced by working-class people. As scholars and writers, the three of us also share a deep interest in literary history and the awareness that projects such as this anthology can impact the formation of that history.

Italian American Writers on New Jersey combines fiction, poetry, memoir, oral histories, and journalistic pieces to offer a chronicle of the Italian American experience in New Jersey from the late nineteenth century to the beginning of the twenty-first century. It features writers who are natives or residents of New Jersey or whose writings focus on Italian American life and the distinctive culture of the Garden State, which has long been home to a large and vital Italian American community. A fertile site for the aspirations of this community, New Jersey has produced Italian American artists, scholars, chroniclers, and participants in the public life of the state and the nation. The pieces in this anthology collectively represent a document of a literature that has been in the making for over a century, a literature that both maintains distinctly regional traits and fully participates in the national American literary project. At a time in which the literary and publishing world are showing an interest in Italian Americans that transcends the sensationalist interest in mob culture, this anthology documents the present condition and traces the origins of the body of work produced by authors who maintain deeply diverse ties to their Italian ancestry and to the Garden State.

New Jersey is a fitting setting for an exploration of American identity and the place of Italian Americans in the American mosaic. This state has been fruitful ground not only for writers, but also for the growth and intermingling of various ethnic American cultures. The variety of New Jersey communities is complemented by the diversity of its topography. From the shore to the Pine Barrens, from the northeastern cityscapes to the southwestern farmlands, and all the suburbs in between, New Jersey represents America in microcosmic form. Similarly, New Jersey's Italian American communities and their experiences of what it means to be marked as "hyphenated" embody the complexities of American identity as it is rooted in geography, ethnicity, class, gender, and sexuality.

Like many ethnic groups, Italian Americans have often found themselves confronted with cultural, linguistic, and psychological challenges that grow out of the experience of being different from the standard Madison Avenue and Hollywood conceptions of American identity. The poems and stories in *Italian American Writers on New Jersey* depict situations and convey emotions that will resonate with people who trace their ancestries to other ethnic groups and to working-class people. Indeed, these works articulate cross-cultural themes of alienation, dislocation, and passing that permeate the histories of marginalized and disenfranchised groups in the United States.

The writers in this anthology explore the condition of being caught between "typical" American and Italian American culture. Maria Laurino poignantly depicts her sense of displacement as a byproduct of her family's attempt to "pass" after relocating from a city neighborhood to what she calls the "ghetto of Short Hills." Remembering life in this affluent New Jersey suburb, she speculates that "perhaps any child who is poor among the rich learns to kowtow to the needs of the wealthy, and in doing so carries a deep sense of shame over her inadequacies." Locations, relocations, and dislocations resulting from migrations of various kinds are the subject of several of the other works featured in this anthology. Maria Mazziotti Gillan's "Daddy, We Called You" evokes the movement between the Italian world inside the home and the American world of the street where "Papa" became "Daddy." As the speaker recalls, "we spoke of you to our friends/ as 'my father'/ imagining we were speaking/ of that 'Father Knows Best'/ TV character" with his "dark business suit" and his "frilly-aproned wife." Noticing the same disparities, Bill Ervolino humorously compares his family's beach outings with those of "cute little blond families." The latter families bring only tanning lotion and towels, while his family lugs along a silver cooler filled with potatoes and eggs, peppers and eggs, and eggplant parmigiana. These writers articulate a negotiation central to American self-fashioning between American popular culture and the values and the culture of the community of origins.

While sharing some of Ervolino's humorous recollections, Tom Perrotta in "Race Riot" reveals a more troubling undercurrent to the insularity of a

1970s town as well as the suburban teen rituals of the decade: cruising in a Camaro, hanging out in a Burger King parking lot, and protecting limited suburban turf from teenage trespassers. Perrotta delves into the turf wars waged between Italian Americans and African Americans and addresses the history of racism within Italian American communities. Such a history must be understood in the context of the history of access to citizenship in the United States. Such access made it possible for Italian Americans, a group that suffered terrible forms of discrimination in the early stages of its immigration, to pass as "white." Thus, they internalized and displaced onto other ethnic groups the racism and discrimination to which they themselves had been subjected. Such a response can be better understood if one considers the status of southern Italians, who represented a majority of Italian immigrants, as the "blacks" of Italy. While Perrotta focuses on intercultural tensions, other writers included in this anthology articulate the creative tensions connected with their biculturalism and binationalism: Agnes Rossi's work, for instance, emerges from the intermixture of her Irish and Italian families, while Susanne Antonetta's work is shaped by her multiple ethnic/racial/cultural origins, which are Italian, English, and Barbadian. Even if they do not share this internal bicultural struggle, many of the writers included in *Italian American Writers on New Jersey* explore issues of competing identity claims. When read together, the works in this anthology attest to different levels of denial, acceptance, but also to creative transformation of one's cultural inheritance. Carole Maso's approach to place as a disembodied metaphor in her postmodern fiction, for instance, is complemented by Maria Mazziotti Gillan's portrayal of place as an embodied character in her poetry.

The anthology is divided into four sections that comment on various aspects of the Italian American experience in New Jersey:

Part One: Looking Back
   In Depth: Paterson, the Alpha & the Omega
Part Two: Blending In
Part Three: Crossing Bridges
   In Depth: Interstate Commerce, New York & New Jersey Bound
Part Four: Changing Direction

We begin with "Part One, Looking Back," a section that deals with connections to the past, whether figured in terms of the initial experience of immigration, village rituals re-created in immigrant kitchens and gardens, or the memory of ethnic enclaves in New Jersey's cities. Grace Cavalieri captures

Introduction

how a child's sense of self is defined by her street and neighborhood: "Trenton had no meaning until I did. . . . We thought Trenton was a street with sidewalks, and telephones with party lines." This birthplace, this Trenton, this city of memory shapes her thoughts, thoughts that "are not divided the way rooms are, the way roads are. They burn like hot grease on the stove smoking in us forever." Writings and oral histories of late-nineteenth- and early-twentieth-century factory workers, labor leaders, and anarchists address the literal experience of having a city's smoke seep into the body. Recalling the physical residue of factory labor—from soot-covered to scarred or broken bodies—the writers in this section chronicle the industrial and modern eras in New Jersey's urban centers.

In an inspiring essay published in 1905 in the Paterson-based radical newspaper *La Questione Sociale* and reprinted here, the activist Maria Barbieri writes: "We have been forced, like human machines, to stay trapped in the immense industrial prisons where one loses strength, health, and youth, where our rights are shattered." Barbieri is one of the women anarchists active in the early-twentieth-century labor movement who are at the center of Jennifer Guglielmo's essay "Rebel Girls." Combining intimate recollection and critical reflection, Guglielmo connects the radicalism of these women with her own rebellion and scholarly risk-taking in writing about them. Guglielmo's essay and William Harry Harding's fictional re-creation of the life of a 1915 Paterson silk mill worker open a spotlight section on Paterson that offers perspectives on that city from the nineteenth century to the present. "Looking Back" re-creates Paterson, Jersey City, Hoboken, Trenton, and Newark, the industrial centers with which Italian Americans have maintained close ties since the immigrant settlements of the nineteenth century.

While Pietro di Donato recalls the tenement where a variety of new immigrants—Jews, Irish, Italians, and Armenians—lived together and shared a vast, urban, multicultural neighborhood in turn-of-the-century Hoboken, Louise DeSalvo, in her memoir *Vertigo*, dramatizes the struggles of readjustment resulting from one family's move in the 1940s from Hoboken to a blue-collar suburb in Ridgefield. In the excerpt of "Combat Zones," included in this volume, DeSalvo offers a unique perspective on World War II as experienced by the wives and the children of the soldiers in a working-class Italian American community in Hoboken. The author juxtaposes the unruly, festive life of a world no longer overseen by the authority of husbands and fathers to the deep-seated trauma caused by the sudden loss of those husbands and fathers, men who left to fight against their ancestors' motherland, some without ever coming back. The families of the little Italian enclave would be forever marked by that loss, as would the men who did return. World War II also appears in the oral history of a Montclair resident, Marge Galioto. Her narrative is part of a cultural project to document the history of the Italian Americans of the Pine Street and Glenfield Park neighborhoods of Montclair initiated by Marisa Trubiano, herself a New Jersey native and resident.

Moving farther south, Gay Talese chronicles the arrival of his immigrant father in Ocean City in 1918. Talese recalls that the life of his parents always seemed "strange and baffling" to him: "I felt unrelated even to my parents, especially my father, who was indeed a foreigner—an unusual man in dress and manner, to whom I bore no physical resemblance and with whom I could never identify." Trapped between two worlds, Talese feels he bears no resemblance either to his parents or to his friends. Not only is he "olive-skinned in a freckled-faced town," he is also saddled with the secret knowledge that his Italian relatives, known to him only through their airmail letters and attached military photographs, are enemies of the United States. He feels a profound sense of difference and dislocation: "I saw myself always as an alien, an outsider, a drifter who, like the shipwrecked sailors, had arrived by accident. I felt different from my young friends in almost every way, different in the cut of my clothes, the food in my lunchbox, the music I heard at home on the record player, the ideas and inner thoughts I revealed on those rare occasions I was open and honest." Talese's reflection on how difficult it was for Italian Americans to blend in with the communities of white, middle-class America is juxtaposed to Rachel Guido deVries's description of this process of assimilation in 1950s Paterson. In her story "The Tangerine Plymouth and the Gilded Cage," deVries depicts an Italian American girl whose fondness for Verp's Bakery, orange NeHi, and Nabisco cookies exists alongside her love for prosciutto, salami, and provolone.

Such mixing and other aspects of the complicated process of negotiating two cultures is the subject of Part Two, "Blending In." Edvige Giunta's poem, "Quench a Plant's Thirst," captures this duality in its representation of the slippage between a late-twentieth-century Sicilian immigrant's position as an American daughter to an Italian mother and as an Italian mother to an American daughter. Echoing Talese's poignant rendering of his desire to fit in somewhere, other writers in "Blending In" suggest that for the second, third, and fourth generations the relative ease with which assimilation is sometimes achieved is proportional to the degree of guilt, loss, and nostalgia that accompanies it.

This section, along with the others in the book, includes works that reflect on the experiences of those mid-twentieth-century Italian Americans who were taught to deny the past and work toward the promise of a shimmering, yet often ever-retreating vision of the great American future. In Carole Maso's rendering of an Italian American man's response to the Futurama exhibits at the 1939 and 1964 World's Fairs in her novel *Ghost Dance*, an excerpt of which is included in the anthology's final section, she depicts the destructiveness of such linear thinking that denies the interconnectedness of the past, present, and future, of cultural practices, and of personal and national identities. Delving into her experiences growing up lower middle class and ethnic in a rich suburb, Laurino writes of her realization that shopping at a national department store such as Saks Fifth Avenue would enhance her personal status as an American and help her to shed the shame associated with her Italian American self. The right clothes, the young Laurino learns early, can help to make one the right kind of American. Thus she costumes herself in these "American" clothes and tries to exude their pleasing smells, hoping that imitation will translate into social acceptance. Other schoolmates who, in her perception, feel more entitled to American identity, persist in labeling her "smelly Italian girl." Commenting on the irony inherent in her attempt to emulate the rich Jewish girls in Short Hills, Laurino recalls: "Decades later, when I told my Jewish husband that in high school I tried to assimilate by imitating his culture, he laughed." As an adolescent, she "didn't understand that the Jewish girls who zealously booked plastic surgery appointments with Howard Diamond, the Manhattan doctor famous for creating identical pug noses in Short Hills and Great Neck, Long Island, were undergoing a similar identity struggle." This is one of the many examples of how Italian American identity can be better understood in relationship to what it means to belong to an ethnic minority in the United States and in relationship to the placement of various ethnic groups in changing social hierarchies.

Depicting the complexities of the process of blending in, both Laurino's memoir and Maso's novel mix social and cultural history. These two texts reflect in their very forms the difficult process of sifting through stereotypical and stultified notions of Italian American life, but they also question misguided notions of a romanticized ethnicity. Clearly, the rush to assimilate and become part of an American monoculture represents a denial of the complex reality of most Americans' bicultural or multicultural heritage. As children conform to those monocultural standards, their own enriching differences are flattened out. In an ironic consequence of this rush to assimilate that characterized the 1950s and early 1960s, third-generation Italian Americans tend to be nostalgic about those markers from which their parents were so eager to dissociate themselves. Of course, such nostalgia is easier for later generations, those who were coming of age in an America seemingly more open and accepting of their diversity. For earlier generations, no matter how difficult the experience of trying to blend in might have been, the pains associated with that process were preferable to the agonizing shame of standing out, especially in school. It is only later in adulthood that these authors and their characters come to recognize the richness of their cultures and the substantiality of their cross-cultural inheritance. Susanne Antonetta suggests that her memory is inflected by a nontraditional life lived in New Jersey suburbs; she figures the brain as a map with "Cul-de-sacs and straight-aways. All that mazy motion." She seems lost in the winding and interconnecting streets of New Jersey's developments from which, at times, there seems to be no exit. At other times, she sees possibility in all these exits and entrances: all the alternatives to which she has been exposed are the source of her strength, a realization obliquely reflected in the title of her piece, "Nevertheless, It Moves." The loss and recovery of one's culture, but also the revisiting of that culture on new terms—creation of new imaginary, "literary" sites—underlies much of the literature we have chosen to include here.

Exits and entrances, movement toward and away from, locations and re-locations, are all themes addressed in Part Three, "Crossing Bridges," which considers various movements between states, between cultures and cultural demands, between family and societal expectations. The narrator in Agnes Rossi's "Hungry Dog" lives in an interstitial space. A teen frequenting a truck stop in the shadow of Stag Hill, home of the Jackson Whites, she learns what it is "like being in the middle"; the experience scares her, but it also thrills her, and marks her for life. Rossi writes of traveling between spaces within the state, but this section also includes writing about traveling between and around the tristate area. Writers such as Frank Finale, Bill Ervolino, Sal Buttaci, and Rosette Capotorto depict the most frequented route, over the bridges and through the tunnels connecting the states. While often these are commuter paths, tourists also travel these routes. Taking the tourist's perspective and demonstrating how New Jersey can be a traveler's natural paradise, Diane di Prima and Mary Ann Mannino, in their respective poems on Greenwood Lake and Wildwood Beach, represent the Garden State as an oasis from the noise and bustle of a city home. In contrast, New Jersey was not always a safe haven for Frank DeCaro. In an excerpt from the memoir *A Boy Named Phyllis*, he uses humor to explore just how much he had to keep crossing borders as a gay teenager in the aluminum-sided, blue-collar world of a New Jersey town in which "to be anything but ordinary was a mistake." Yet, DeCaro also describes how throughout his childhood his Italian American family provided a shelter for him from his "enthusiastically malicious" peers staring him down from across "inhospitable" manicured front lawns.

Janet Zandy explores the crossing many children of immigrants experienced, from home to school—a sort of crossing from Italy to America, and almost always an experience of separation from home and family. Looking back as a college professor, she suggests, in "Class Quartet," that she exists in a gap between her actual family and her chosen academic "family," feeling both affiliation with and distance from both communities. Zandy's gradual recognition that her academic family encouraged her to sever herself from her history and culture is followed by a moment of transformation, which comes with the realization that "it was time to cut in another direction." Politicizing her history, "Liberating Memory" documents how she began "to connect lived working-class experience to the study of literature and how to organize and struggle for change." This connection was vital to Zandy's groundbreaking work in working-class studies. This autobiographical essay is included in "Changing Direction," Part Four of our anthology, that features other writers and characters who recount of analogous realizations that "it was time to cut in another direction."

A number of writers reexamine the pain they suffered as children because they were different, and they transform it into a source of creativity: their Italian American voices speak with renewed power, a power rooted in the understanding and revisiting of the very stories within which they were once silent. This final section includes work that involves a change of attitude toward aspects of one's heritage or community rituals, a reconnection to identities that earlier had been denied, or a revisiting of mental and physical landscapes that had previously been abandoned. In "Elizabeth" Susanne Antonetta recuperates Elizabeth, one of those cities so often associated with the excesses of pollution and urban decay. The author creatively intertwines death and pollution by connecting the radio announcements about the unacceptable air quality in Elizabeth and her accidental inhalation during a cremation ceremony of the ashes of the fourth wife of her Italian grandfather. Antonetta's compelling implication is that she cannot stop the inevitable process of absorbing her birthplace and her ancestors into her body. No matter how toxic they would later be found to be, all that she has literally and figuratively swallowed becomes an intrinsic part of her. Other writers return to places that they had renounced in their early years, only to embrace them in adulthood. Michele Linfante's "Circolo" offers a poetic take on this process. As an adult, the speaker collects "distant memories" of smells, tastes, and sounds that were hieroglyphs to her child self and gathers them "in a ritual task," an attempt to bring together all the "dis-membered" parts of herself.

This final section turns to the discovery of such connections between one's origins and one's present, between a writer's New Jersey roots and the source of his or her creative work. The various selections bring to life New Jersey's vibrant Italian American cultures and the communities of the past that still live in the memories of Italian American writers in spite of cultural and geographical migrations and dislocations. Carole Maso associates those memories with the city of her birth, Paterson, "one of the great American poems: From the beginning home for me is a poem. I was born in the modernist masterpiece by William Carlos Williams." If the works included here testify to the fact that their authors have been collectively engaging, at times unwittingly, in the creation of Italian American literature, these authors also maintain profound ties to other authors, and view themselves as part of the larger U.S. literary tradition, even as they often maintain a problematic relationship to that tradition, which has for too long excluded them.

Paterson, the "masterpiece," is the home and inspiration of many other Italian American writers, including Agnes Rossi and Rachel Guido deVries. Maria Mazziotti Gillan views Paterson as her birthplace, but also the wellspring of her creative art: for her, Paterson is "the Alpha & the Omega." It is also the city in which in 1980 she founded the Poetry Center. Given that the idea for this anthology blossomed at the symposium *Speaking of Jersey*, held at the Poetry Center, we felt it was fitting to include a spotlight section, "In Depth: Paterson: the Alpha & the Omega" to highlight the centrality of this city in the Italian American imaginary. Some of the members of the audience and participants at our symposium had relocated from New Jersey to New York City; others had relocated from New York City to Paterson's artists' housing. This housing, along with the Paterson Museum, schools, and offices, is located in the converted old mills in which Italian Americans worked for much of the twentieth century. Because Paterson is the birthplace of two foundational American poets, William Carlos Williams and Allen Ginsberg, many writers make pilgrimages to the city and travel long distances to attend the readings and conferences at the Poetry Center. For some, it is a re-crossing of sorts, since they or their parents, grandparents, or even great grandparents grew up in this city.

Our second spotlight section, "Interstate Commerce: New York & New Jersey Bound," includes pieces that reflect on the productive traffic between

Introduction

New Jersey and New York as well as on the exchange of people and ideas between New Jersey and the city which much of its coastline faces. It also features creative works that represent earlier migrations of families from Ellis Island to various cities in New Jersey and from New York City to those cities and, later, its suburbs. Focusing on that special connection between New York and New Jersey, this section concentrates on a variety of crossings, migrations, and homecomings. Framed by these two spotlight features, on Paterson and the productive crossings between the peoples, poems, and creative works of New York and New Jersey, this anthology proposes new entrances into the interior of New Jersey, its Italian American communities, and their creative work. This book is intended as a map to guide you through the winding and interconnecting paths of the Italian American literary production of New Jersey. We hope it offers a fresh perspective on the depth and complexity of the writing of a state that has been most often associated with the stale witticism, "You from Jersey? What exit?"

Jennifer Gillan, Cambridge, Massachusetts and Hawthorne, New Jersey
Maria Mazziotti Gillan, Paterson and Hawthorne, New Jersey
Edvige Giunta, Jersey City and Teaneck, New Jersey
November 2002

PART ONE

Looking Back

COMBAT ZONES
Louise DeSalvo

What do I know of my parents' lives before they became my parents, before they married on Sunday, July 6, 1941? Not very much at all.

We were not a family inclined to sit for hours talking about ourselves, sharing intimacies, sharing personal histories. What I learned about my parents' histories came to me piecemeal. Usually, it was something I overheard when I entered a room, when I walked past an open door, or when I listened to an argument.

What do I know about my mother's life? I know that her proudest moment was when she won a prize in high school in 1929, for writing. I know that she wanted to go to college, and that she had been awarded a scholarship to attend one in New York State, but that she couldn't go because her parents were too poor to send her. I know that my mother worked as a salesperson for W. T. Grant's in Hoboken, New Jersey, after she graduated high school, before she married my father. (She stands on the edge of a group portrait of Grant's workers in 1940, wearing a tweed jacket, sweater, and short skirt, looking tense.) I know that she sold shoes. I know that she developed a strong, lifelong friendship during her years at Grant's. I know that she taught herself to become a fine seamstress.

I know that my mother adored her father, and that she had a very difficult childhood. That her mother died during the influenza epidemic of 1918, when she was two years old. That her father, an Italian immigrant, who spoke no English, who worked for the railroad as a day laborer, had a difficult time finding adequate childcare for her, and that he farmed her out to neighbors or relatives who probably either abused or neglected her. I know that she nearly died after her mother's death and that her father remarried a peasant woman newly arrived from Italy, primarily to provide a mother for his child. I know that my mother hated her stepmother. And that, at some point in her life, my mother experienced a depression so severe she had to be hospitalized.

Much of this I learned from my father as an adult. It was not something my mother talked about. As a child, I was never told that my grandmother was my mother's stepmother. This was a secret, although it was alluded to by my parents and other relatives in close whispers, or by my mother and step-grandmother in heated arguments.

I was told of my mother's birth mother, and shown her picture, only after I had married. I was astonished to see that I looked just like her. Same heart-shaped face. Same small eyes. Same wide brow and upturned nose. Same dark, wavy hair. Same prideful look on her face as on mine.

Learning that my stepgrandmother was not my mother's birth mother was a great shock I experienced as a young bride. The other, that my mother had taken the $5,000 I had saved during my years of work from our joint bank account to pay for my wedding reception. I had worked hard, lived frugally, denied myself material pleasures to save enough money to feel financially secure and to be independent. I was furious when I discovered she had spent it on my wedding without asking me.

For years I have wondered why no one told me that my mother's birth mother was dead. It would have explained so much. Why my mother and grandmother always shouted at one another in Italian about love, and about respect. Why our household was always a pitched battleground after my grandmother came to live with us after my grandfather's death. "You're not my blood," the mysterious words my stepgrandmother flung at my mother routinely.

Sometimes I think that my mother's mother's death was kept a secret from me because she hadn't died from influenza, she had really killed herself. I have no evidence for this. But what else could explain this shroud of secrecy? Why else would they have tried to obliterate her memory?

The greatest gifts I get from my mother are her fierce loyalty to family, her sense of justice and fairness.

And what do I know about this man who became my father? I know that his being the only son in a family with four daughters was a source of irritation to him. That, as a boy of six or seven, he helped his mother at her piecework job by buttoning the buttons on the shirts that she folded. I know that my father was required by his parents to drown the kittens that the family cat would periodically deliver. I know that this disturbed him. I know that, as a teenager, he was caught stealing copper pipe from a construction site and put in jail. I know that his mother, not his father, came to bail him out.

I know that my father graduated from eighth grade when he was sixteen years old because his family moved around so much that he was always getting left back. (He lived in Italy, Brooklyn, New York City, North Bergen in New Jersey.) I know that my father was dyslexic, and that going to school was agony for him. I know that he wanted to go to high school, but decided that since he would be more than twenty years old when (and if) he graduated, he would quit school to work to help his family. That his father was a barber, and that he owned his own shop, but that he was irresponsible—he would return to Italy periodically after the family moved to the United States, leaving his wife and five children behind without an income.

An early memory: I am on a pier in New York City waving good-bye to my paternal grandfather who is in the bow of the ship waving a white handkerchief. He is off on another of his jaunts to Italy. I wonder why we have come to say good-bye to him because I have heard the family arguing heatedly about these periodic sojourns of his. When I am older, I think that he must have had another woman, perhaps even another family, in Italy. Only this can explain to me why he comes and goes, comes and goes.

I know that my father had a spectacular untrained operatic voice, that he wanted to become a singer (he had the raw talent, and the temperament, to become a star), but that he couldn't afford the lessons, and, besides, he didn't have sufficient schooling to make that possible. I know that my father, without much formal education, had decided that he could get the training he needed to become a skilled laborer if he enlisted in the service, and so he did, spending the years from 1935 to 1939 in the Navy. I know that he was good at fixing things. I know that he loved to travel and that that's another reason why he joined the Navy. In the Navy, his secret ambition was to become a pilot, but he soon learned that he didn't have the necessary education to fulfill his dream. Throughout his life, he will read hundreds of books on flying. Whenever there is a space launch televised, he will sit in front of the screen watching the entire event intently. He will try to get the rest of the family to join him, but we're not as interested in these things as he is. I know that when my father left the Navy the first time, he had become a gifted machinist, and that he could figure out how to fix just about anything, an ability that was put to good use by the Navy during the war.

The greatest gifts I get from my father are his capacity for finding joy in whatever comes his way, his engagement with life, and his voracious curiosity for discovering how things work.

I saw a movie once, in which a character played by Humphrey Bogart said, "The world is inhabited by two classes of people. Those who are alive. And those who are afraid." My father was alive. My mother was afraid.

Combat Zones

❧

1943

I am fourteen months old when my father goes away to war. I have no memory of this event. In the pictures that are taken of me just after my father goes to war, I look shell-shocked. The real father whom I experienced has been wrenched away from me and will be replaced by a father whom I will know only through my imagination.

I know that children who lose caregivers at this young age can become withdrawn and there is something of that look about me. I have the feeling that I experienced the loss of him profoundly, that I mourned his loss as surely as if he had died, and, to protect myself, I locked him out of my heart.

As I grew older, I told myself stories about how we were happier without him, better off without him, about how all the mothers and children were better off without their husbands and fathers, and that all the trouble started in my life when my father came back from the war a changed man, an angry man, a man against whom I will wage my own war. But I know my stories aren't all true.

From time to time, during the war, my mother shows me a picture of my father so that I won't forget him, so that I will remember what he looks like.

He is standing in his Navy uniform, on deck. Giant coils of rope are behind him. He is clowning around. His cap is pulled back on his head so that you can see his curls. He has a silly grin on his face.

Now, so many years after this picture has been taken by one of his buddies, so many years after my mother has received it, so many years after she has shown me this picture of my father in his bellbottoms for the last time, before he returns home from war, I detach the tape that holds it in place, and take it out of the album, carefully, and turn it over, wondering whether, so many years ago, he has written any message to his wife on the other side.

"Me trying to look funney," he writes, misspelling that word, as he has misspelled it throughout his life.

I experience an almost unbearable surge of love for him, for his ability to feign happiness, to try to look "funney" for the family he has left behind, for the family that he knows he might never see again.

Louise DeSalvo

1943–1945

This is how I remember the war years, though I know that it is not altogether true, and, maybe, that it is not true at all. Maybe this is the story that I tell myself about that time in my life because it is too difficult to remember what I really lived through.

Soon after all the husbands in our working-class apartment building in the Italian section of Hoboken, New Jersey, left for the war, the geography of the place changes so completely that life itself took on an antic, festive, tribal quality. Anarchy prevailed, and it was good.

Before, each family was locked together to carry on its claustrophobic life in its tiny three-room cell. There was a funeral-parlor-like quiet to the building, though if you listened closely enough, you could hear raised voices or howls or sometimes even smacks and screams behind closed doors. Parents and children were stuffed together in single bedrooms in the apartment's center; meals were taken at predictable hours at kitchen tables; laundry was done on Mondays in kitchen sinks with washboards (and, always, no matter how careful the mothers were, there were far too many suds, that made the rinsing a horror) and hung outside to dry on lines strung like a giant's version of cat's cradle, one of our favorite games played with string.

Before the war, hellos between women and children were exchanged, politely and briefly, as we passed one another on the stairs, or on the streets outside (the men merely grunting, or nodding in grudging recognition). Families went to church on Sundays when everyone dressed up in their best to show how affluent they wished they were, and parents trundled their children in perambulators or strollers up and down sidewalks.

But after the men left for war, the women, who were left behind to raise their families single-handedly, threw open all the doors to their apartments, and children began to clatter up and down the five flights of stairs at all hours of the day and night. Women and children wandered from one apartment into another without ceremony or invitation. Children played together on landings, and in the weedy enclosed courtyard behind the apartment, which was completely off limits when the men were in residence—the sound of shrieking voices was too trying for them after their long, hard day's work.

Meals were taken, picnic-style, in the strangest places—on fire escapes and parlor floors, in the cellar where my grandfather made wine at Easter, on the stoop out front, or in other people's kitchens. Bedtime, naptime, came whenever you were tired and you fell asleep wherever you were, and not necessarily in your own bed.

Mothers ducked into churches for prayers for the safe return of their husbands on their way to and from markets or playgrounds and they generally avoided the place on Sundays.

Children, even girl children, were allowed to play hard enough to get dirty and rip their clothes. Heads, examined for lice regularly, were found to contain them more often than not; children with infestations were gathered into one kitchen or another and lined up for the gasoline shampoos that were guaranteed to kill the lice. Skating contests were held routinely on the sidewalk out front. Mr. Albini, the owner of the drugstore on the corner of Adams Street, where we now live, too old for the war, tended to our cuts and bruises with neither panic nor warnings that, next time, we should be more careful.

Gangs of women—five, six, or more—gangs of children—nine, ten, or more—would gather together in the tiny parlors of apartments during birthday parties (which seemed to occur weekly) or holiday celebrations or for no good reason at all, except for the pleasure of being together.

The children, when they think of these years, will remember the happy press of hordes of bodies in one tiny place or another; they will remember drinking juice without being afraid they will spill it; they will remember licking the icing off the cake before it was cut and not getting yelled at for it; they will remember their mothers' thinking that jumping up and down on someone else's bed was the funniest thing in the world.

After the party, the women scrunch together, happily, on the sofa, for a picture-taking session. They have had their sherry; they are very happy. They lean against one another's knees, lean into one another's bodies, caress one another's shoulders. They are all smiling; they are always smiling. They decide to have six copies of the picture made to mail to their men at war.

(In various combat zones, on battlefields and battleships throughout the world, six men will later open their letters, look at this picture, and wonder to themselves, what is going on, and why on earth these women look like they're having such a good time.)

Then, it is the children's turn to take pictures to be sent off to their darling daddies away at war. The four smallest toddlers stand in front, holding hands. The bigger children stand behind, making faces. The tiniest babies hang off their mothers' laps, their mothers aglow with female talk and companionship. One child decides to walk out of the picture; something else has captured his fancy. No mother bothers to stop him. The mothers do not care whether he appears in the picture or he doesn't.

Although the women say they miss their men (and try to teach their children to miss them as well), and although they spend hours of every day penning long accounts of their brave and unhappy lives alone to their husbands in combat, their lives, and those of their children, are far happier than either before their husbands go to war or after their husbands return home.

This is my story about the war, and, as I have said, I'm sure it can't be all true. Yet, in many photographs that my mother sends to my father during the war, she smiles broadly and she seems happy. In one, deeply tanned, hair atop her head, she is gathering me close, as she kneels next to me in the surf of a beach. In another, on a snowy winter day, in winter coat and scarf, she kneels behind me; I am all bundled up, sitting on my new sled, my Christmas present. In still another, I am perched atop her knee in an armchair in our parlor and I am wearing my sailor dress; again, she smiles (though I do not).

It may have been that she doesn't want to show her sorrow, which would demoralize him, and so she feigns her wide smiles. Or, released from wifely responsibilities for the duration of the war, she is, from time to time, truly satisfied.

∾

At regular intervals throughout the war, my mother rounds me up, washes away my scruffiness, clothes me in my best clothes, arranges my banana curls perfectly, and poses me for a picture to be sent to my father so that he can see how well I am doing and how big I am growing.

It is Christmas Day, 1944, and I am standing in our parlor, in front of the tabletop Christmas tree, in my brand-new pajamas with feet attached to them. They are way too big for me—so big that every time I try to walk in them, I fall down. My mother has already begun what becomes a habit with her—buying clothes a size too big for me so that I'll grow into them. Under the tree, on the fern-patterned carpet, there are four Christmas presents. Under my right arm and in my right hand I clutch two more. I am neat, clean, and my hair is combed. I am as clean and neat as if I am going to church, or to a party.

Behind the chair my mother sits in, against the fern-patterned wallpaper, is a bookcase filled with a set of books, all with the same blue-gray binding. I think it is my mother who has bought them, on time, from a traveling salesman, either for decoration or to establish the image of her household as literarily minded—neither she nor my father reads them. Yet, ours is the only parlor I know with books in it.

When I am little, I take one of these books down from the shelf and pretend to read it. Often, I hold the book upside down, but my mother corrects my mistake. "Don't bother Louise, she's reading," my mother jokes to a friend when I do this. Later, in my early teens, I read each of them—the first of my many self-imposed reading programs. They are a strange agglomeration: Oscar Wilde's *Picture of Dorian Gray*; Samuel Butler's *The Way of All Flesh*; Sir Walter Scott's *Ivanhoe*; Fyodor Dostoyevsky's *The Possessed*; some plays by Yeats; some poems by Frost. I am the only one in my family to read these books; I am the only one of my teenage friends to read books like this, even though I don't really understand all of what they're about.

Less than a month after Christmas, my mother fixes me up to pose again. This time, I am standing in our kitchen, dressed in my sailor dress, feet crossed, demurely, bow in my hair. On my chalkboard, my mother has penned the message "HELLO DADDY. WE LOVE YOU." On the counter behind me is our new telephone.

After the photo is developed, my mother writes a message on the back of it from me to my father.

"January 17, 1945. Dear Daddy:—How do you like our telephone. Gosh mommie & I are just wishing we get a call from our favorite sailor real soon. We love you daddy. Louise."

Easter Sunday, 1945. I am standing next door to our apartment in front of Albini's Drugstore in my Easter finery. Behind me, there is a prominent display of Kotex napkins and an advertisement for a special sale on Ex-Lax. I am wearing a new baby blue coat with a Peter Pan collar that my mother has made for me and a wonderful hat with a feather that is drawn down onto my forehead. I am very proud to be wearing it because it is such a grown-up hat. I am wearing white gloves and carrying a little pocketbook. My socks have little embroidered hearts on them.

"It won't be long now," my mother tells me when I ask her when my father will return. "Daddy's coming home soon. And then we can all get back to normal."

August 5, 1945

When my mother heard about how we had dropped the atom bomb on Hiroshima, she wept. She did not join the people celebrating in the streets sure, now, that the war would soon be over. All she could think about was all of those innocent people dying. She was ashamed of what her country had done, even if it meant that her husband would be coming home soon. She couldn't look at the newspapers.

1945

When the men came storming back from the war, I remember staring at them in their uniforms as they walked down the street, and I remember not liking what I saw. From as far back as I could remember, the streets of Hoboken were inhabited only by women, children, and old men. Men my father's age were a species I hadn't grown up with, didn't remember, wasn't familiar with, and now, there was an invasion of these men into what I had come to consider my private territory.

Everything changed for me when the men came home from the war. It was harder to see my friends. Gangs of cheerful women and exuberant children stopped getting together for the impromptu potluck suppers that were a mainstay of the war years. All the doors in our apartment building were, again, closed. All children were cautioned to play quietly, if we were allowed to play at all, because the fathers needed their peace and quiet after what they had been through. Nighttime story hours were shortened or curtailed altogether. Snacks were forbidden. Mothers hushed their voices, and hushed us, to listen with deference and awe to whatever the men had to say. And, as if it weren't bad enough that we had lost our mothers, that our fathers had displaced us, a year or two years later, there was a spate of squalling babies who came along to complete the separation of us wartime children from our mothers. Many of us wartime children tried our best to pretend that our fathers and those babies weren't really there.

I can remember my mother telling me "Daddy is coming home soon," but I can't remember what I felt when I heard those words. I can remember her taking me to the movie theater on Washington Street to see the newsreels showing jubilant sailors waving frantically, tossing their caps into the air, as they stood on the decks of naval vessels as they sailed past the Statue of Liberty, making their way home, at last, to the wives and children they had left behind a very long time before, to resume their lives.

My father is lucky to be coming home alive and unharmed. Although he was in constant danger from submarine attacks on the way to where he was stationed, he spent the war on an island in the Pacific at a seaplane base after the Japanese had left the island. His job was to repair seaplanes that had been damaged in battle or maneuvers. And, although he saw a man crushed by a truck, rescued a buddy engulfed by flames from a gasoline fire, and watched a ship transporting munitions explode, killing all four hundred men aboard, he himself made it through the war years without injury. He knows he has gotten off easy.

Of the several hundred daily letters that my mother wrote to my father in the evenings after she had put me to bed, none have survived. She penned them at the kitchen table, or in an easy chair in the parlor, the blackout curtains preventing the overhead lights from being perceived by the enemy, or sitting in her rocking chair in a corner of the kitchen.

Of the several hundred daily letters that my father wrote to my mother at nighttime after his duties for the day were completed, hunched down on the beach, by the flickering light of a gasoline-soaked pail of sand, none have survived.

Years later, when I ask my father what happened to this correspondence, he tells me he doesn't know. He tells me that he thinks my mother had saved the letters for awhile—he remembers a box of some kind, stored in the top of some closet or other—but thinks that at one point my mother destroyed them because she didn't think they were worth saving, that they were "only collecting dust," as she would have put it.

OCEAN CITY
UNTO THE SONS
Gay Talese

The beach in winter was dank and desolate, and the island dampened by the frigid spray of the ocean waves pounding relentlessly against the beachfront bulkheads, and the seaweed-covered beams beneath the white houses on the dunes creaked as quietly as the crabs crawling nearby.

The boardwalk, that in summer was a festive promenade of suntanned couples and children's balloons, of carousel tunes and colored lights spinning at night from the Ferris wheel, was occupied in winter by hundreds of sea gulls perched on the iron railings facing into the wind. When not resting they strutted outside the locked doors of vacated shops, or circled high in the sky, holding clams in their beaks that they soon dropped upon the boardwalk with a splattering *cluck*. Then they zoomed down and pounced on the exposed meat, pecking and pulling until there was nothing left but the jagged, salty white chips of empty shells.

By midwinter the shell-strewn promenade was a vast cemetery of clams, and from a distance the long elevated flat deck of the boardwalk resembled a stranded aircraft carrier being attacked by dive-bombers—and oddly juxtaposed in the fog behind the dunes loomed the rusting remains of a once sleek four-masted vessel that during a gale in the winter of 1901 had run aground on this small island in southern New Jersey called Ocean City.

The steel-hulled ship, flying a British flag and flaunting hundred-fifty-foot masts, had been sailing north along the New Jersey coast toward New York City, where it was scheduled to deliver one million dollars' worth of Christmas cargo it had picked up five months before in Kobe, Japan. But during the middle of the night, while a number of crewmen drank rum and beer in a premature toast to the long journey's end, a fierce storm rose and destroyed the ship's sails, snapped its masts, and drove it into a sandbar within one hundred yards of the Ocean City boardwalk.

Awakened by the distress signals that flared in the night, the alarmed residents of Ocean City—a conservative community founded in 1879 by Methodist ministers and other Prohibitionists who wished to establish an island of abstinence and propriety—hastened to help the sailors, who were soon discovered to be battered but unharmed and smelling of sweat, salt water, and liquor.

After the entire thirty-three-man crew had been escorted to shore, they were sheltered and fed for days under the auspices of the town's teetotaling elders and ministers' wives; and while the sailors expressed gratitude for such hospitality they privately cursed their fate in being shipwrecked on an island so sedate and sober. But soon they were relocated by British nautical authorities, and the salvageable cargo was barged to New York to be sold at reduced prices. And the town returned to the tedium of winter.

The big ship, however, remained forever lodged in the soft white sand—unmovable, slowly sinking, a sight that served Ocean City's pious guardians as a daily reminder of the grim consequences of intemperate guidance. But as I grew up in the late 1930s, more than three decades after the shipwreck—when the visible remnants at low tide consisted only of the barnacle-bitten ridge of the upper deck, the corroded brown rudder post and tiller, and a single lopsided mast—I viewed the vessel as a symbol of adventure and risk; and during my boyhood wanderings along the beach I became enchanted with exotic fantasies of nights in foreign ports, of braving the waves and wind with wayward men, and of escaping the rigid confines of this island on which I was born but never believed I belonged.

I saw myself always as an alien, an outsider, a drifter who, like the shipwrecked sailors, had arrived by accident. I felt different from my young friends in almost every way, different in the cut of my clothes, the food in my lunchbox, the music I heard at home on the record player, the ideas and inner thoughts I revealed on those rare occasions when I was open and honest.

I was olive-skinned in a freckle-faced town, and I felt unrelated even to my parents, especially my father, who was indeed a foreigner—an unusual man in dress and manner, to whom I bore no physical resemblance and with whom I could never identify. Trim and elegant, with wavy dark hair and a small rust-colored moustache, he spoke English with an accent and received letters bearing strange-looking stamps.

These letters sometimes contained snapshots of soldiers wearing uniforms with insignia and epaulets unlike any I had seen on the recruitment posters displayed throughout the island. They were my uncles and cousins, my father explained to me quietly one day early in World War II, when I was ten; they were fighting in the Italian army, and—it was unnecessary for him to add—their enemy included the government of the United States.

I became increasingly sensitive to this fact when I sat through the news-reels each week at the local cinema; next to my unknowing classmates, I watched with private horror the destruction by Allied bombers of mountain villages and towns in southern Italy to which I was ancestrally linked through a historically ill-timed relationship with my Italian father. At any moment I half expected to see up on the screen, gazing down at me from a dust-covered United States Army truck filled with disheveled Italian prisoners being guarded at gunpoint, a sad face that I could identify from one of my father's snapshots.

My father, on the other hand, seemed to share none of my confused sense of patriotism during the war years. He joined a citizens' committee of shore patrolmen who kept watch along the waterfront at night, standing with binoculars on the boardwalk under the stanchioned lights that on the ocean side were painted black as a precaution against discovery by enemy submarines.

He made headlines in the local newspaper after a popular speech to the Rotary Club in which he reaffirmed his loyalty to the Allied cause, declaring that were he not too old for the draft (he was thirty-nine) he would proudly join the American troops at the front, in a uniform devotedly cut and stitched with his own hands.

Trained as an apprentice tailor in his native village, and later an assistant cutter in a prominent shop in Paris that employed an older Italian cousin, my father arrived in Ocean City circuitously and impulsively at the age of eighteen in 1922 with very little money, an extensive wardrobe, and the outward appearance of a man who knew exactly where he was going, when in fact nothing was further from the truth. He knew no one in town, barely knew the language, and yet, with a self-assurance that has always mystified me, he adjusted to this unusual island as readily as he could cut cloth to fit any size and shape.

Having noticed a "For Sale" sign in the window of a tailor shop in the center of town, my father approached the asthmatic owner, who was desperate to leave the island for the drier climate of Arizona. After a brief negotiation, my father acquired the business and thus began a lengthy, spirited campaign to bring the rakish fashion of the Continental boulevardier to the comparatively continent men of the south Jersey shore.

But after decorating his windows with lantern-jawed mannequins holding cigarettes and wearing Borsalino hats, and draping his counters with bolts of fine imported fabrics—and displaying on his walls such presumably persuasive regalia as his French master tailor's diploma bordered by cherubim and a Greek goddess—my father made so few sales during his first year that he was finally forced to introduce into his shop a somewhat undignified gimmick called the Suit Club.

At the cost of one dollar per week, Suit Club members would print their names and addresses on small white cards and, after placing the cards in unmarked envelopes, would deposit them into a large opaque vase placed prominently atop a velvet-covered table next to a fashion photograph of a dapper man and woman posing with a greyhound on the greensward of an ornate country manor.

Each Friday evening just prior to closing time, my father would invite one of the assembled Suit Club members to close his eyes and pick from the vase a single envelope, which would reveal the name of the fortunate winner of a free suit, to be made from fabric selected by that individual; after two fittings, it would be ready for wearing within a week.

Since as many as three or four hundred people were soon paying a dollar each week to partake in this raffle, my father was earning on each free suit a profit perhaps three times the average cost of a custom-made suit in those days—to say nothing of the additional money he earned when he enticed a male winner into purchasing an extra pair of matching trousers.

But my father's bonanza was abruptly terminated one day in 1928, when an anonymous complaint sent to City Hall, possibly by a rival tailor, charged that the Suit Club was a form of gambling clearly outlawed under the town charter; thus ended for all time my father's full-time commitment to the reputable but precarious life of an artist with a needle and thread. My father did not climb down from an impoverished mountain in southern Italy and forsake the glorious lights of Paris and sail thousands of miles to the more opportunistic shores of America to end up as a poor tailor in Ocean City, New Jersey.

So he diversified. Advertising himself as a ladies' furrier who could alter or remodel old coats as well as provide resplendent new ones (which he obtained on consignment from a Russian Jewish immigrant who resided in nearby Atlantic City), my father expanded his store to accommodate a refrigerated fur storage vault and extended the rear of the building to include a dry-cleaning plant overseen by a black Baptist deacon who during Prohibition operated a small side business in bootlegging. Later, in the 1930s, my father added a ladies' dress boutique, having as partner and wife a well-tailored woman who once worked as a buyer in a large department store in Brooklyn.

He met her while attending an Italian wedding in that borough in December 1927. She was a bridesmaid, a graceful and slender woman of twenty with dark eyes and fair complexion and a style my father immediately recognized as both feminine and prepossessing. After a few dances at the reception under the scrutiny of her parents, and the frowns of the saxophone player in the band with whom she had recently gone out on a discreet double date, my father decided to delay his departure from Brooklyn for a day or two so that he might ingratiate himself with her. This he did with such panache that they were engaged within a year, and married six months later, after buying a small white house near the Ocean City beach, where, in the winter of 1932, I was born and awoke each morning to the smell of espresso and the roaring sound of the waves.

My first recollection of my mother was of a fashionable, solitary figure on the breezy boardwalk pushing a baby carriage with one hand while with the other stabilizing on her head a modish feathered hat at an unwavering angle against the will of the wind.

As I grew older I learned that she cared greatly about exactness in appearance, preciseness in fit, straightness in seams; and, except when positioned on a pedestal in the store as my father measured her for a new suit, she seemed to prefer standing at a distance from other people, conversing with customers over a counter, communicating with her friends via telephone rather than in person. On those infrequent occasions when her relatives from Brooklyn would visit us in Ocean City, I noticed how quickly she backed away from their touch after offering cheek for a kiss of greeting. Once, during my preschool day I accompanied her on an errand, I tried to hold on to her, to put my hand inside the pocket of her coat not only for the warmth, but for a closer feeling with her presence. But when I tried this I felt her hand, gently but firmly, remove my own.

It was as if she were incapable of intimate contact with anyone but my father, whom she plainly adored to the exclusion of everyone else; and the impression persisted throughout my youth that I was a kind of orphan in the custody of a compatible couple whose way of life was strange and baffling.

One night at the dinner table when I casually picked up a loaf of Italian bread and placed it upside down in the basket, father became furious and, without further explanation, turned the loaf right side up and demanded that I never repeat what I had done. Whenever we attended the cinema as a family we left before the end, possibly because of my parents' inability or unwillingness to relate to the film's content, be it drama or comedy. And although my parents spent their entire married life living along the sea, I never saw them go sailing, fishing, swimming, and rarely did they even venture onto the beach itself.

In my mother's case I suspect her avoidance of the beach due to her desire to prevent the sun from scorching and darkening her fair skin. But I believe my father's aversion to the sea was based on something deeper, more complex, somehow related to his boyhood in southern Italy. I suggest this because I often heard him refer to his region's coastline as foreboding and malarial, a place of piracy and invasion; and as an avid reader of Greek mythology—his birthplace is not far from renowned rock of Scylla, where the Homeric sea monster devoured sailors who had escaped the whirlpool of Charybdis—my father was prone to attaching chimerical significance to certain bizarre or inexplicable events that occurred during youth along the streams and lakes below his village.

I remember overhearing, when I was eleven or twelve, father complaining to my mother that he had just experienced a sleepless night during which he had been disturbed by beachfront sounds resembling howling wolves, distant but distinct and reminiscent of a frightful night back in 1914 when his entire village had been stirred by such sounds; when the villagers awoke they discovered that the azure water of their lake had turned a murky red.

It was a mournful precursor of things to come, my father explained to my mother: his own father would soon die unexpectedly of an undiagnosed ailment, and a bloody world war would destroy the lives of so many of his young countrymen, including his older brother.

I, too, had sometimes heard in Ocean City at night what sounded like wolves echoing above the sand dunes; but I knew they were really stray dogs, part of the large population of underfed pets and watchdogs abandoned each fall by summer merchants and vacationers during the peak years of the Depression, when the local animal shelter was inadequately staffed or closed entirely.

Even in summertime the dogs roamed freely on the boardwalk during the Depression, mingling with the reduced number of tourists who strolled casually up and down the promenade, passing the restaurants of mostly unoccupied tables, the soundless bandstand outside the music pavilion, and the carousel's riderless wooden horses.

My mother loathed the sight and smell of these dogs; and as if her disapproval provoked their spiteful nature, they followed her everywhere. Moments after she had emerged from the house to escort me to school before her mile walk along deserted streets to join my father at the store, the dogs would appear from behind fences and high-weeded yards and trail her by several paces in a quiet trot, softly whimpering and whining, or growling or panting with their tongues extended.

While there were a few pointers and terriers, spaniels and beagles, they were mostly mongrels of every breed and color, and *all* of them seemed unintimidated by my mother, even after she abruptly turned and glared at them and tried to drive them away with a sweeping gesture of her right arm in the air. They never attacked her or advanced close enough to nip at her high heels; it was mainly a game of territorial imperative that they played each morning with her. By the winter of 1940, the dogs had definitely won.

At this time my mother was caring for her second and final child, a daughter four years my junior; and I think that the daily responsibility of rearing two children, assisting in the store, and being followed, even when we children accompanied her, by the ragged retinue of dogs—a few of which often paused to copulate in the street as my sister and I watched in startled wonderment—drove my mother to ask my father to sell our house on the isolated north end of the island and move us into the more populated center of town.

This he unhesitatingly did, although in the depressed real estate market of that time he was forced to sell at an unfavorable price. But he also benefited from these conditions by obtaining at a bargain on the main street of Ocean City a large brick building that had been the offices of a weekly newspaper lately absorbed in a merger. The spacious first floor of the building, with its high ceiling and balcony, its thick walls and deep interior, its annex and parking lot, provided more than enough room for my father's various enterprises—his dress shop and dry-cleaning service, his fur storage vaults and tailoring trade.

More important to my mother, however, was the empty floor of the building, an open area as large as a dance hall that would be converted into an apartment offering her both a convenient closeness to my father and the option of distance from everyone else when she so desired. Since she also decorated this space in accord with her dictum that living quarters should be designed less to be lived in than to be looked at and admired, my sister and I soon found ourselves residing in an abode that was essentially an extended showroom. It was aglow with crystal chandeliers and sculpted candies in silver holders, and it had several bronze claw-footed marble-topped coffee tables surrounded by velvet sofas and chairs that bespoke comfort and taste but nonetheless conveyed the message that should we children ever take the liberty of reclining on their cushions and pillows, we should, upon rising, be certain we did not leave them rumpled or scattered or even at angles asymmetrical to the armrests.

Not only did my father not object to this fastidiously decorative ambience, he accentuated it by installing in the apartment several large mirrors that doubled the impression of almost everything in view, and also concealed in the rear of the apartment the existence of three ersatz bedrooms that for some reason my parents preferred not to acknowledge.

Each bed was separately enclosed within an L-shaped ten-foot-high partition that on the inside was backed by shelves and closets and on the outside was covered entirely with mirrors. Whatever was gained by this arrangement was lost whenever a visitor bumped into a mirror. And while I never remember at night being an unwitting monitor of my parents' intimacy, I do know that otherwise in this domestic hall of mirrors we as a family hardly ever lost sight of one another.

Most embarrassing to me were those moments when, on entering the apartment unannounced after school, I saw reflected in a mirror, opposite a small alcove, the bowed head of my father as he knelt on the red velvet of a *prie-dieu* in front of a wall portrait of a bearded, brown-robed medieval monk. The monk's face was emaciated, his lips seemed dry, and as he stood on a rock in sandals balancing a crosier in his right arm, his dark, somber eyes looked skyward as if seeking heavenly relief from the sins that surrounded him.

Ever since my earliest youth I had heard again and again my father's astonishing tales about this fifteenth-century southern Italian miracle worker, Saint Francis of Paola. He had cured the crippled and revived the dead, he had multiplied food and levitated and with his hands stopped mountain boulders from rolling down upon villages; and one day in his hermitage, after an alluring young woman had tempted his celibacy, he had hastily retreated and leaped into an icy river to extinguish his passion.

The denial of pleasure, the rejection of worldly beauty and values, dominated the entire life of Saint Francis, my father had emphasized, adding that Francis as a boy had slept on stones in a cave near my father's own village, had fasted and prayed and flagellated himself, and had finally established a credo of punishing piety and devotion that endures in southern Italy to this day, almost six hundred years after the birth of the saint.

I myself had seen other portraits of Saint Francis in the Philadelphia homes of some of my father's Italian friends whom we occasionally visited on Sunday afternoons; and while I never openly doubted the veracity of Francis's achievements, I never felt comfortable after I had climbed the many steps of the private staircase leading to the apartment and opened the living room door to see my father kneeling in prayer before this almost grotesque oil painting of a holy figure whose aura suggested agony and despair.

Prayer for me was either a private act witnessed exclusively by God or a public act carried out by the congregation or by me and my classmates in parochial school. It was not an act to be on exhibition in a family parlor in which I, as a nonparticipating observer, felt suddenly like an interloper, a trapped intruder in spiritual space, an awkward youth who dared not disturb my father's meditation by announcing my presence. And yet I could not unobtrusively retreat from the room, or remain unaffected or even unafraid as I stood there, stifled against the wall, over-hearing during these war years of the 1940s my father's whispered words as he sought from Saint Francis nothing less than a miracle.

HOBOKEN
THREE CIRCLES OF LIGHT
Pietro di Donato

Our third-floor-right flat had four high-ceilinged, narrow rooms: the meagerly furnished front room with two windows looking out to Central Avenue, two bedrooms that received stale glimmers of day from an ever-dank light shaft, and the kitchen.

The kitchen was the heart of our home. On its Italian cooking smells alone one could have been nourished. On the wall between the wood- and coal-burning Richardson-Boynton black stove and the iron sink with only a cold-water tap was a garland of garlic and dried hot peppers. An open pantry held the jug of olive oil, sheaves of herbs, crocks of conserves, the twenty-pound box of spaghetti, salami and grating cheese wrapped in cloth, the round loaf of bread that had to be picked up with two hands, and the bottles of Pluto Water, Brioschi, and Fernet-Branca. On the opposite wall were an Italian calendar showing King Umberto and illustrated Saints' Days, the calendar of Ruppert's brewery and the coffee grinder. On a shelf were the glass-encased painted statue of the Madonna and Child and votive lights; above it the crucifix wreathed with palms. There was a gaslight, couch, and slate washtub, and on the floor was cheap linoleum, worn to its bare and tarred last layer. The two windows looked onto the clothesline, fire escape, and back yard.

Father's jacket was draped over a chair by the upright piano in the front room. In a pocket I found his straight razor. I tried to imitate his shaving, and sliced my cheeks. There was a sudden hot, red dripping from my face. I toddled through the shadowy railroad flat to my mother in the kitchen. She screamed, then quickly bathed my face from a bowl of water and salt. The salt burned wrigglingly in my wounds.

The vast tenement contained Jews, Irish, Italians, and Armenians. The labyrinthine hallway where the bogeyman hid was rank with the woolly smell of lamb-tail fat, onions, garlic, cabbage, cats' leavings, and garbage. Upstairs by the Armenian's door there were flat, wheel-like bread and leaf lard in a bag. I sent the bread rolling down the stairway, urinated through the balustrade like the big kids did, greased the banister with the lard, and rode the banister.

Father was in the front room with the piano teacher. She had fish-net black stockings, high-heeled shoes, a big-brimmed hat, and long earrings. She was sitting on Father's lap. He was kissing her and running his hand up and down her leg.

He barked at me: "I told you to stay in the kitchen. What the hell are you doing here?"

Pasty, dirty kids and clean, well-dressed kids snarled at me: "Wop, guinea, dago, Tony-Macaroni, Hey!—paesano!"

I did not know why they called me those names. I became aware of the people called paesanos whom I saw in our flat, in church, and in the food markets. It grew on me that I belonged to them, a people of Father's and Mother's own, a kind distinct from the cold American. And I felt a possessive, clinging love of my paesanos.

Father and Mother took me to someone's flat. There were people crying: "The job killed him, on the job he was killed. The job!"

There were flowers. A man was in a box. Everyone kissed him. They closed the box and took it downstairs to a carriage. We rode in a carriage to church. Outside the church they put the box with the man in it down in a hole and covered it with dirt.

Mother shouted to the women: "With our men building high walls for bread and wine we at home live in the shade of their death. Say we each day: 'Will my man come home this night alive?'"

I then acquired the word Death. It was a new word.

Summer meant sneakers and overalls, and long, smelly, sunny days with sweat-stained face and shaven head, and crowded streets, and brawling kids, and cuts and bruises, and horses' tails flicking flies, and at night the tormenting bed-bugs.

One itchy hot night the gaslight in the bedroom made leaping shadows on the yellow walls. Mother, her stomach large and swollen, was on the bed shouting. Father nudged me from the bedroom. The midwife La Smorfia, the witch with the twisted mouth, came to Mother. Mother gave out eerie yells and then was quiet. La Smorfia left a squalling new baby with Mother.

Winter meant white daggerlike icicles, frostbitten ears and stinging feet, and dashing to the cold, drafty seat in the unlighted hall toilet, and in the coal stove–warmed kitchen the sweetish lacteal manger fragrance of baby-soil and steaming, drying diapers that Mother made from rugged bags that said Atlas, Hercules, cement.

I slipped down the ice-covered tenement stoop, my head bounced stunningly on the stone steps, and my voice came from me with inarticulate alarm. High above me were Father's godlike cherry-olive face, jet waving hair, black eyes, and gleaming white teeth, and Mother's long brown hair and brown eyes, and fine gentle voice calling: "My son, get to your feet. Fear not and come to your mother."

People, places, and things were forming larger identities. From the veiled kaleidoscope of recall they appear on the screen of my mind, each claiming the importance of having lived.

Mother dragged me to the chicken store. There was sawdust on the floor; the windows were bleary with fowl spatterings, and the cages filled with white, speckled, brown and black, noisy cock-a-doodling, muttering, feathery-smelling chickens.

Mother poked about in a cage and pulled out a protesting chicken. She pinned its wings, blew the down apart from its breast and scrutinized and smelled its bottom.

Pleasant, round-faced, and silver-spectacled Mrs. Liebman weighed the cackling bird on a flimsily suspended scale. She spoke to Mother in Jewish, and Mother answered in Italian, but they understood each other. The market was cold. Mrs. Liebman wore men's work shoes, overalls, an army jacket, a shawl over her wig, and a man's fedora over the shawl.

Mr. Liebman was a titanic man with long, curling sideburns, a black silk skullcap, and a beard to his waist. He cut the chicken's throat with a shining razor; its blood polka-dotted the wall and its life was convulsively stopped. I was sorry for the chicken and rebelled sadly for it. When I was older I used to receive coins from Mr. Liebman at Shabbos sundown Friday evenings for turning on the gaslight and stoking the coal stove in the Liebmans' bare flat next to the market.

In the hand laundry, the Chinaman Mr. W. R. Wang gave me crinkly-paper-shelled lichee nuts that had exotic meat within. In Bachauser's pork store they gave me slices of rosy baloney and spicy liverwurst. Father drank bock beer in Tony's saloon, and I would stand on the brass rail and reach to the basket of crisp, salty pretzels. Goldberg's stationery had myriad penny candies under the curved glass showcase.

The store with the painted wooden Indian in front sold Father his corncob pipes, and his Prince Albert tobacco, and Royal Bengal Tiger Virginia cheroots. Sometimes he smoked a clay pipe and switched to Honest or Ivanhoe tobacco.

I was the despair of my parents for I was a daily and famous stray. When Mother forgot me during her ceaseless chores the door beckoned. I would quietly leave the flat, and wander and wonder at the world that everywhere awaited my eyes and ears. To the firehouse I would go, the firehouse with its wonderfully fancy brick walls, wide arched openings, shining red and brass wagons with ladders, canvas hose, pole hooks, tall rubber-tired wheels, the rich harness suspended in readiness, the magnificent white Arabian horses in their stalls, the alert Dalmatian, the ruddy firemen in their navy-blue suits, the polished brass sliding pole, all awaiting the alarming clang!-clangety-clang! that would send daring men rushing, hitching, and, reins in hand, shouting: "Let's go, boys!" and the spirited horses galloping and wagons careening to save flame-threatened lives and flats.

Time meant nothing. Many were the hours I stood on Lincoln Boulevard looking into the automobile salesrooms at the skinny, invincible, black Model T Fords, the great Winstons and Chandlers, the sporting Stutz, and the modest Chevrolets, seeing myself driving, driving, driving. I would watch the Assyrian with the parasoled cart cook hot dogs covered with kraut and mustard. He wore a straw hat, apron, arm-garters, and had a pocked face and white mustaches. For a penny the hokey-pokey man would give me a scoop of teeth-chilling lemon ice in a wax cup. When I saw a woman suckling her baby, I would stop to peruse, and after the baby had had enough I would continue my unplanned journey.

I would look into the Turnverein where the clean, pale, silent Swiss from the embroidery mills seriously lifted bar bells and flipped through gymnastics. And I was curious about the Turkish Social Athletic Club on Central Avenue with its lazy, fat, mustachioed, fez-topped Turks drinking coffee, smoking water pipes.

I wondered why the pawnshop had three golden balls, and what the candy-striped barber's pole was for. I would linger outside the Jews' church and the Turks' mosque, but was afraid to peek in. I had to check on the trolley barn, the reservoir, St. Michael's Monastery, the Palisades.

I could never find my way home; dusk would come and fearsome night, and I would be hungry, tired, and weeping in Union Hill, or Weehawken, or down near the meadows, or among the hurly-burly of ships and docks by the Hudson River in Hoboken, until some man or woman or officer kindly took me back to West Hoboken to our tenement where under the roof cornice raised letters said, "OMNIA LABOR VINCIT," and separating the words were naked tin caryatids on brackets with hands above heads upholding scrolled and tabled ornamentation.

Some scenes stay hidden, and then steal through my mind like recurring dreams.

I was near our tenement on Central Avenue, eating olive oil–soaked stale bread sprinkled with salt and oregano. The summer street was lined at the curbs with pushcarts, and there were stands outside the shops. On the steps of the Armenian coffee and nut store, the bushy-haired, mustachioed owner Mr. Saroyan sat remorsefully smoking his water pipe. Bowlegged Zio Camilli was basking before his grocery which displayed dried cod, an open cask of floating lupino beans, cylinders of lemon ice, cold watermelon, and wicker baskets of snails. The Turk Callipygian was sitting in front of his carpet and linoleum store chewing sunflower seeds. A fashionably dressed woman went into the curtained store where the fortune-telling gypsies lived.

On one corner was our dilapidated frame church and the cemetery of San Rocco. Opposite it on the other corner was Tony's paesano saloon. Vadi, the old fish peddler, stood by his seascape-painted cart wearing his tattered sea-captain's cap, apron, and leather cuffs. The umbrella man carried a grind-stone upon his back, ringing a large hand bell and crying that he would mend pots and sharpen knives. Mr. Smolensky stood out in the gutter before his rag and bone shop wailing that he would buy old clothes and junk. The music store a block away blared Victrola music from a megaphone. Vendors sang out singly and then in vying concert:

> "Garlic, delicious is my garlic-O!"
> "Peppers! Peppers to make your mouth dance, peppers!"
> "Ba-nann-as! Yes! Ba-nann-assss!"

Swiss cyclists from the Turnverein wheeled by. A Bulldog Mack truck with chain drive rumbled over the cobblestones, and then a brewery wagon pulled by immense Percherons. Mr. Nash, the friendly, stout policeman with the gray walrus mustache, plodded slowly along. Old women leaned elbows upon pillows and cushions at windowsills. Seminude children lolled on fire escapes by potted plants and draped pee-painted mattresses. Mothers squat-ted on stoops and chairs and boxes, suckling babies.

Beautiful Stella L' Africana, in a white blouse, red skirt, and yellow canvas slippers, saw me. She pinched my cheek. "Paolino, would you like to keep me company?"

I went with her to Zio Camilli's grocery, where she shopped and bought me a lemon ice. I carried the bag for her and followed her home.

TRENTON

Grace Cavalieri

Trenton had no meaning until I did. From mortality the city rose, a creative force from streets, an eminent domain following me the long way home. Did we dream we could live without streets always changing? Can we forget the silent suppers of the family, the sweep of a bridge outside of town? TRENTON MAKES THE WORLD TAKES. Hard rubber, steel wires, fixed systems, shining objects, smoke stacks of brick, interrupting a flow in the hurry toward my own motion. I left its streets determined by need, and was taught the world, the flesh, and the devil in the Blessed Sacrament Church—begging for permission to take part in the rites, a body aching to sing its own prayers. Cadwalder Park, Junior Three, the Strand Theater, the Hermitage Library. We were safe everywhere we went, except within. A family, a bank, an Italian restaurant on South Warren Street were the human commitments. Seeing from there, who were those grandparents we came through who would not speak the language, and, what is a house, or a business but a consciousness which goes outward. The courage of childhood filled the crown of my head . . . pantries, stale bread crusts for stuffings, sewing machines, dust, buckets on the back porch, one for starch. What is the heart of it since everything assigned will soon be forgotten—japonica, snowball, forsythia, hyacinth, in the back yard, middle-class flowers—Queen Anne's lace by the tracks carried in a basket, in a scarf, in a bottle, for the Virgin Mary's altar in May. We didn't know it was a journey. We thought Trenton was a street with sidewalks, and telephones with party lines. A bus took us everywhere all week, for a dollar pass, on roads not under construction, on a trip without interruption. Streets go farther and farther when we change our position, like a story that exaggerates each time we tell it. Time was just a notion, a layer to go through for Aunt Rosie, who wasn't allowed to marry the soldier from Ohio, or the policeman from Chambersburg, because they weren't Italian. What is left of her now that time has collected her, digging the self out of the body, leaving her soul still singing in its wheelchair. Then who *should* we be talking about, saying, always saying more than we're asked. My great uncle took a fall for the crooks so he could live in a rich house on the river, near a tree stuttering with cherries on a hill. Little Al ran in from the playground to suck on Aunt Maggie's breast. Uncle Joey was drunk again on New Year's Eve, listening to *Amapolla* seeing facets of himself in different people, thinking it was himself. They are angels riding the crest of my porch wearing plaid shirts and high-topped shoes dazed with their own light, endowing, even now, our lives with meaning. My father was an honest banker, Jesus Christ to the Italians. He'd stop his work to read them mail from the old country. My mother was as natural as the breath that comes from sleep. She never sang but was the sweetest sound I'd ever heard. Did they know they were part of my blueprint—my father, with his code of perfection, from whose reduction, I learned freedom—my mother who had no walls, from whom I'd learn form . . . Shad and Moon Mullins ran numbers on Broad Street. They won't remember you, they are our plebiscite of spirits and ghosts. While we wait for their voices only the chimney hears the wind. How can something as dark as death give off so much light? These thoughts are not divided the way rooms are, the way roads are. They burn like hot grease on the stove smoking in us forever, like a message to be delivered. Then, what is there to keep on this map with old folds—voices, storms, the wind, the silence, the sun, worn clothes, dead people, rooms sealed off, wallpaper with roses dripping blood on the bed. To make our lives matter, we create cities which are holy. We create Trenton as memory. So that we can be awake before we die, we build the city as a place for thanks. Then we invent eternity so we will always have a home.

MONTCLAIR MEMORIES
PERSONAL REFLECTIONS AND
AN ORAL INTERVIEW

Marisa S. Trubiano

Everyone called him Benny, but his name was Baldassare. He would work outside on the front lawn, pruning the bushes, or he would barbecue striped bass out back, basting it with the savory *ammogghiu*, oblivious to that heavy, humid air of Ocala that weighs down on you and makes you gasp for breath sometimes. Central Florida always seemed to me to be a strange place for my grandfather to have chosen to retire, with its temperamental weather and warily cheerful residents, its isolated and airless feel. I can still picture his smile, the crackle of his dentures when he laughed or chewed, and his taut, wiry muscles as he worked. Though some of his acquaintances might underestimate him because of his broken English, Baldassare was a perceptive man with sharp business acumen, who could spot a swindler, even amongst his own kin.

Baldassare had survived a French concentration camp during the Second World War, and had been a bricklayer for years. He was tireless, unbeatable, indestructible. In the Florida heat he wore khaki pants and a white undershirt, and I remember that with his big, rough hands, he would point out some new surgical scar on his dark red-brown chest, tracing it as though it were a precious mark on a treasure map. That scar was proof that Baldassare, determinedly cheerful, had weathered yet another stormy voyage. Upon coming to this country after the war, my grandfather traveled wherever the construction jobs were most plentiful, laying bricks in Brooklyn, Long Island, even out in Arizona. He would always give my father, a bespectacled chemist-turned-handyman, advice on home repair jobs, like the placement of bricks on the front steps, the pouring of cement for the sidewalk, the pruning of the rosebushes from Brooklyn or the big pine tree in front of the house. I still remember the laughs we had when, because of their enthusiastic efforts, the pine tree almost ended up half shorn of its branches. When I go home to central Jersey, I always notice that some of my grandfather's rosebushes still manage to weather the elements and the neglect. One winter, in January, two roses bloomed defiantly above the snow.

Montclair Memories

Though he lived in Florida, while I was growing up, I used to think about my grandfather when we visited other relatives in the old Italian neighborhoods in the Bronx or Brooklyn. It might have been because I knew that the carefully laid brick façades of those apartment buildings had been built by hands like his. I think of him now, when I look at my brother who so much resembles him as a young man, and as I listen to the stories of the Italian American residents of my new home, Montclair, New Jersey. They speak about their great-grandparents and grandparents who built the buildings on and around Pine Street and Glenfield Avenue, since the late 1880s, a working class Italian neighborhood. "Life is work," say the parents' gesturing hands in Felix Stefanile's poem "Wedding Photograph, 1915," and like all the other ethnic groups whose contributions built this country with their bare hands, the Italians played an important role. I feel particularly fortunate to have the opportunity, through this oral history project, to accompany the Montclairions of Italian descent as they revisit their families' histories and experiences. The project was aligned with my Italian American Experience Course from Spring 2002. It is also an important part of the Montclair State University Community Outreach Partnership Center initiative, whose community heritage documentation component aims at recording the history of the Pine Street and Glenfield Park neighborhoods of Montclair.

Many Italian American women quite literally created and tended the fabric of the community: Ruth Kunstadter's grandmother was an accomplished seamstress, Maryann Zecchino's grandmother sewed and took in boarders, Lena Ostella's and Mary De Carlo's mothers worked in a sewing factory, Alda Francalancia's mother worked at the flag company, and her sister was a dressmaker. The first Italian men to arrive in Montclair worked on the public works projects, like the excavation of the town's water supply and sewer lines, and the laying of track for the railroads. Italians were involved in the construction of Montclair, from its foundations up. Anna Chevralotti's grandfather worked in the quarry, and later lit the gas lamps in Glenfield Park. Her father was a contractor, truck driver, and laborer, doing cement work, and later, he joined a union, as did Angelina Marzullo's father and Mary De Carlo's father, a mason. Donato Di Geronimo's grandfather was a laborer and worked for the Township, and Marge Galioto's grandfather was a gardener, a landscaper, and worked for the Immaculate Conception Cemetery on Grove Street.

Marge Galioto recounted the story of her family during the summer of 2002 to Pasquale Pontoriero, a student of Montclair State University. Numbers in parentheses refer to page numbers in the interview transcript.

In the late 1880s her maternal grandfather, in his twenties, came to the United States from Acri Cosenza, in Calabria. He was first accompanied by his wife, but then they returned to Italy. Eventually, he came back alone to Poughkeepsie to work on the railroad. Some of his stepbrothers settled in the Northeast, others in Colorado. Marge recalled that her grandfather dug ditches and dragged stones, and that, as a foreign unskilled laborer, he was not, to her knowledge, represented by any union. When he called his wife and daughter over, they settled in an apartment on Bay Street in Montclair, New Jersey, by the railroad tracks. They later bought the apartment, along with other property. Her grandfather was to live in Montclair for the rest of his life.

> They [my grandparents] probably had cousins, somebody that they knew from back home settled there, and they would come and my grandfather must have rented a room in someone's house when he was here by himself, somebody that he knew, a relative's friend, cousin, whoever that was here before him would rent a room. He would work until he saved up enough to bring his wife over to get their own apartment. That's how that was done.
>
> They came here with nothing. My grandmother knitted and crocheted and made beautiful lace tablecloths and curtains and bedspreads. She made a separate one for each of her daughters. And now we still have it. We have a lot of plates that she made.
>
> [My grandfather] was a laborer. When he came over here, what he finally did was landscaping and he worked at the Immaculate Conception Cemetery on Grove Street in Montclair, and then he had a little side business. He would maintain people's lawns and flowerbeds, so to say that he was a gardener would be the best that I could do at this time. That's what he basically did. He was a landscaper.

An important point of reference for the Italians of Montclair was the parish of Our Lady of Mount Carmel, their place of refuge after they had been turned away from the other predominantly Irish Catholic parish.

> They would have the feasts. It was a big thing. He [my grandfather] would participate, he would help carry the saint and go for the entire

day walking around. He and my grandmother, my aunts, my mother, of course, all participated too, because I was born and raised for the most part on Bay Street. We all participated. I still go to that church, my grandparents went there, my mom still goes there, and I still go there. It's a rebuilt church on the grounds that was taken down and about seventy-three years ago they built the church you see today, and my grandfather, as did the other members of the church, donated their time . . . whatever they could do, whatever skills they had to help build that church as well, so he did participate in that church.

The children's education was important, and Marge recalled her school years and the camaraderie among classmates that has endured through time. Her memories of growing up in Montclair revolve around those friendships and parish activities. The feast came up frequently during the interview.

I started out at Glenfield School, which is right across from Bloomfield Avenue. And in second grade, they started early to Mount Carmel School, but they hadn't bought a school. They had an apartment building on the parking lot where you see it now, it has since been knocked down so in second and third grade, I think, we attended school with the nuns in an apartment building. . . . They didn't have enough nuns so second and third grade had a school together and first and kindergarten and every year they would add another grade.

I have friends then that I still have now, which is pretty unique. I grew up with them and they all kind of stayed, not in the Montclair area, but in the surrounding towns, so I went to kindergarten with people that I still see today.

Saturday afternoons we helped out at home first, cleaning and stuff; the afternoons, a lot of the time, we would go and set the church up, the altar, help the nuns change the linens and get everything ready for Mass on Sunday. The feasts were very exciting for us. It was a big time because they had the rides and games, and food, and everyone got together. They had a singer at night and they'd start to put the decorations up in the street a week or two before and people would be getting all excited. A lot of people would have family over on that Sunday of the feast; everybody had their own family party, so there was a lot of cooking and baking involved. It was good. I don't have any bad memories.

Communicating in English was essential, and Marge's grandfather learned English from his five daughters. Communication among some family members in many instances may have been limited, but the transmission of affection and respect never was.

Whatever they learned they picked up from their children; my mother, who was the youngest of the five daughters, spoke Italian at home and didn't learn English 'til she went to kindergarten, at which time that's where they all learned English; being so young they picked it up right away. And whatever they brought home and tried speaking to them, that's what they picked up. My grandfather would read the Italian newspapers and tried to read the English ones as well, and that's how they learned. From people they worked with, people they went to the store to buy something, you just picked it up as you went. They had no formal education or anything available to them to learn, other than from their children, for the most part. . . . And we could communicate—I communicated with my grandfather. He spoke broken English, but he knew what we were saying and we knew what he was saying. . . . I had other grandparents that did not speak as well and there was a communication barrier, as in particular with my father's father, but we were able to communicate with him.

For the most part, Italians did not venture forth toward the center of town, and their activities were restricted to the Bay Street, Glenridge Avenue, Pine Street, and Sherman Street area. There were some limited interactions with other ethnic groups. In Marge's accounts, they appear to have been motivated mostly by commerce and trade.

At times [Italians interacted with other ethnic groups]. There were some Jewish people: Jewish store owners, which was pretty amazing, and anyone who lived in my areas will tell you there was a store on Bloomfield Avenue called Welenskis': Louis Welenski, and he had brothers. They had a dry goods store; you can go get all kinds of clothes there: work clothes, pajamas, anything you needed, and they were Jewish, they spoke Italian, fluent Italian. My grandmother spoke no English, or very little because she stayed home and raised the kids, so she didn't have co-workers where she would pick up a little more of the language; of course, from her daughters she did. . . . But they spoke fluent Italian so there was no communication problem in doing business with those people and they were wonderful people. They just closed their doors not long ago. But, yes, and then there was Mr. Kohn's, who was the grocer on Glenridge Avenue. He had a dry goods store, he and his wife, and I remember going down there with my mother buying his fruits and vegetables—and there was the chicken. Every Saturday you go there to get your chicken for Sunday dinners. Bakeries were all over. There was a Greek man who owned a bakery—Chris was his name—and there were other bakeries as well. It was an area, mostly made up of Italians; there were black people as well, and everybody kind of got along. Everybody minded their own business, there was nobody trying to break in your house because you didn't have any more than they did, so it wasn't a problem.

From the interview with Marge, the coordinates of the little Italy of Montclair start to delineate themselves and one can formulate a mental map of the area.

Pine Street ran parallel to Bay and the church was there, the convent was there, and the school was there for a short time. The people were the same on Pine Street as on Bay, or any other street. There were mostly apartment buildings on Pine Street, so you had all families living there and their children playing in the street, because nobody really had a big backyard. There was a park where Mountainside Hospital parking lot is now. It was a lovely park. We used to play there a lot. And the trains would always be going by.

We went to Glenfield School, but never ventured that far up [Glenfield Park] to go to the park to play. We played in our backyards or in front of the houses or in the park right on Bay Street. But no, we never went to Glenfield Park to play. Never had to. We couldn't go that far from home. Get hit by a car or someone could steal you.

Certain traditions remained constant throughout the family's development, especially the Christmas gathering and the feast days of Saint Joseph and Saint Anthony. Some traditional recipes were a cornerstone to the commemorative holidays.

Well, the usual macaroni, homemade pastas, stuff like that, certain baked goods, although my aunts did a lot of baking and that tradition has come down to us. The usual, nothing different than anyone else would have had. We made gravy because my grandfather had a large tomato garden so that was a fun thing. My grandfather made wine every year.

Italy had a particular significance for Marge Galioto, as the source of those recipes and traditions, and the mythical homeland to which she returned many times. In her family's case, she and her sister were the first to start to address the trauma of separation first felt by her grandparents so many years before.

[Italy] was wonderful, it was a good feeling [to visit] because you just felt connected to the land, because that was where your grandparents came from so there was a connection. . . . I loved it, can't get enough; I would have loved to live there for a couple of years just to travel around and just soak in the whole culture of it all, because there is so much that you lose when the people came over here, I think. A lot of them maintained certain customs and certain traditions, but in their quest to Americanize, they must have dropped certain things or discontinued them, or maybe it wasn't their particular taste or fondness to do things that disappeared through the years. So you go back there and you see things and experience things that, you know, you connect to.

Sure, poverty abounds, a little wealth and beauty, but there is that need to survive and you need to do better. I'm sure they would have been okay out there, but maybe they didn't want okay. Maybe they wanted to do better, maybe they wanted to provide a little better, and the opportunity is here, though, you know, before the streets were paved with gold. . . . So they had these very high hopes and dreams and felt that they could go there and become millionaires . . . while it wasn't true, they wanted to do better for themselves and for their families, and why not? If you're a healthy person and you got to have a brain . . . you would like to improve your lifestyle, who wouldn't? I think that might have been a driving force.

Memories of the Second World War, experienced directly by Marge's family, were unforgettable. Such recollections call to mind the strange destinies that befell many Italian Americans: some returned to the idealized homeland which their predecessors had left behind, healing the original wounds of separation, while others died there, compounding the sense of loss that had been suffered generations before.

I was actually talking about this last night, as a matter of fact, with my parents. We were talking about how they would practice the air raids. People would go up and down Bay Street and all over, a couple of times a week. You'd have to shut your lights out. My mother said they'd have to just sit in the dark and wait for them. The sirens, she said, were scary and frightening. That she remembers and there was rationing, that they didn't have everything that they had before, people had to do without.

[My father], well, he traveled extensively. He worked for the engineering division and he drove trucks and what they would do is, they would fix the bridges after they were blown up or bombed and whether they were the ones to blow them up or the Germans blown them up, they would go there and prepare the bridges. And he spent, like I said, three or four years in France, Germany, and England and he tells his stories. . . . He never went back. My mother was afraid to fly. And now my dad is eighty-three and . . . [he] never went back after the war and he never went to Italy, and my father was born here, so he never saw Italy. The war did not take him into that area, it was very difficult for him. He never even visited there, unfortunately. He's Sicilian. His family comes from Sicily. I visited there as well and met his family and different people. . . . His family is from towns outside of Palermo: my grandfather from one town, and my grandmother is from another.

The conversation turned to the present oral history project and whether in Marge's estimation there is still a significant Italian American community in Montclair and what factors caused its transformation.

For the most part, it's not like it used to be, of course, but all things do change and it was awhile ago. . . . [The Italians of Montclair] didn't move out. Some of them just moved into a better area of Montclair. Why? Because I'll tell you why, they wanted their children to have better than they had. They had that area of Montclair—a lot of them were homes, like I say—the want on those people's part was to have their children educated and to go out and have their homes and whatever they wanted, and have a better life for themselves. And that's exactly what took place. So while a lot of people stayed in the Montclair area—Verona, Caldwell, Cedar Grove, Glenridge—a lot of them are in Montclair as well, but not in that area. That area was a little Italy and it was the poor part of town. If you were from the Fourth Ward, you were poor people. And then there was Montclair, and there was Upper Montclair and there were definite minds even, and I'm not that old, I'm forty-seven, no, I'm forty-eight, when I was going to high school, a lot of people, a lot of your students defined you by where you came from, and if you came from that part of Montclair, well, I don't want to call it labeling, but in a way it was. I had that experience; some of my friends didn't have that experience.

They wanted to raise their children in a single-family house kind of thing so you got away from the multiple dwellings, the apartment buildings, and everything else and that's what happened. Like I say, [in] the general area, there are single-family homes, but there are not a lot. There is two-family and multiple-family, some of them since have been knocked down, and condos have been put up or whatnot, but it dissipated because people improved their lifestyles. That's what I can tell you.

Marge expressed satisfaction that the history of the Italians of Montclair is finally being transcribed and recorded. The preoccupations with work, learning a new language, and striving for advancement had left little time for the luxury of indulging in reminiscences about humble, everyday living.

I think it's very good. I think it's nice. I think it's a special part of Montclair and I think that it was a special time and I think they [the Italians] were instrumental in how Montclair proceeded because they were an integral part of the town. They sent their children to school, they participated, they paid their taxes, they went to town council meetings, they tried to make their homes and their lives better. And thereby, I think, contributing in a positive way to Montclair . . . the people that came from that area, a lot of them became judges and doctors and many success stories for most people have gone on since bettering their lives and the lives of those they touch.

The interview concluded with Marge's observations about what remains of a person's life of work, and what it can mean for subsequent generations. Marge's simple words echo profound philosophical considerations about life's mysteries and the sense of immortality. The lives of our ancestors have never really ended; they are imprinted in every tree, every brick, and every word.

You should never forget where you came from. You should never let go of traditions your family has, because now they might not mean as much to you and you might think you may want to get away from a lot of them because they're old-fashioned, but you will notice that they become dearer and dearer to you and they have a significant meaning, because they are a part of your backbone and they are. They tell the story of what you become and you can't exclude the fact that if your parents were poor, whether they were this, whether they were that, you are because of them and so you always have to remember that. And you should be proud of who you are and where you came from . . . even the laborers that built the railroads and dug the ditches for the cemetery and that planted, put in trees—their work is still here as a testament to the fact that we're here, and what little labor they had, what little knowledge they had, their hearts are in that little tree, and in that little bush . . . and so it has its worth, and it's *all* to me. It's a very large part of the improvement to this world and I'm proud of it.

LITANIA FOR MY MOTHER'S HANDS
Edvige Giunta

Sewing the hem of her dress
knitting a sweater
with blue-and-white wool
in a Norwegian pattern for a Sicilian girl
writing a letter to daughters now *Americane*
to the granddaughter they no longer know
washing plates the ones for special occasions
with gold lines
the plates she keeps in the *sparecchiatavola*
(the chairs of the dining room falling apart)

dusting Capodimonte porcelain in the *salotto*
where her youngest practiced endless scales
on the piano she could not touch
the wedding gifts
luscious and preposterous
slicing eggplants for the evening's *parmigiana*
purple skin grace on the open garbage bin
wiping her forehead after spreading the sweet *astratto*
for the ragù reddish condensation of women's sweat

grating fresh pecorino on a steaming plate
(I no longer remember the smell)
spreading *nutella* (always Ferrero) on my brother's bread
thin generous slices of *pane di casa* from the bakery in the alley
wiping tears after he fell one story
broken head after dancing with the birds
blood spilling out his ears magnificent fountains

Litania for My Mother's Hands

picking oranges and tangerines parsley and basil
grading *dettati di prima elementare*
guiding the hands of first-graders
tracing awkward consonants and vowels on the lines
(how can English vowels be so different?)
paying bills
paying for an Alitalia ticket only to come back
dialing always new numbers zero one one three nine
(but that's what I dial, I don't know her numbers)
carrying her suitcase bus train plane

straightening her dress
fixing clothes fixing rooms fixing their lives
stirring the past simmering its smell
wrapping a packed box of almond pastries
for Catania Miami Southampton Schenectady North Brunswick
Jersey City
still sending their bounty
without restraint with sorrow
squeezing between sheets of rough brown paper
DO NOT SEND BACK IF UNDELIVERED
wringing the water from a silk Rinascente blouse
wringing sorrow
holding me rough softness on my face
a craving of their touch.

GARDENER
Edvige Giunta

for Cuciuzzo

He left
everything in order.
Neanche un filo d'erba, not a weed,
not a thread of grass.
Mother mourns the Sicilian garden.
Father hides behind words
that never betray.

Sixty-five years old when you died.
You were always sixty-five
and looking at your wrinkled face
I believed you were everybody's father,
including your wife, Carmelina,
who looked fifty at twenty,
withered by all those brothers
and clothes she washed in the *pila*
at the back of the house
with hard soap they don't sell in America.

In my aseptic condominium in Jersey City
washing machine and dryer
hide coyly behind white doors.
Carmelina's arms would be useless
in this country where clothes never
dance to the wind and clothespins
make only a rare, shy appearance
on a wooden rack in the bathtub
that quickly disappears into secret corners.

Gardener

I am one of the old Italians dying
in the poem, trapped
between the half-life of chromium
sites beneath my house,
the flowers of New Jersey and the peaches of Gela
that turned black in my youth.
Yes, I am one of the old Italians,
and the fumes are taking my breath away.

In America you always die young,
whether you're fourteen, forty-four
or eighty-four, all deaths garnering
equal grief.

I spell birthday in my head
and a voice chants: the old Italians are dying.
My birthday a deathday.
One week after your funeral:
I blow out the candles and thirty-eight worms
court your flesh in the old cemetery,
where the old dead make room for the new
in tight alcoves.

You tricked me, he says.
But who is the trickster, who, the magician?
And what if you don't know
the words that will undo your spells?
What if in the solitude of the Garden State
all you can smell is the aroma of death
and the only guests at your party
are the old Italians dancing
a tarantella inside your heart?

A TRIP HOME

David Della Fera

He stood at the back door collecting drizzle on his hat brim and overcoat, bulging K-Mart bags dangling from his hands. He had forgotten bus fare for the ride home; was my father around?

We wound through Branch Brook Park, the cherry blossom trees bare and shiny with rain. The crackling of plastic bags buried the low hum of the radio as Italo pulled out each item and checked it against the long receipt: Tylenol boxes, film containers, jumbo Hershey bars, Marlboro cartons, economy packages of Wrigley's. With pride he had told me the details of the flight, proved them by taking the ticket out of his coat pocket several times to show me: Alitalia flight 832, leaving Newark at 9:30 p.m. next Friday. Bags in lap, he was poised to curry favor with the natives by awing them with this bounty of American purchasing power.

"Thirty-two years I waited," Italo said. "That's longer than you've been alive. *Dio mio*, I'm old." He cackled at his quip and sent a volley of spittle onto the windshield and my right arm.

I pulled a right at Franklin Street since the old way through North Sixth was no longer safe because of angry kids in hateful neighborhoods. Before I started kindergarten my father had moved us out of Newark and across the river to Arlington as part of the exodus following the riots. We used to live next door to Italo and his sister, my father's paesani.

"Everything will be different. *Il Terremoto* destroyed the whole town. They say I won't recognize it."

I had never heard any of the old men call Italo by his name when he wasn't around. He was known as Giofecco, a nickname I think means the junk at the bottom of a bottle of bad wine. My father had grown apart from him during the past few years. Italo had remained on North Twelfth Street, never bought a car, never married. We had moved to a nicer town and spoke English at home; we had made it to the middle class on a machinist's salary.

"Do you remember living on Twelfth Street?" he asked.

"I remember little things. I remember our apartment, Zia Carmela's apartment"—he crossed himself—"I remember the bonfires in the yard for San Giuseppe."

He waved me silent. "You were small, a little boy. It used to be nice. Everybody's dead." He laughed. "That's life, you know."

We crossed Bloomfield Avenue and entered the North Ward with its two- and four-family apartment houses crouched together with little room to breathe. We passed my old house, a red brick fortress that was more familiar to me from home movies than from memory. I parked the Cavalier in Italo's driveway and helped him out. He winced at the tight squeeze between the door and the bushes and brushed down his overcoat with his hands. Outside of summertime I never saw him dressed in anything but tie, vest, and jacket, an old-time tailor's proud stance against the conquest of casual clothes for adults. He turned to me and grabbed my hand. "Leave the bags in the car," he whispered. He answered my puzzled look with a finger to his lips and a nod toward the front door. His sister stood partially concealed behind it, eyeing us both. Her hair was still a rusty red with only a hint of gray, her round pale face splashed with freckles, characteristics I imagined passed down from some Vandal invader raping an ancestral plebeian centuries earlier.

I followed Italo barehanded. He walked slowly, as though her gaze weighed him down until his chin grazed his chest.

We stood in the lobby, his sister forcing a rectangular smile over clenched dentures.

"*Come sta*, signora?"

She clasped her hands in front of her. "*Bene.* I haven't seen you in so long. How is your family?"

"They're fine."

The smile disappeared as she turned to Italo, his hands tapping the sides of his thighs.

"And you? Where have you been?"

"At Angelo's house. I took the bus."

Her face tensed. Italo looked down at his feet, over to mine, to the bottom of the door. She smiled again.

"And he made you take him here? He's a crazy old man."

I chuckled. "No, signora. He has pictures I want to see. Pictures of Calabritto. When he and my father were boys."

"Ah yes, pictures."

Italo held his hat in his hands, examining the inside as if he were looking for a place to hide.

"You can give him something to eat?" Her voice stung. Italo looked up, surprised and slightly angered.

"Of course. Of course."

"I'm not very hungry."

She ignored me. "Go upstairs, then. Go get the pictures." She stood in the lobby as the pounding of our footsteps echoed through the stairwell. I heard her apartment door close after we went around the first landing and put my hand on the small of Italo's back to support his climb.

The apartment appeared exactly as I had remembered it: the rabbit-eared television in the corner, the ashtray on the coffee table, the brown couch bracing the blank white wall. I followed him into the kitchen and sat at the table as he removed his hat and overcoat in the adjoining bedroom. "I don't have too much to eat," he shouted to me. "You like tomatoes?"

"Yes." I opened the mini-venetian blinds behind me and watched underwear and t-shirts waving on the lines above the concrete backyards.

Italo shuffled into the kitchen, leaning slightly to the left, excited by his role as host. He pushed some strands of gray hair onto the top of his long oval head and stood with indecision.

"You sure you want tomatoes? I don't have too many things."

"I like tomatoes. With bread."

He nodded and instantly the kitchen swirled with the clanking of plates and knives, drawers open and shut several times, cabinets slamming closed and glasses clinking on the table. In his flurry he used three knives to cut one tomato and gave me four glasses for the wine, each a different size and shape, all coated with water spots and an occasional speck of dried food on the rim. As he hunched over the counter dousing the tomato slices with oil and oregano, I cleaned a small glass with my shirt and filled it halfway from the green gallon bottle of Carlo Rossi.

"Your father and I have known each other since we were kids." He held one hand parallel to the floor at his waist to show their actual size as the other slid the plate of tomatoes onto the table. I forked some into my plate as Italo stuffed a napkin into his shirt and pushed the bread and provolone my way. "One year apart. He went to work for the locksmith, I went to learn from the tailor. That was all there was. Unless you were an idiot. Then you learned to be a barber." He shrugged and bit into a hunk of bread and tomato, still speaking with a piece of crust pushing out of his cheek. "He was smart, your father. All the kids liked him. He had respect."

I nodded at the familiar boast I had often heard at home.

"Listen." His face became severe as he held his glass over the table. "We had nothing. *Nothing*. Then the war came." He shuddered theatrically and let out a moan. "Terrible." He gulped his wine. "Nineteen forty-four. The worst year. I'll never forget it. Ask your father. We had to climb the trees at night on the farmer's property to get figs." He cackled loudly. "Ask your father. We were hungry all the time. We climbed up the tree and ate the figs and there were ants all over them. Nobody cared!" He coughed as he laughed. "*Che miserabile! Che miserabile!*"

His laughter died down to hiccups after another glass of wine. "Have you ever been back?" I asked.

"Nineteen sixty-four, when my mother died. I was here for six years. My sister took care of her while she was sick. I sold the property and brought my sister here. She didn't want to come." He shrugged. "Now it's different. The earthquake destroyed everything. It's all new, except for the mountains." He paused. "If it wasn't for work, I never would have left."

When the tomato plate was empty I declined his offer to make coffee. He cleaned the table as noisily as he had set it, wrapping the tablecloth and unfurling it out the window to free it from crumbs.

I followed him through the living room. He drew open the folding doors to another room and turned on the single bare bulb in the ceiling. Cardboard boxes and black trunks were stacked waist-high around the walls, some covered with white sheets. I watched as Italo put on his glasses and bent over the boxes, touching their sides to divine their contents, then moving on. He pulled out one and dragged it across the floor to my feet, excitement spreading across his face. He brought two folding chairs over and we sat opposite each other looking down into a box filled with papers and loose photographs. He seemed to forget about me as he quickly peered into folders and envelopes, discarding each on the floor before digging in again. He plucked a little green book and flipped through the pages before handing it to me. "My passport when I came to America." I caressed the leather cover with my thumb and flipped it open. The script in it was faded. I stared at the picture of Italo, here a young man in black-and-white, an aura of darkness around his head like you see in many old photos. His face was serious and somber, possessing the cocksuredness that with age transforms into a sort of comic criminality. "You were handsome," I said. "Like a mafioso."

He laughed. "Like a donkey." We sorted through many photos of unsmiling people whose names and relations to us both were rattled off and quickly forgotten. I was eager to see a picture of my father as a boy. The earliest one I had ever seen was his own passport photo, taken when he was twenty-two.

Italo's face brightened behind his bifocals. "Here he is." He handed me a creased square of cardboard with a yellowed scalloped border. A vaguely familiar boy stood in front of a doorway wearing Our Gang knee-highs and a dirty ruffled shirt. He frowned distrustfully into the camera. I loved it.

"He was twelve years old. 1945. The war just ended. The American soldiers took pictures. I don't remember how I got this one. Take it."

We spent another hour poring over the contents of that box, Italo bringing a story to every new face. The doorbell rang several times. Italo let it continue without getting up, then dropped a handful of pictures into the box. "That's my sister. Excuse me." I helped him out of his chair. "Take anything you want."

I paced around the room, glancing into boxes, poking behind chairs and trunks. I found a small parcel of newspaper clippings on a shelf, tied together with string like a cake box. The carefully cut articles were brittle and brown with age. Headlines celebrated the 1982 World Cup team; a dozen or so announced the devastation of the 1980 earthquake. Others went further back: Joe DiMaggio at the Newark Columbus Day parade in 1976; a profile of my father's and Italo's social club, dated June 7, 1969. In the center of the papers I felt something hard, about a quarter-inch thick. I pulled out a stack of long cards tightly bound with a rubber band. I flipped through them with my thumb. Some were fairly new, some faded, but all contained the same type of information: Alitalia flight 773, departing from Newark June 6, 1994; Alitalia flight 467, departing October 14, 1993; flight 1061, July 12, 1990; 277, August 20, 1987; June 1983; May 1981; 1979; 1976; 75; 71; 68. All unused. I stroked the edges gently with my fingers. The buzz of his sister's angry voice rose in the stairwell. I rewound the rubber band around the tickets and placed them back on the shelf, covering them with a newspaper page screaming "*Moro Assassinato.*"

Italo walked through the front door, sagging with the weight of the K-Mart bags. He turned into his bedroom without looking my way. I heard a closet door creak open and shut. He reappeared in the living room, pale and frowning slightly, eyes averted like a boy just scolded for stealing the neighbor's figs. He seemed to shrink into himself, fading into the heavy silence.

"These pictures are great."

He looked up and smiled. He walked into the room and stood over me.

"I knew you would like them. Take whatever you want."

"Just this." I held up the picture of my father as I rose.

"Those were different times. When I go back I'll remember everything."

A Trip Home

He stood outside his door to watch me leave. "Come again. Next time I'll have a nice lunch for you." I waved before turning down the next flight. The steps creaked as I approached the door of his sister's apartment. I could sense her body pressed behind it, listening for my exit, all that heat and anger impossible to conceal. I hurried out into the light rain and tucked the photo in my jacket pocket before making a dash for the car.

Paterson, the Alpha & the Omega

1915

MILL SONG

William Harry Harding

It wasn't paved with gold. It wasn't even clean. America was smokestacks.

Great clouds, as dark as the burning coal that made them, spewed from brick chimneys one hundred feet tall. Those round red towers got ever narrower from base to top, like giant fingers of a woman's hand, so slender and graceful any sculptor would have been proud to have carved them. Letters had been painted one below the other down the full height of the tallest chimney:

M
A
S
T
E
R

It was the right one. The one he had come so far to find. In places here along the river, summer sky leaked through, as if winking in the smoke. So different from the pale color of his home sky, this blue was dark and cold. Even in the late June heat, America's sky made him shiver.

And cough. His best suit of clothes, his only white shirt, his only tie, would be grimy with soot in less than an hour if he stayed outside on the streets. He wanted to go back to his mountains in Campania. He fought tears. He cried too easily. His father had told him that and his mother had said nothing to dispute it. Twenty years old and he still cried like a little boy. The Americans would laugh at him. It was a mistake to come to this filthy place.

From his jacket, he took the letter his uncle the mayor had written inside the train station at Avella. He had read the short note hundreds of times— on the train to Naples, on the boat across the Mediterranean and the Atlantic, on the hot island in the harbor where the Americans kept everyone from everyplace, on the train from New York to here, Paterson—and by now, he could recite the words, but he could no longer enjoy them. By now, reading the letter only meant more waiting. He would be glad to get rid of it, as grateful as he had been months before to receive it. He matched the letters on the paper to those on a sign nailed to the mill: MASTER DYE & FINISHING. He crossed the wide street, his note bending in a breeze off the water, and opened the front door.

The skinny woman at the desk inside asked him the same thing every officer had asked at every point in his travels: "Your papers?"

He reached for his wallet, then stopped. He would not show this woman his papers. She didn't wear a uniform. He held out the letter and tried to sound like the mayor: "Mr. Galli, please." Not a question, an order. "Give orders to those who take orders for a living," the mayor had told him, "and ask questions only of those who give the orders." The woman squinted and snatched the letter from his hand. Her eyebrows got busy. She shook her head, as if she couldn't read Italian. She must have been able to, because she handed back the letter without looking up and said in an accent he could barely understand—Piedmontese?—"Upstairs in the office."

The stairs had not been swept. Halfway up, noise from machines came through the walls. At the head of a long hall, he found another desk, but no one sitting behind it. He knocked on the first door. Inside, someone grumbled. He turned the knob and walked in. "Mr. Galli?"

Salvatore Galli didn't get out of his big chair. He wasn't fat like the mayor. He had a young man's body with an old man's face. He took the letter. He read the signature first, and his surprise turned into a sour smile. He studied the rest of the letter, and that smile did not get better. Finally, he folded the note. "So, August Zorzoli, what is the service your uncle claims you did for my niece?"

It had been a long time since August had heard anyone speak the dialect of his home. It made him smile. It made him want to like this man. He cleared his throat. "I escorted her home one night, when some soldiers were giving her trouble."

"You are a hero, then? All of Avella cheers you?"

He shook his head. He had done nothing more than take the girl by the arm and lead her out of the town, and the soldiers had been too drunk to follow or want to, those soldiers had thought the whole thing called for another drink.

Galli's shoes had been freshly shined. His palm smacked the little table beside his chair. "What was she doing out at night?"

"An errand for your sister."

The thin man laughed. "My sister could have sons if she married right."
He eyed the letter again. "Your Uncle Carlo is not the mayor of Paterson. I
don't have to do this."

Even when his uncle the mayor was asking a favor, it sounded like an
order. He had been the mayor too long. August nodded at the man in the
chair and turned to leave, happy he didn't have to put that letter back into
his pocket and protect it any longer.

"You read and write," Galli said, "like all the Zorzolis?"

The Zorzolis had been the town recorders ever since records were kept,
and in time, the townspeople had become dependent on the family for
everything from deeds to wills, and a Zorzoli had been the mayor as long
as anyone in Avella could remember. Even Zorzoli women were taught to
read and write. It used to be a town joke. Now it was only an oddity, of no
real importance. "Our language," August said, "and some Latin for the
law."

That smile again, as if those thin lips had touched wine too young to
drink. Small hands unfolded the letter, carefully, thoughtfully. I have two
sons. A few years older than you, I think. My mill goes to them. They must
agree before I give you a high position here."

"I only ask for a job."

Galli waved the note. "I'm not the stupid man your uncle the mayor
thinks. You work for me, I use your talents." He let his arm drop, and his
smile showed yellowing teeth. "And Galli pays you what you're worth."

He pushed out of his chair, told August to wait where he stood, and went
out and down the hall. It was hot up here. Through a dirty box window, he
could make out the summer river, low and full of silt. Moments later, Galli
came back. He fingered the letter. "My wife will like to keep this."

August made a shallow bow—his father's gesture anytime a woman was
mentioned in conversation. It made Galli cock his narrow head. He pock-
eted the letter, stepped to a low desk in a corner, moved papers to uncover a
tin box. Paper money inside, and coins. He picked out a large circle of silver,
put it in August's hand. "You get paid by the day, like everyone else. Go see
the girl downstairs, she'll show you the work. You have somewhere to sleep?"

The money felt warm. He shook his head.

"You sleep here, then. She'll find you a spot." The old man turned and
went back to his desk. "Find someone to teach you to read and write English
and you'll get two dollars a day instead of one."

1915: Mill Song

August couldn't move. He opened his hand, saw the shine of silver. Paid already, and he hadn't done a minute's work. It wasn't possible. He couldn't find his voice to say thank you.

"Be quick, Zorzoli," Galli told him without turning around. "Go earn your pay."

He ran down the stairs, eager to find paper and pen to write home and tell everyone, especially the mayor, about America, knowing they would not believe him.

It wasn't even work. It was numbers. And names that looked impossible to pronounce: Lawrence-Massachusetts, Harrisburg-Pennsylvania, Chicago-Illinois, Poughkeepsie-New York. It was like stealing. A dollar a day.

And the English everybody spoke was not the same language they wrote. One could be learned from anyone—mill workers, cooks, even children—or from books with drawings in them to show what the words meant in Italian and in English, and how they should sound. But the written language could be learned only from someone who knew how to read, write, and speak both English and Italian, because all the books on how to read and write English were in English. There must have been such people, but no one knew where to find them, no one had any use for them or the money to pay them.

For bills and orders, Galli had made up a system that got around the written language: he numbered the colors of his dyes. If the written order called for silk in "champagne beige," it was still color 08 to Galli, no matter what the Americans called it or how they spelled it. Simple. And it worked. There would not be a need to learn how to read and write English, only a need to copy the letters and match the numbers.

August got good at copying and matching, good enough to convince Galli that his new worker had learned to read and write the new language. August got a raise. Another dollar a day.

The corner of the upstairs hall of the mill Galli let him sleep in was fine for sleeping, but not for living. Inside of a week, August found a room in a house on River Street, twenty minutes by foot from the mill. The woman who owned it, Mrs. DeMatto, cleaned it daily, changed his sheets weekly, fed him twice a day, and for a small additional charge, washed his clothes once a week. The room was brown, with one small window facing the street. The curtains came from the mill, a gift from another worker who had lived here before he moved out for something bigger and better. This room, with its cot and chair and standing wardrobe, was bigger and better than the corner of the house August had called his own in Avella: this room had a door.

He kept his silver dollars in a box on the floor of the wardrobe. By winter, when the hot breeze off the street turned cold, he knew he would have to buy another box or a bigger one. He solved the problem by going to a storefront downtown where, for a fee, they would take his silver dollars and send them back to Avella. Galli had been doing it for years with no problems. August handed the clerk sixty dollars and the clerk gave him a receipt for fifty-four dollars that would be sent to Ferdinandi Zorzoli of Avella and should arrive within four months. August sent a letter to his uncle the mayor, advising him to watch for the money, but not to tell August's father or mother it was coming. It was to be a surprise. The letter would only take two or three months to reach the mayor. August couldn't wait to read the proud man's reply.

On the shiny table in the hall, catching light through the lace undercurtains, his name stood out on an envelope from home. The mayor's handwriting was as bold and careful as ever. Black lines from the post office ruined the large stamps. The letter felt dry, almost brittle. He worked a finger under the flap, pulled out the note.

The money had arrived safely, much sooner than expected. It had come at a time when his mother would need it. Ferdinandi Zorzoli had died in his sleep. Avella mourned him. If August had any money, he should send it to his mother. And if he had enough money, he should return home, where he was needed.

He took the letter up the stairs, unable to see the words. He saw his father dead in bed, his mother's steady tears, the priest and his cage of incense, the mayor leading the march to the grave. He saw his mountains. He wanted to go home, but knew he could not, it cost too much. If he could save enough, it would be better to bring his mother over here. America had been her idea. Her dream, for the last of her four sons. America did not have wars. Young men did not die there. But she would not come. He could beg her and she would not come. She would not leave the spot beside her husband's grave empty, she would fill it with her own body when the time came. His father was dead and August knew he would never see his mother again. This is what the mayor's letter meant.

He stared down at the black street the snow had broken, listened to the spring river race away from the rumble of the Great Falls. He wondered why he couldn't cry.

REBEL GIRLS
Jennifer Guglielmo

In September 1897, Maria Roda, an immigrant weaver in a Paterson silk mill and self-described socialist-anarchist, issued a statement in the local radical newspaper: "It is time that we also agitate and organize, to prove to the world that accuses us, that we too are capable of something." Addressing herself to "*le operaie,*" her sister-workers, she declared: "They say we are frivolous, that we are weak, that we are incapable of supporting the struggle against this intolerable society, that we cannot understand the ideal of anarchism. . . . But they are the cause of our weakness, our undeveloped intellects, because they restrict our instruction . . . and ignore us." The solution she proposed was for women to come together, "because we feel and suffer; we too want to immerse ourselves in the struggle against this society, because we too feel, from birth, the need to be free, to be equal."

I come across Roda's treatise in an archive in Minneapolis. I am working here to pay my way through graduate school, and in my off hours I sit atop a twelve-foot ladder in the back recesses of the storage facility and pore through boxes of delicate, yellowing letters, photographs, newspapers, poems, books, pamphlets, maps, and drawings—the belongings of another generation now long gone. I am in search of immigrant women's political culture, some trace of their activism, some history of visionary rebellion. This building, which used to be a coffee warehouse, is now home to one of the largest collections of archival materials in Italian American history, and especially radicalism.

It's Salvatore Salerno that finds Maria Roda. He comes to the archive daily too. He is the only other Italian American I really know in this city, and we share this obsession with tracking immigrant radicals, though not like the feds. Having grown up in one of the few Sicilian working-class families in Chicano East L.A. in the 1950s and 1960s, he revels when he finds out that Paterson's Italian immigrant anarchists not only hid out in Mexico to avoid and protest the draft during the First World War, but that the Mexican Revolution's radical newspaper *Regeneración* had only one page that was not in

Spanish, and it was in Italian. He notices Roda while uncovering this history of collaboration between Italian and Mexican anarchists because she was a part of this transnational radical world.

Sal finds me in my cubicle with a copy of her essay in hand, and another by Maria Barbieri, titled "*Ribelliamoci!*" (Let's Rebel!). We look at each other, speechless. He takes me to the microfilm he's been reading. There they are: Italian immigrant women's revolutionary testimonies, manifestos, letters, and essays. They begin with dramatic calls to action: "*Alle donne, emancipiamoci!*" (To women, we must emancipate ourselves!); and "*Alle mie sorelle proletarie*" (To my proletarian sisters). They are writing from their hearts, with little formal education. Many had immigrated as young women to work in textile mills and garment factories. As one woman by the name of Alba Genisio wrote, "I am not an intellectual, but the daughter of a discredited and oppressed people." This torrent of creative, powerful, and inspired radical prose by Italian immigrant women exists in only two U.S.-based newspapers: the "anarchist-socialist" Italian-language weeklies *La Questione Sociale* and *L'Era Nuova*, both from Paterson, New Jersey.

I take Barbieri's essay with me to my night job, waiting tables at a greasy spoon. When there is time in between tables, I translate the essay in the back, behind the wait station so the manager can't see me: "To my women comrades, these thoughts are dedicated to you, from another woman worker: It is the thought and palpitation of my soul in which I feel all the social injustices, that for centuries we have been humble and obedient slaves; I am a rebel who rises up against all these inequities, and I also invite you to the struggle."

I cannot contain my excitement. I start to read aloud to the other servers standing behind the station, and they laugh as my voice rises, "We must cast off these servile chains that a family, a society, a church have made us drag from remote eras!"

Later on I would learn that Barbieri was from West Hoboken, that she and her lover Sante (anarchists did not formally marry since they believed in *amore libero* or free love; that passion should not be corrupted by the state or the church) had buried a young son in 1903, after a pot of boiling water fell on him while she was out working in the mills. She would write about this, calling on her fellow "*madri proletari*" (proletarian mothers) to unite against the entire system of capitalism, which, she argued, took mothers away from their children, valued profit over human well-being, and filled one with hatred. "A struggle continues," she wrote, "each and every day, to pull out the deep roots that a false education has cultivated and nourished in my heart."

I have read these women's words aloud in a number of settings. The restaurant was the first, then over the phone to friends and family, and then before large glowing audiences. These rebellious "Jersey girls," with names like Teresa Ballerini, Ninfa Baronio, Gilda Bartolucci, Maria Teresa Brocca, Amalia Canova, Tobia Tavecchio, Maria Caruso, Adele Castelli, Ernestina Cravello, Anna De Gigli, Marietta Durante, and Maria Lucia Esposito, seem to fill the room whenever I say their names.

Telling their stories is for me all about recovery. When I went to college in the 1980s, I was told that these women did not exist. Yes, Irish immigrant women were feisty and rebellious, and Jewish women had a deep, rich, and vibrant tradition of radicalism. In these histories, and those of African American, Mexican, Chicana, Chinese, Korean, Puerto Rican, American Indian, Dominican, Jamaican, Japanese, and other women's struggles against the brutalities of colonialism, slavery, racism, and patriarchy, I learned a vision of liberation that was large enough to include all of humanity. But there were no Italian American women. In book after book I was told in polite *academese* that we did not have a history of revolutionary activism or culture. Sadly, Italian immigrant women and their American-born daughters had been largely dominated by excessively patriarchal men—or so the story went. They had not devoted lives to political activism, but instead to raising dozens of children, often attired in dark black clothes, and frequently whispering prayers to the Blessed Mother.

I know these women. I grew up all around them. Certainly they had been busy raising children, but they were also pretty fierce. They were nothing like the passive, reticent women I saw depicted within historical narratives. My eighty-two-year-old grandmother doesn't wear all black, at least not without her Versace shades, an eye-catching brooch, and an elegant, colorful scarf around her shoulders. When I comment on her sunglasses she says, "I treated myself. I never treat myself! I figured it was time. Right?"

She grew up in the Bronx, the daughter of Antonia and Francesco Paolo, immigrants from a small hill town outside Naples who sold fruit and vegetables, and took in boarders, to make ends meet. My grandmother would later write that her mother Antonia was "a non-conformist, a rebel." One of her many acts of resistance was "refusing to adhere to the traditional custom of wearing black mourning attire for months a time, which would have been incessant due to the numerous deaths of the family members in the twenties." As with many women of her generation, Antonia expressed her creativity with food, and my grandmother's memories of her culinary magic and their shopping sojourns, which often took them across the city and back, are vivid to this day. Antonia died suddenly from pneumonia when my grandmother was only thirteen. Soon after, she dropped out of school to work for her family, married at nineteen, and gave birth to eleven children. I was raised with her many stories of the intense, backbreaking labor it took to cook, clean, and care for so many, three of whom were in diapers at once.

The story that has always stayed with me, though, and taught me much about women's resistance, is of her collapse when she turned fifty. She would write about this during her period of recovery, when she returned to school: "I walked the streets of upper Manhattan for hours one night. I threw away my wedding ring. I had lost my identity. I finally phoned home and I was brought to Saint Vincent's Hospital to recover my sanity. I remember sitting in the recreation room reciting to myself the names of my children, one by one, so I wouldn't lose my hold on reality." Her breakdown occurred after a series of events that began with a visit from a friend. A Chinese-Hawaiian professor, who was a friend of my father's, came to spend several days with us one summer. A huge garden party at my grandparents' house was arranged in his honor: "The backyard was not a yard anymore—it was transformed into a beautiful garden with tables covered with red cloths, vases of flowers, and lighted candles. Thirty-five guests including the family and friends were dressed in their finest and after dinner the garden was filled with laughter, someone playing a guitar and all of us singing. It was like a story from a book—a memorable evening, never to be forgotten." In the course of the evening, the professor turned to my grandmother and asked a simple question: had she ever read Katherine Mansfield's *Garden Party*? After they saw him off at the airport, she came home and cried: "I had never communicated with anyone like that. I joined the library—for the first time in years. I couldn't wait to read *The Garden Party* and all the other authors my friend had suggested—Willa Cather, Virginia Woolf, and Cervantes among others. Reading would become a big part of my life. Besides cultivating my mind, I was cultivating my garden. This encounter led to the most important turning point in my life."

It was 1966. Everything was changing. She had five teenagers: a sixteen-year-old son in Vietnam, another struggling with his sexuality, and others also in deep crisis. She needed someone to talk to, someone to listen and help. "It took all my courage to visit a psychotherapist as someone suggested," she would recall, and Saturdays became her day to herself. She took the subway into the city in the morning to see her therapist, and then spent the rest of the day walking through the city. It was the first time in over sixteen years that she had a day to herself. It was, she remembers, "a whole new world, an awakening." She visited galleries and museums, and sat in the Metropolitan Museum of Art for hours, often with entire rooms all to herself. She especially loved going to thrift stores, and would arrive home in the late afternoon, her arms filled with bags of books that she found for a dime. She read voraciously. She devoted more time to her garden. And later, she would begin to paint and write. She took the high school equivalency exam, enrolled in the local community college, studied art history, women's literature, and began to travel.

I was born in 1967, just as my grandmother's healing began. I saw firsthand her determination to have her own creative life and the effects this had on the entire family. The value she placed on nourishing herself taught us to do the same. Yet, it also meant that she had to take on the men in the family, and anyone who questioned the time she took to care for herself. Often she did so with a quick statement, "Enough already!" Ten years ago she stopped cooking for large gatherings altogether and announced that she was fed up with being solely responsible for the regular feasts. Today, whenever someone pulls some tired authoritative patriarchal shit around us, she and I always look at each other and smirk before we let loose our vocal opposition. I learned from her how to stand up for myself, how to give to myself.

My grandmother also prays each morning, throughout the day, and into the evening. And she tells me her dreams. When I stay at her house, in the morning we congregate in the kitchen with my aunt and recount our dreams, discussing what they might mean and how they provide us with guidance for our lives. My grandmother always reminds us that Antonia taught her the importance of this ritual. She even kept a dream book, though she could not read or write, and had her daughters read to her various interpretations. We too have become so familiar with each other's dreams.

When I devote my life to going in search of Italian immigrant women's dreams, I find endless ruptures and contradictions embedded in stereotypical myths: "silent" women ignored employers' threats and took to the streets; "ignorant" women smashed industrial factories with rocks; and "hopeless" women organized revolutionary political circles. I find hundreds like my grandmother, women who struggled with cultural expectations, poverty, and tragic loss, to create a life of her own. And I find many like Maria Roda, anarchist and socialist Italian immigrant women who were far from invisible or hidden in their own day. Yet early on I decide that I am not interested in documenting a romantic history. My intention is to engage the historical evidence to document a usable past.

The importance of remembering fully was something I learned before I ever knew how to write. I watched my mother wither away from cancer when I was four. She had a strange sensation in her leg, fainted, and soon after discovered that she had a tumor in her brain. She was twenty-seven years old. She tried valiantly to fight it with rounds of chemotherapy and surgery, but the cancer metastasized ferociously. She wrote me a letter in those final days, telling me how sweet our relationship was, how she'd give anything to see it grow, how I would understand her love for me only when I have a daughter of my own. I can feel her sorrow, her sense of helplessness and disbelief that she has to go. It takes root in me.

Kindergarten was a nightmare. The separation from her was terrifying and I could not focus on anything. I surprised myself when I smacked another kid in the head with a block and pinched the neighbor's baby until she cried. I walked home each day wondering if my mother would be alive when I arrived.

She died in March of 1973 when I was five years old: that same year the U.S. federal government occupied Wounded Knee in an attempt to destroy the emerging freedom movement on the Pine Ridge Indian reservation in South Dakota. The two events are always connected for me. It wouldn't seem to make sense, a girl born to Italian and Irish working-class immigrant families in New York City linking the loss of her mother to Wounded Knee. It must have occurred when I learned of Anna Mae Aquash. She had been active in the American Indian Movement (AIM), and soon after the occupation of Wounded Knee, she was found raped and tortured in a ditch with a bullet hole in her head. The F.B.I. cut off her hands and sent them to Washington, D.C., for identification because she was a radical, a subversive, someone questioning if freedom even existed in a country founded on colonialism and slavery. She was someone imagining and working for a world free from oppression.

Nineteen seventy-three feels catastrophic. All I remember of that year is being awoken in the pitch black of night, and standing at the foot of my parents' bed where my mother lay. With my two little brothers at my side, we were told that she was dead. My mother's sister will later tell me that in the morning I sat with my brothers on the front stoop trying to explain what "dead" meant. "She's never coming back, I think."

I can't remember much of 1974 or 1975 either. When my mother died my father began sexually molesting me. A deep, endless sorrow filled the house. Photographs of the four of us in these years are hard to look at. I see one unexpectedly when I am twenty. I am home from college for Christmas, and we are looking at some old slides my father had found in the attic. I cannot breathe. I am being swallowed alive by terror. I am having my first major panic attack. In these photos my hands are always clenched. In some I look weary, ready to get the fuck out myself and follow my mother. In others I look defiant, ready to kick somebody's ass. My hair is always matted, and my face is almost always dirty.

A woman across the street invites me into her house every so often to feed me lunch, wash my hair, and brush out all the knots. I'm so thankful for her tenderness. I do my best to care for my brothers, who are only two and four years old, while my father loses and tries desperately to regain his sanity. I tell myself that I cannot forget the abuse, that to remember would be the single most important thing I could do for myself. I almost tell my best friend in fourth grade. But the words don't come out. I don't tell a soul until I am twenty when the panic forces me to get help. But it came out in other ways.

I grew up just north of the Bronx. My dad was the first in his large family to complete college, get a master's degree, and leave the city. His father had worked three jobs to put food on the table while his mother gave birth to and cared for him and his ten siblings. He too would work many jobs to go to college, become a teacher, and move his young family to a place with many trees and birds, far from his poor and working-class Corona, Queens, neighborhood. My mother was also a teacher, and an artist. She loved her new home, having grown up in poverty in Flatbush, Brooklyn. But she struggled with feelings of isolation as she adjusted to living in a suburban setting far from her family and friends.

The town then was mixed-class—primarily Italian, Jewish, and Irish. After my mother died, our second-hand clothes, broken-down cars, furniture from other people's garbage, dilapidated house, and loud screaming matches made our devastation feel shameful and obvious. This particular feeling was one we seemed to share only with other low-income families. Yet, we owned our own home in the middle-class section of town, our dad was a professor, and we lived in a very different world from our cousins in Queens who were on welfare. Moreover, our father's extreme frugality with his modest salary enabled us to not only live in this town, but to have a summer home on an island off the coast of Maine (though one of the few without electricity and running water) and some property in Canada. It was entirely confusing.

My closest friends were, of course, other inconsolable and angry girls. When Janine Caruso and Lisa De Luca weren't beating the shit out of each other in the girls' locker room, or when we weren't fried out from too much weed, we shared our war stories. Most of us were living in single-parent households where we were the ones raising our siblings. We were mostly Italian, but also Irish, Polish, Jewish, Puerto Rican, and Black. And we all wanted to be darker. When summertime came I was teased endlessly for my fair, freckly Irish complexion that did not take on the deep dark brown tones that theirs did. We were heavy into disco, learned every word of the first crossover rap hit by the Sugarhill Gang, and got our sense of style from what we saw going on with the Italian, Black, and Puerto Rican girls in the Bronx. Our parents may have left the ghetto behind, but it still spoke to us more deeply than middle-class WASP culture ever did.

We hated school, but showed up if only to convene outside, plan our adventures for the day, and cruise. When we did choose to stay we spent the majority of the day in the girls' bathroom smoking cigarettes and talking trash. In ninth and tenth grade we'd pool the cash we stole from our parents and made babysitting, buy beer and snacks, and sit up in the woods or down by the river getting loaded with the kids who had dropped out of school altogether. Janine could sing something fierce. She'd always start belting it out and we'd all join in. I can see us now, fucked up, singing our hearts out. Often we'd drink until we threw up, but you could always count on one of your girls to hold your hair for you and rub your back while you got rid of all that shit. Lauren Butler and I started hanging out a lot in those days. She hated her stepfather so much she peed in some brownie batter before bakin' them up for his union meeting. I loved this. We all prided ourselves on being tough, on giving teachers the finger, lighting up cigarettes in class, grabbing our crotches like the boys, and looking out for each other. Our rebellion was so many things: inspired, self-destructive, courageous.

Fights did break out. They usually began as very public verbal battles which would draw large crowds to see who could humiliate with the most skill and act the least scared. Then it turned ugly. I managed to avoid getting beat down by having a valuable trade. I could forge any parent's signature with ease. All I needed was an original and I could get all my friends out of class for days on end. One summer I had to sit in the principal's office for two weeks after school ended to make up for all the detentions I skipped.

By the eleventh grade I moved beyond my clique of primarily Italian girls. I liked crossing the lines between groups, and the Italian boys wouldn't give me the time of day since I didn't put out. I started hanging out in one of the other bathrooms, with some of the older girls. Most were artists and many were Jewish. Sarah Levinsohn and I became quick friends because we both hated school and wanted to be in the city instead. We went down to Manhattan regularly. I was taking dance classes and she was studying sculpture, each with her own money. Many years later, when I told her of my first panic attack, she confided in me her own struggle with paralyzing anxiety, having internalized her mother's depression.

There was also Anna Webb. Her father had disappeared when she was a kid, and her mother worked as a counselor for Vietnam vets, many of whom she'd end up sleeping with and let live in their home. Anna was the first poet and openly bisexual young woman I had ever met. Often she would run away, sometimes for weeks at a time. Once she even made it all the way to California by assuming a new identity.

We all had our stories. We never shared the details, but we knew we shared suffering.

I barely graduated high school since I rarely attended. But I made an extra effort toward the end since I was determined to get out. I worked as a secretary in Manhattan, since all I had really learned in school was how to type, and the guidance counselors told me I was definitely *not* college material. Maria Angela Gallo and I had tried to take Advanced Placement History in our junior year, thinking we might get something out of it, but the teacher laughed when we showed up to the first day and told us to get out (we had him for homeroom two years earlier and had made torturing him our sport). The only classes I liked were Theater Arts, since I was into performance, and this one class on foreign affairs. The teacher let me interview my Aunt Yesenia about her childhood in El Salvador. When I presented my report and told the class how the U.S. had waged war against a popularly elected government there, a student in the back yelled, "Fucking communist!" Having been weaned on antiwar rallies, rebel music, and a certain political radicalism within my father's family, I didn't mind the charge. My rebellious attitude carried over into my secretarial work. I hated taking orders, but I could smoke at my desk and make enough money to get my own place. Within nine months I had enough to get out and I went to Italy. Another migration of refuge, though this time in the opposite direction.

It was the combination of being very far away yet also at home that pulled me across the ocean. It was like being at my grandparents' house. They had kept me alive in the rough years, and my trips to Italy would deepen my connection to them. My mother's parents weren't there. Her father had died when she was a child, and her mother disappeared from our lives after my mother died. I would later learn my mother's mother was an alcoholic and had lived a life filled with bitterness and anger, in part because her own mother had died when she was five. She and my maternal grandfather had come from Ireland, but I would learn nothing of this culture or history.

Like me, my mother and both of my grandmothers all lost a parent in their childhood. My dad tells me it was more common then: "everyone was losing someone." I later learned that many of the women who immigrated from Italy as young women in the early twentieth century did so not only because they followed family or were in search of better jobs, but also because their own mothers had passed away. There was nothing to keep them rooted anymore.

My grandmother understood my anger and sorrow. I lived to go to her house. We went every Sunday, and sometimes more. I loved walking in the door and being greeted by a house packed full with loud, boisterous, passionately expressive kin. The warm smells of a sauce with sausages simmering on the stove. The parade of wild characters. The drama of it all. My grandmother also came to our house. She scrubbed our floors, and cooked us meals. She too found my father insufferable in those years and it felt good to have an ally.

There were a lot of boys. My grandmother had nine sons, and I was the only girl in my family of four. So I was always in search of the feminine. My mother's brother, who is a Catholic priest and remained close to us, gave me a *Madonnina* right after my mother died and taught me how to pray to her. I wore this little gold medallion of the Blessed Mother around my neck religiously, and She and my own mother Maryloretta became one.

When I went to Italy this last time, I went in search of Her. Yet, my purpose was specific: to understand what kinds of protest southern Italian peasant women were up to at the turn of the last century. I wanted to know how they fought back. How they claimed dignity. How they turned their own personal struggles into powerful tools for change.

I am in need of inspiration and guidance. I stay at the house of a woman whose mother also died when she was a child. My brother Marco comes with me and we marvel at what we find there: She is everywhere. *Maria Santissima.* We all fill our houses with her, and it seems we always find each other. She is in every room at my grandmother's house. My friend Mary has a room devoted to Her in her house in Weehawken. Kym and I always marvel at the ways our altars to Her resemble one another. When I meet Stephanie for the first time, we talk incessantly about our grandmothers, *le nonne.* She tells me about her altar to the Black Madonna. Even some of the men I know are fascinated by her, the Divine Mother and this ancestral worship of an earthy Goddess.

Rebel Girls

Whenever I travel through Italy I am drawn to the sanctuaries. I especially love the small chapels made from clay and stucco that women in the neighborhood maintain separately from the church. They are almost always filled with fresh flowers and votive candles burning desires. She is always front and center. I didn't go to Catholic school, and wasn't forced to attend church since my father believed we should find our own sense of spirituality, and that the institutionalized church was corrupt. But my grandmother's faith, which was also my mother's, is in my flesh. I am named after the Blessed Mother with my middle name, and I was born on her birthday. Without any sense of scripture, as a kid I always made up my own stories to explain the imagery. While Jesus seemed pretty cool, it was all about Mary.

I enter every *santuario* I encounter. My brother and I hike the six-mile pilgrimage up San Pellegrino in Palermo to be in the woods where Santa Rosalia lived when she fled an arranged marriage and hid in the hills. I learn that Sicilian women revere a pantheon of female saints who struggled against patriarchy: Santa Lucia, an early Siracusan Christian martyr under Diocletian's persecutions, who was forced into prostitution by her husband, protects vision; and Sant'Agata of Catania, who refused the advances of a senator, who then tortured her, in part, by cutting off her breasts, protects against Etna's volcanic eruptions, fire, and lightning. In each story female power is transcendent in the end.

I go to my great-grandparents Antonia and Francesco Paolo's village outside of Naples with my brother and uncle, and look into the eyes of my kin. They marvel at how they see their own children in our faces. *Americani. Napoletani.* I walk through the cemetery to find the graves of my ancestors. Many stones bear portrait photographs. I see much weariness. Sometimes there is horror, and sometimes defiance.

I visit many archives—everything from the massive Archivio Centrale dello Stato (Central State Archive) in Mussolini's EUR district in Rome, where I comb through police files on Italian refugee antifascist anarchist and socialist women in New York City, to the attics of Centri Sociali, social centers in abandoned buildings that have been appropriated by students and workers to create sites of subversive culture.

I learn that between 1892 and 1894, a wave of popular unrest washed over Sicily. In town after town, peasants mobilized labor strikes, occupied fields and piazzas, and looted government offices. While the island had a long history of this kind of revolt, this marked a new era of social protest. Women took the lead of this mass-based radical social movement, and they infused the struggle with their own mixture of socialism and spiritualism.

Their activity began in the towns surrounding Palermo, and then spread across the island and onto the mainland. In Monreale, women and children filled the central piazza shouting *"Abbasso il municipio e viva il fascio!"* (Down with the municipal government and long live the union!) After attacking and looting the offices of the city council, the women marched toward Palermo crying *"Abbiamo fame!"* (We are hungry!), waving banners with slogans connecting socialism to scripture. In Villafrati, Caterina Costanzo led a group of women wielding clubs to the fields where they threatened workers who had not joined the community in a general strike against high taxes and the repressive local government. In Balestrate, thousands of women "dressed in traditional clothes" and also armed with clubs, marched through the streets, demanding an end to government corruption and high taxes. In Belmonte, Felicia Pizzo Di Lorenzo led fifty peasant women through the town and then gathered in the *palazzo comunale*, demanding the abolition of taxes, the removal of the mayor, and the termination of the city council.

This is just the beginning. The women formed unions and celebrated them as they would a religious festival, with music and food, and they wove their political and spiritual ideologies together in their speeches. In the words of one woman, "We want everybody to work as we work. There should no longer be either rich or poor. All should have bread for themselves and their children. We should all be equal . . . Jesus was a true socialist and he wanted precisely what we ask for, but the priests don't discuss this." Their blending of spiritualism and socialism would continue when they came to New Jersey. Maria Roda devoted much of her life to organizing workers and studying anarchism, socialism, and syndicalism. But later in her life she would turn to Rosicrucianism, with the intention of connecting to the divine through deep meditation and contemplation, while remaining deeply committed to political activism.

I focus on Maria Roda because there are records that document her life. I learn that her rebelliousness developed in her childhood and only deepened with her migration. She crossed the Atlantic in 1892, at the age of fourteen, with her father and younger sister, just after an arrest for singing seditious songs during a strike in the Milan silk factory where she worked. After she was released, the Rodas came to Paterson to find work in the city's silk mills. Like other Italian immigrant women, she and her sister arrived in the U.S. having developed skills for the industrial marketplace, and with the day-to-day experiences of resistance and struggle in Italy. The daughter of an anarchist father, Roda had been active in radical circles in Milan as a young teenager, and studied revolutionary theory and practice with Ada Negri, known widely to radicals as the "ardent poetess of revolt." I cannot find her mother. She is nowhere in the records.

Upon her arrival in the U.S., Maria Roda joined the radical circle Gruppo Diritto all'Esistenza, which met on Straight Street in Paterson, and included over one hundred other Italian anarchist migrants, similarly committed to connecting their struggles in the U.S. to other workers throughout the world. Their political beliefs rested on their conviction that no one was free until all were free. Revolution was not something they waited for—it was the daily act of bringing about the society they envisioned. At only sixteen years of age Maria Roda began speaking before large assemblies of workers, where she immediately impressed seasoned radicals and rank-and-file workers with her ability to rouse audiences.

She fell in love with the celebrated Catalan anarchist Pedro Esteve, and while raising eight children, both became part of a community of intellectual working-class leaders that extended beyond Paterson and across the United States. A charismatic and powerful speaker, Roda often traveled with Esteve to assist and support the collective struggles of Cuban, Spanish, Puerto Rican, Mexican, African American, East European Jewish, Italian, and other workers on the docks, in the mines, and at work in the cigar and textile factories in the U.S. While they were based in Paterson until at least 1908, at different times they also set up home in Weehawken, Brooklyn, and Tampa in order to connect the revolutionary activities of these different communities. Often they did so by opening their home on Gregory Avenue in Weehawken, which became a central meeting place for local radicals, especially on Sundays. It is for this reason that Italian women's writing makes it into these two anarchist newspapers: they were published during the years that Esteve served as editor.

This commitment to women grew out of Roda's belief that they were foundational to revolutionary anarchist and socialist movement. As she stated, "*Chi conosce la miseria più della donna?*" (Who knows misery more than women?). In order to accomplish this, she helped to found a *gruppo anarchico femminile* (anarchist women's group), called the Gruppo Emancipazione della Donna (Women's Emancipation Group), in 1897, which met once a week at 90 Straight Street in Paterson at Ninfa Baronio's place. Their purpose was to create a place for women to inform the revolutionary culture with their own philosophies and perspectives. The Paterson women's group met over a period of at least seven years, and involved women who worked in the city's silk mills. They also met regularly with *compagne* across the river in Manhattan. Together, they announced their intention: "to defend the large number of women workers in the city," . . . "to contribute to the cause of women's emancipation," and "to educate the new generation in the sublime principles of anarchism."

As with Roda, most anarchist immigrant women were deeply rooted in the radical culture through their families. Ninfa Baronio, her husband Firmino Gallo, her sisters Serafina, Divina, Anetta, and Jennie, and her brothers Egisto and Abele, were all active anarchists in Paterson. Ninfa's son recalled that she "did a lot of reading and a lot of deep thinking." She believed "that the church was dogmatic and authoritarian, cardinals living like princes, crusaders stealing and looting and raping—all in the name of the Vatican." "Father felt the same way," he remembered, and together, they ran a small radical bookstore/library on Straight Street in Paterson that was collectively owned by the local workers. Ninfa also became active in performance art, where she, Ernestina Cravello, and other radical women used plays to educate and mobilize audiences in revolutionary principles. Cravello often drew a big crowd, especially when she made the local daily newspapers at only nineteen years of age as the "Queen of the Anarchists."

Her claim to fame developed in 1900, when Gaetano Bresci, a local silk weaver and comrade in her anarchist circle, assassinated King Umberto I of Italy, which some believed was in retaliation for the unarmed workers who had been gunned down by police during the 1898 hunger riots in Milan. In the aftermath, a wave of repression and anti-Italian sentiment washed over Paterson. Police and newspaper reporters combed the city, labeling it "the capital of world anarchism." In their search for a conspiracy, the press fixated on Cravello, an outspoken anarchist. When questioned by reporters for her support of Bresci, she stated, "I am an anarchist. This is because I am moved by the suffering of hundreds of thousands of workers and I struggle for a world in which such exploitation is no longer possible."

I learn that a central component of the radical culture women created overall was to imagine, discuss, and bring about the world they desired: a world without exploitation, humiliation, and oppression. Revolution was the daily act of bringing about a society without coercive authority or unequal distribution of community resources. This led them not only to meet on their own, but to publish and circulate women's radical texts. Their feminism was "not in the manner of the bourgeoisie," as they wrote, but a movement in which working-class and poor women's struggles, concerns, and strategies informed revolutionary practice. "Being women, we believe that feminist action is essential," they argued, "just as we believe that the working class must take action in unions, congresses, and strikes."

The evidence for these women is everywhere. I found it in my own lived experience, in tracing my own responses to trauma, and watching the girls and women around me deal with theirs. I found it in these radical New Jersey newspapers. But it is in few other documents. And it is all in Italian. Because of this, many historians have not seen these women. Even political activists of their own time could not see them. In reflecting on her career as a radical labor organizer, for example, Elizabeth Gurley Flynn proclaimed, "There were practically no women in the Italian movement—anarchist or socialist. Whatever homes I went into with Carlo [Tresca] the women were always in the background, cooking in the kitchen, and seldom even sitting down to eat with the men." Yet, ironically, during the famous 1913 strike in Paterson, Flynn slept for several weeks at Ninfa Baronio's house. Moreover, Italian women were described by local newspapers as "the most ardent in the struggle," since they were central actors not only in workers' uprisings in Paterson that year, but also in strikes that took place in Manhattan, Hoboken, Newark, and dozens of other cities across the U.S.

Even when they made themselves as conspicuous as strikers, or as Ernestina Cravello, Maria Roda, and Ninfa Baronio, they were always behind the scenes and in the kitchens. What was going on in that kitchen? That's what I want to know. A classic female space and site of women's retreat and collaboration, the kitchen is not only the heart of family and community, it is at the very core of revolutionary political struggle. By not looking in such spaces many have not noticed these women. But maybe that was the point. Away from watchful eyes, and in a space of their own, they were able to nourish these movements and themselves.

When it felt right, they also took it into the streets. In the springtime of 1902, anarchist and socialist women across northeastern New Jersey and New York City came together in what they called a *festa*, "to begin a new era of stimulating activity among the female element." Indeed, it did mark a turning point, one in which radical Italian immigrant women created autonomous spaces to facilitate female participation within revolutionary struggle. In 1913, they would lead a strike of 25,000 in Paterson that would change the course of the American labor movement.

One hundred years later, my friend Mary invites me to a *notte delle streghe* (night of the witches) at her home in Weehawken, just blocks from Maria Roda's home. I am the last to arrive. We are nine women total around the table, with ancestors from Italy, Croatia, Ireland, Africa, and many other places as well. Among us are a few writers, some performance artists, and two civil rights attorneys. We eat dinner, speaking in Italian and English, and then retire upstairs to Mary's sky blue room with the tower, the one entirely devoted to the Blessed Mother.

The room is filled with artifacts from all over the world, images of Mary in all her forms, as the dark mother of the Mediterranean, as the brown Guadalupe, as pre-Christian Goddess. She is from Italy, Africa, Palestine, Mexico, and beyond. We form a circle and share spoken word poems, music, and laughter. We click our castanets and learn ancient dances that bring together these traditions from the four corners of the globe.

Three of us get up the next morning and walk the block toward the Hudson River, where you can see all of Manhattan. Leaning over the wall, high on Weehawken's cliff, we talk about the women we met, the city before us, and the world all around us. Maria tells us about the prisoners she's been defending, mostly people of color. Some men, most of whom are mentally ill, are kept in solitary confinement for over seven years. She talks about how they lose their minds because they are deprived of human contact, and when they turn on themselves and attempt to end their misery through suicide, they are given only more time. She talks of the women she's defending, who are organizing to protest and end the sexual violence of guards whose acts of atrocity go unpunished.

Mary talks about her own struggle locally to organize residents in Weehawken. They are protesting the construction of high-rise apartment buildings along the coast. The buildings will not only require the removal of several acres of dense foliage and trees, which process toxins in the air, they will also obstruct the view of mostly working-class people and be built on top of chromium-filled soil. The developers' plan is to lay plastic over the sick soil and then just build the homes on top. They don't listen to the environmental and medical experts who warn that living on such land will be devastating to the families, and that widespread cancer, birth defects, and other illnesses can be counted on.

Watching the world unfold before us, we measure our losses, count our blessings, and imagine the world that will most certainly come. We talk about the way capitalism, nationalism, racism, and patriarchy endanger our lives and those we love, but also our conviction, shared by our revolutionary foremothers, that such systems and ways of living are not sustainable. They are collapsing before our very eyes. It is for this reason that I continue to track and map the worlds of these visionary Jersey girls: to feel the continuum, the inspiration, and the wisdom of those who went before, those who had both the courage to stand up and the ability to see through their own pain. They chose for their rallying cry *Emancipiamoci!*—let's emancipate ourselves. Because they knew that freedom is something we have the power to give ourselves.

It feels ironic that this recovery happens in Jersey. For a New Yorker like myself, Jersey was the place my family always got lost whenever we dared to cross the river. It was, I would later joke with my New Mexican and Californian friends, my boundary between the East and the West. It is a place with its own trauma. Today I teach women's studies and history in northern Jersey, and I listen to my students make meaning of their own histories in this space. They tell me of their parents who have cancer because the soil they grew up on was soaked with toxic chemicals. They complain of the thick, dense, brown air that floats above their homes. They reflect on their families' histories in the state, as poorly paid workers in the factories and fields, with few rights and resources. The massive brick factory buildings are still everywhere. The sweatshops continue. The fact that revolution develops from such spaces doesn't surprise me. I have felt with my own heart how beauty can grow from devastation, and how in loving those places most severed we learn how to be there for ourselves and each other.

WE MUST REBEL!

Maria Barbieri

Translated by Edvige Giunta and Jennifer Guglielmo from the Italian-language "anarchist-socialist" newspaper La Questione Sociale, *November 18, 1905.*

To my women comrades, these thoughts are dedicated to you, from another woman worker: It is in the thought and palpitation of my soul that I feel all the social injustices that have humiliated and subjugated us for centuries. I am a rebel who rises up against these iniquities, and I also invite you to the struggle.

It is necessary that we cast off these servile chains that the family, society, and church have forced us to drag from remote centuries. It is necessary that we too rise up to reclaim our rights and challenge the duties that a false upbringing has inculcated in us. It is time for us to awaken the fire of rebellion, join the immense proletarian masses, and fight for our deliverance.

Only when we are free from all the social and religious superstitions that have been instilled in us shall we be redeemed. We must study with passion, and read the newspapers that our comrades are publishing with enormous sacrifice. There we will learn of their ideas, of the evils that afflict us, and the means to rid ourselves of these evils. We must get a hold of those pamphlets from which we can learn all about the hypocrisy and foulness that religion contains. When we rid ourselves of this terrible evil, we will become women with a consciousness and we will work for our emancipation, for today we have realized our need for it.

We have been forced, like human machines, to stay trapped in the immense industrial prisons where one loses strength, health, and youth, where our rights are shattered because of the greed of the bourgeoisie. Will we not rebel when faced with this attack on our right to live? Will you not shake with rage before the pompous and contemptuous lady who walks by you, lifting her silk skirt so as to avoid the contaminating touch of the humble skirts of workers?

While we exhaust ourselves from morning to night to procure all that is beautiful and comforting in life for a handful of pleasure-seeking people, while we are bent over our work, overwhelmed by a torrent of grief over the future of our children, the grand ladies chat in the perfumed sitting-rooms, proposing banquets, balls, theater, and walks, all with the gold they bleed from us and our children.

When disease tears a loved one from us because of inadequate treatment and deprivation, or when a loved one dies in the factories or mines, should we choke our grief in tears or mumble a prayer and beg for resignation?

Oh no, no! We must rebel in the face of so much injustice. We must break the shackles that bind us, and become free and redeemed. We must fight to gain our rights and to create happiness for our children.

Come then, comrades of suffering and struggle. We must rise against our oppressors. We must unite, all of us. If the faith in a better future still shines in us, if the flame of redemption still burns in our hearts, then we must show ourselves to be strong and rebellious. In this way we will attain the dream that so many have long desired, and for which many generous people have lost their lives!

TO THE WOMEN WORKERS
Maria Roda

*Translated by Edvige Giunta and Jennifer Guglielmo from the
Italian-language "anarchist-socialist" newspaper* La Questione Sociale,
September 15, 1897.

Dear women comrades: It is time that we too rise and organize ourselves to
prove to the world that accuses us that we too are capable of something. Let
this be known to the men who stifle our will, who do not allow us to use our
minds, and act according to our natural impulses, those who consider us to
be inferior and impose on us their authority as fathers, brothers, and husbands, those who believe themselves to be stronger, while they step on and
oppress us. Sometimes their violent hands slap us, and because we are
weaker, we have to subject ourselves to this. They also use us as objects for
their pleasure, but we too want to enjoy our rights and our liberties.

I have heard men, and you have also heard them, dear women comrades,
say that we only know how to gossip and malign, that we worry only about
fashion and knick knacks, and that we are incapable of understanding serious matters, that we don't take to heart the miseries of our society, that we
don't concern ourselves with fighting against the infamy of our class, which
condemns us to pain and fatigue. They say that we are frivolous, that we are
weak, that we are incapable of sustaining the struggle against this unfortu-
nate society, that we cannot comprehend the anarchist ideal.

What you men don't realize is that you are the only ones responsible for
our weakness, for our inadequate intellectual development, because you
alone forbid us education. Your accusations are slanderous. Instead you
should teach us what we don't know. You should encourage us to participate
in the noble struggle for the oppressed of humanity. You should instigate us
to assert our rights. Instead you are proud to keep us ignorant and to treat
us as your slaves.

Let's instead demonstrate, women comrades, that we are capable of something, that we too feel the shame of this abominable society, and that the idea
of rebellion also rises within our hearts. We are tired of being subjected to injustice; we too want to abolish servitude; we want to rise to freedom. We also
want to abolish the prejudice that the church has been able to plant in the
hearts and brains of our fathers. We too want freedom and equality.

To the Women Workers

We too have a have a heart that beats, that suffers when facing so much misery. The pain of the working masses affects us too. Who knows misery more than women?

Oh, you tell them, you mothers who raise your children, how much anxiety, how much torment you have suffered. Tell them, tell them how many sleepless nights you have spent working to feed them. Tell them how much pain you feel when this society tears you away from the children that you raised with so much love and care. Tell them how much you suffer when you learn of yet another disgraceful deed that the bourgeoisie has committed against the working masses.

It is exactly because we feel and suffer that we too want to become involved in the fight against this society, because we also feel from birth the need to be free, to be equal.

With this purpose in my mind, we have organized a group of women comrades in Paterson, who plan on spreading the sublime idea of anarchist Socialism among women workers. We hope to see good results and we shall see how our numbers grow.

Maria Roda

Editor's note (*La Questione sociale*)
The activities and conviction of Maria Roda and other women comrades are well known. Thus we wish them much success and offer our support of their initiative, in the hope that it will be followed in every town.

PATERSON: 1913

Josephine Stifano

Believe me when I say the whole city was starving, the whole city of Paterson was haunted in 1913. No one was working, everyone was on strike, everyone was hungry. Not like now, no relief, welfare. I was ten in 1913. We had to leave, my uncle in West Virginia said there was work and we came back to Paterson when I was twelve. They say to me, how can you remember? I say, when you had pain, you remember. I started to work in the mills at twelve. I didn't use my name. I had to get false working papers. We had no choice. I was working ten hours a day, six days a week. Any money could help us eat. I worked in the mill across from School Two, a dye house. They had to put me up on a box to work. I would hear the recess bell from the school and cry. I would watch the children playing at the school from the window and cry. I wanted to play with them. The foreman told me I couldn't stand by the window anymore. But the owner heard him once and said let her stand by the window. I learned all could, all phases. I ended up being a weaver. I was proud of my work. I can remember so clearly, everything so clearly.

Editor's note (*Italian American Writers on New Jersey*)
Shortly before her death in 1988, Josephine Stifano shared her memories with journalist June Avignone in an interview from which the above is excerpted.

TIME'S END

Arturo Giovannitti

To my martyred brother, Carlo Tresca,
who dreamed thus with me.

Thus shall it be. When after this long night
The Rebel Fiend at last clasps hands with God,
And his black wings become great fans of light;

When the last tyrant has been slain and trod
Into the loam with the last cursing priest,
And every liar lies in his foul blood—
Judge, soldier, legislator, journalist—
Life shall then burst into a gale of fire
And cleanse Man from the taint of saint and beast.

Beauty rued at last to man's desire
Will make all laws her handmaids and will strip
Them naked of all weapons and attire

Like lovers and athletes. Strong hands will grip
Soft hands in freedom's pact and there will rise
New orders with the rule of brethernship.

Then will the meek stand girt with boundless ties
Of strength, and strength will boast a humbler name,
Then power will be a servant in disguise,

And pride will be the better side of shame;
Then art and thought will take the place of strife
And only toil will wear the wreath of fame.

DYE HOUSE STRIKE, 1933

Arturo Mazziotti

When the dye house went on strike in 1933, I was living in an old farmhouse at the top of Lafayette Avenue Extension in Hawthorne so I got up at three o'clock in the morning to give myself enough time to walk to Fifth Avenue in the Riverside Section of Paterson. The workers congregated on Fifth Avenue and marched to Market Street in East Paterson to the spot where Marcal Paper Company is now located.

We picketed that dye house until we were chased away by police. Carrying the American flag, our group of workers marched to the United Piece Dye Works on Fifth Avenue and picketed that shop. Our demonstration was a peaceful one, but the police came and threw tear gas bombs at us and hit us with their clubs.

Our union was Dyers Union Local 1733, United Textile Workers of America. Under the leadership of Anthony Amirato, president of the Dyers Local, the Local grew from 1,800 members in 1933 to 13,000 in January of 1935. We fought for the rights of the textile workers, rights people today take for granted.

DOWNTOWN PATERSON
Tom DeBlasio Carroll

The sky was open and bright, and the city lay quietly nearby beneath the lookout point above Marshall Street. I, too, sat quietly, a feeling of deep harmony overtaking me, but soon there was a distraction in the trees to my left when three young people, Peruvians—two older, one very small—emerged. A soccer ball was clamped under an arm, but the ball rolled out onto the grass and the boys arrayed themselves into positions for an ad hoc game. They played, feinting and kicking, age differences dissolving into the common movement, sky and field merging to encompass it all—their voices, their busy legs, the sound of the ball brushing through the grass, the birdsong drifting from nearby trees, the sun an almost audible presence in the heightened air. In the sheer openness of that moment, the cosmic whole was suddenly, playfully revealed.

Gradually, others entered the scene from the same patch of woods, carrying bags and a blanket. There were women and men, an infant, and young girls, and they spread themselves and their things into the grass space just above the game. And the game grew, billowing into this developing context, and the soccer boys, playing hard, laughed and murmured among themselves. The women reached into their bags and began passing food around—tamales, corn on the cob, meat on the bone. The people ate, some breaking away momentarily from the game, one by one, to obtain bits of the food, then chewing and playing, legs marking the action, and all the while their laughter, their playful voices spiraled through the orchestrated, mindful movements of the now living ball and filled the air, bursting with optimism and the teeming possibilities of life and of hope. All the while the city, my city and theirs, lay just beyond and outside it all, a bundle of temporalities tied with a *taja*.

Later, memory supplied a reference: the opening scenes of an Antonioni movie, because in the blazing sunlight the event had appeared so cinematic, so much like a dream or an oversized reality. In fact, a conjunction had occurred then and, with it, the realization that the lives of those Peruvians—

migrants in the 1990s—were broadly akin to my own life in the 1950s as a grandson of migrants. Both sets of lives, commingling now in my memory, were discovering forms of freedom while coping with daunting and difficult conditions. Knowing this, what else can free people do but act freely against prejudice, against nostalgia, against the would-be monocultures of the non-urban spaces? Or they can make provision for tolerance, for hope, and for the full and ongoing range of human and earthly possibility, in the city and elsewhere, then and now, speaking with our many-colored tongues.

THE TANGERINE PLYMOUTH AND THE GILDED CAGE

Rachel Guido de Vries

Father Valente died in 1954, the same year my father, Little Louie Brancato, bought the tangerine Plymouth. One was pomp, the other circumstance. The first event, Father Valente's death, I remember by the scent of incense, and the second by the taste of a creamsickle. For Father, we all stood on the sides of Trenton Avenue, in Paterson, and watched the procession on its way to Saint Anthony's, where I went to school and church. I was nine. My mother, Delores, kept a statue of the Infant of Prague on the windowsill in our kitchen, and Father Valente looked just like that statue to me. He was clearly a grown man, of course, and not an infant, but he looked like the infant, and he was dressed like him, too, with red robes and a golden crown. It seems to me, thirty some years later, that he was carried in an open casket, framed on all sides with gold, and with clear glass panels, sort of like a gilded cage.

My father needed the tangerine Plymouth because he was a numbers runner and a small potatoes bookie. He had not yet moved up to the Cadillac or Continental school of thought because he was still peanuts, with just a few connections where they counted. Years later, Philly Falcone, a police lieutenant and a *compare* of my father's, would chuckle about those early years. He'd look at my father and bust his balls about the old days, when, as he affectionately said, Pop was ". . . the new kid on the block. Oh, yeah, I remember when I first heard aboutcha. Little Louie Brancato, big shot, cuz we all remembered your brother, Patsy, Golden Gloves winner in '47—had his own trade 'til he was shot, and there was plenty who that pissed off. Then along comes Louie with his bow-legs and his busted schnozzole. Skinny and already going bald, and a tough little bastard you were, Louie."

By then, Pop was completely bald and pretty stocky, but he was still bow-legged and tough as nails. A regular wise guy, he was. By then, he had also graduated to a pale blue, brand-new Cadillac. Philly, always known as a good cop, drove a Ford, not even a Thunderbird, but an Escort. My mother drove a Thunderbird. She'd graduated, too, and at sixty, she had a license plate frame that said "over forty and feeling foxy."

But my father never loved a car the way he loved that tangerine Plymouth. I used to wait for him to come home, sitting on the stoop of the house we lived in then on Alabama Avenue, up on the third floor. We rented from Uncle Tommy Giordano—he was my godfather, not a blood relation—and his wife Irene, whose brother, Mario, lived with them. Mario had, as my father said, just come off the boat, a real greenhorn. But Mario was nice. He had slicked down curly black hair and a big cleft in his chin, and eyes so dark they never just looked, they always gleamed. He worked at Uncle Tommy's fruit stand, and sometimes, when I was waiting for my father, Mario'd come home first, and he'd give me a peach or an apricot or an orange, depending on the season. Mario always smelled like an orange. Not like a creamsickle, more like an orange with cloves stuck in it. Once in a while, my father and Mario arrived within minutes of each other. My father would turn into the driveway and slowly pull the tangerine Plymouth right up to the door of the green garage, but never into it, at least not in the summer or fall. He liked to sit out on the stoop and look at it, and when Mario was there, we'd all three sit on the stoop, eating fruit and gazing in the direction of the car.

Every Saturday, I helped my father polish it with Kiwi car wax and a chamois rag. The last step was cleaning the mirrors: side view, rear view, and then we were off, just me and Pop, off to the Italian store for prosciutto and salami and provolone. Then we'd stop at Uncle Santo's Buffalo Bar and Grill, where he and my father would do a little business, and where I played the shuffleboard game and drank birch beer with my cousins Little Santo and his sister, Franny. Little Santo runs the bar today, and both Santo and Franny still live in the old neighborhood.

Me and Pop would get back home right around suppertime, around six. Mamma'd be in the kitchen breading the veal cutlets we always had on Saturday night, and my sister Bernadette, three years younger than me, would be in a corner playing with her washrags. Louis Junior would be in his playpen in the kitchen, where he could watch Mamma. Bernadette had about three of those washrags, and she'd fold them and unfold them, sometimes for hours. Nobody thought it was strange then, but when I think about it now, it seems very strange.

Father Valente's funeral was my first ceremony, not counting my brother Little Louis Junior's baptism, which, although it was said in Latin, and although Father Valente was bathed in incense, did not strike me as too mysterious. I was more caught up in a sense of relief for Louis Junior's soul not having to gamble on Limbo, which I imagined as a bunch of baby heads floating aimlessly on the clouds. I was eight when Louis Junior was baptized, but even then, the sort of aimlessness that couldn't be changed alarmed me.

The year of Father's death was the beginning of my fascination with ritual and ceremony. He died in April, and in May, I received First Communion, wearing a little bridal dress and clutching a white patent leather pocketbook where I could store the dollars my relatives gave me. In May, also, Ray Ann Del Guidice saw the Blessed Mother move. The statue moved; the lips moved, and all of the more hopeful girls, myself included, swore we saw it also. *Something* happened. I remember that day very clearly. The afternoon light filtering through the stained glass, the scent of incense, and the pale, pale blue of Our Mother's robes, resplendent to all of us, despite the chipped plaster of the statue, despite the old and rather musty church. And Raye Ann's fervor was something to behold. Of course, Sister Fabia, our teacher, had a fit. She was fond of knuckle rapping and humiliation, and she hated all of the Italian kids. I once had to sing "Yellow Rose of Texas" with Donna Mazzotti, because Sister caught us reading a pop music magazine during arithmetic. I hated her anyway, because she was Polish, not Italian, and because last year I had fallen in love with Sister Claire, who was Italian, and whose hand I always held at recess. I fell in love with her because she had the softest hand I have ever held. Today, that is what I remember about falling in love. For the life of me, I can't remember a single feature on Sister Claire's face, though I know she was slender and delicate boned.

Sister Fabia was fat and burped unashamedly throughout our lessons, and she kept a snot rag shoved up one sleeve of her habit, which always struck me as sacrilegious. She was outraged by Raye Anne's and our behavior with the Blessed Mother, though she had encouraged it by telling us stories endlessly about miracles that young children like us had a part in. There was one she especially loved, about a boy named Johnny, who was very poor. He had a paper route to help his family, kept a ninety-three average in school, and still had time to be an altar boy on Sundays. On top of all this, he managed to make a visit to church every day, no matter how busy he was. He made it quick, she granted him that, but every day he'd go into church, genuflect and cross himself, and say, simply, "Hello, Jesus, this is Johnny." The punch line of this story was, or course, Johnny's untimely death, witnessed by several adults. Johnny was struck by a car on his way out of church after his daily visit, and he died on the spot. All those around him unanimously agreed they heard it: the voice from the heavens, saying simply, "Hello, Johnny. This is Jesus." Well, we were in third grade, and about to make our First Communion, and we knew since we were practicing going to confession that we had reached the age of reason. We were constantly being reminded of the difference between heaven and hell and we knew that you could sometimes get time off in purgatory for things like daily visits, to say nothing of the jump you could be granted for a sign of good grace, such as having the Virgin move her lips in your direction. Donna Mazzotti and I even made a pact about the afterworld. We were all caught up in figuring how to be in touch with each other after our bodies, like Johnny's, died. We agreed to meet on the corner in front of Verp's Bakery, ten years after we died. We must have thought we'd die at the same time, and it didn't strike us at all odd that we chose a Jewish bakery rather than church. Verp's had the best hard rolls. We ate them every Sunday, right after 9 o'clock mass, and they tasted great with my mother's meatballs, which we dug into hours before the macaroni was served. We were starved from the fasting that took place before receiving the body of Christ.

Since my father bought the tangerine Plymouth during the year of my fascination with ceremony, that car has always seemed sacred to me. When I think of it, I picture it with an aura, a halo. The day of Father Valente's funeral, my father dropped me off at the school. He didn't like pomp, didn't much care at all for church, and was particularly suspicious of priests, though he did let Mamma get the house blessed. He considered himself Catholic, but not a churchgoer, certainly not like Donna Mazzotti's father, who worked at Nabisco, belonged to the Holy Name Society, and ushered at mass each week. My father would have never done that. He would have been embarrassed to death. I always sort of liked that about him. But when I watched the tangerine Plymouth pull out of my sight, halo and all, and I stood in the chilly rain that April and viewed my first dead body, and a dead holy body to boot, and was on the fringes of the procession, the incense wafting up through the rain, all the priests chanting Latin, the altar boys waving the incense decanters, I was suddenly and certainly besieged by a feeling of righteousness, a kind of breeze of holiness. I felt as though I were lighter than air, borne up on the wind of a young and violent Catholicism. Though my heart and my physical self wanted to be off in the tangerine Plymouth with my father, my soul or my conscience or my newly acquired reason gave me a shove in a holier direction. I knew, even at nine, that my father's business was shady. When I asked him and Mamma what they were doing at night with the portable radio in the middle of the kitchen table, they said they were listening to the results. I never asked the results of what, I just watched them hunch toward the radio in the center of the table, in the kitchen's dim light, while they wrote some figure down, and shuffled fast through a little stack of tickets with numbers printed on them. "Trestle tickets," Mamma said, when I asked what they were. What trestle? And Pop would laugh, shake his head, say, "You're a pip, Ma." He always called her that.

All of this was in my mind, and despite the loneliness that watching my father's Plymouth vanish from sight brought me, despite the pleasure I knew would come from that car, I had to breathe in the pomp of Father Valente's funeral, and I followed the procession, feeling ancient and pious just the same.

When I was thirteen, my father bought another car. He traded in the tangerine Plymouth for a brand-new Chevrolet. Black, with black vinyl interior. He was moving up, as his color choice showed. That was also the year I received my confirmation. I picked a middle name, Maria, for my father's mother, as my confirmation name, and got to kiss the Bishop's ring.

We still lived in the same neighborhood, but in our own house. It was half a duplex, with a kitchen, living room, and dining room on the first floor, and three bedrooms and a bath upstairs. There was a wrought-iron railing around the three steps that led up to our front door. Uncle Tommy Giordano was gone, moved to Jersey City, and Mario had bought the fruit stand. I still saw him once in a while, but hardly ever in the neighborhood. I ran into him with Mamma a couple of times downtown when we were waiting for the bus. He was a wino, Mamma said, like poor Winnie Glover's husband, Mike, the one who kicked dogs. Mario was still kind of handsome, even though his eyes had lost their gleam. He still had a head full of black, curly hair, and the cleft in his chin, and he still smelled vaguely like an orange.

By the time my father bought his Chevrolet, I'd become a little snooty toward him. I had stayed very Catholic, and I knew by now those were no trestle tickets he and Mamma'd been counting. He didn't use that system any more, but he had a second phone put in, and he hung around with guys with names like Big Sal Polizotto and Twofy Barberio. Twofy was short for Two Fingers. I asked my father once what happened to Twofy. Looking over at Mamma, and not quite laughing, he said that Twofy lost his fingers during an accident in college. "Really," I said, impressed. It had never occurred to me that men like Twofy went to college. Years later, when my father went to college—the Passaic County Jail, for bookmaking, along with my Uncle Santo—I understood. Fortunately, both Pop and Uncle Santo left college with ten fingers each, but they did learn a lot while they were there.

I've learned some things since then, too. Last week I went car shopping. I'm looking at Plymouths, but they don't make them in tangerine these days. In fact, I don't remember ever seeing one other than Pop's. I've been to a few funerals, but I've never seen one like Father Valente's. Last winter, a friend— a Jewish bookie from Manhattan—asked me to help her book bets on college basketball games. I couldn't resist, though I felt a little out of my element. I really did go to college, the first one in my family to do that. I took her offer, and I loved every minute of it. I do not, though, ever go to church anymore. Gilded or not, a cage is a cage, and now that I have really reached the age of reason, I would much rather live my father's life than Father Valente's. I do cherish the memory of his funeral, and every spring, usually sometime around Easter, I rise to the occasion, filling up the house with incense, and trying to remember exactly the way Trenton Avenue looked in 1954. But what I mostly see is the tail pipe of the tangerine Plymouth as it rounded the corner away from me, and I long for summer, when we'd sit on the stoop in silence, eating fruit and gazing hopefully at that car.

PATERSON, NEW JERSEY
Carole Maso

Paterson is one of the great American poems, and it is a place, and it is the place where I was born and lived for a time. From the beginning home to me is a poem. I am born in a modernist masterpiece by William Carlos Williams. And in fact as I am being born he is completing Book Five of that opus, the book of the triumph of the imagination. Mysteriously he is handing this to me as I now begin to breathe. I am not surprised; it seems like destiny to me. And in the times of my illness, I will in fact believe I am the chosen one, handed this directly from him who wrote not for love or fame or because he wanted to say something, but to keep his sanity.

"It's a strange courage you give me, ancient star."

And yes, I am a daughter of Williams, who combined poetry, fiction, fact, criticism, bits of this and that in his work. A strange brew. I am his daughter as you, even if you know nothing of my work except this essay, will see. He has sent me on this charmed path.

"Rigor of beauty is the quest."

And then there is Allen Ginsberg, the other native of Paterson I grew up with. I adored his great heart and hunger, his music and outrage and audacity. His fallibility. How, as a teenager, I howled his *Howl*. I feel thankful to have had these two as my literary fathers. It feels like a much more fortunate literary inheritance than my southern friends who have Faulkner to contend with. Williams, that troubled iconoclast, seems to me a far more benevolent, happy influence simply in terms of what he allows. Somehow Faulkner continues to look best far from home on the Latin American writers. I, as a North American, am grateful not to have to wear his necklace of crows and thorns.

Home is my father playing the trumpet—the music drifting. In Paterson. My grandfather's house has a stained-glass window, and when my grandmother weeps, sick of this life, sick of the burden of simply being herself, there is the stained glass to focus on. My Grandpa Frank on the other side of town—with his Armenia and his wife, who will not live long—worked in the silk mills. Later, he will be beaten nearly to death with the pipe he began to keep under his bed for protection. Paterson, by then, having turned against us.

But not against me, not then.

Cadence was the block I lived on. Language my home. Charmed one, I was born into a poem.

PUBLIC SCHOOL NO. 18, PATERSON, NEW JERSEY

Maria Mazziotti Gillan

Miss Wilson's eyes, opaque
as blue glass, fix on me:
"We must speak English.
We're in America now."
I want to say, "I am American,"
but the evidence is stacked against me.

My mother scrubs my scalp raw, wraps
my shining hair in white rags
to make it curl. Miss Wilson
drags me to the window, checks my hair
for lice. My face wants to hide.

At home, my words smooth in my mouth,
I chatter and am proud. In school,
I am silent, grope for the right English
words, fear the Italian word
will sprout from my mouth like a rose,

fear the progression of teachers
in their sprigged dresses,
their Anglo-Saxon faces.

Without words, they tell me
to be ashamed.
I am.
I deny that booted country
even from myself,
want to be still
and untouchable

as these women
who teach me to hate myself.

Years later, in a white
Kansas City house,
the psychology professor tells me
I remind him of the Mafia leader
on the cover of *Time* magazine.

My anger spits
venomous from my mouth:

I am proud of my mother,
dressed all in black,

proud of my father
with his broken tongue,
proud of the laughter
and noise of our house.

Remember me, Ladies,
the silent one?
I have found my voice
and my rage will blow
your house down.

IN THE STACKS AT THE PATERSON PUBLIC LIBRARY

Maria Mazziotti Gillan

When I was fourteen, I asked my father to help me get a job. So he called the mayor and asked him for help. My father had worked very hard to get out the vote so the mayor owed him a favor. When my father said I wanted a job in the Paterson Public Library, the mayor said, "But that pays only fifty cents an hour." My father told me this, but I still wanted to work in the library. I loved to read, loved the branch library, loved the feel of a book in my hands, so I went off to the Public Library where I was told to speak to Ms. Cherry, supervisor of circulation. I went there after school, walked from Eastside High to the imposing white columned library, through the marble hall with its curving stair and bronze statues and oil paintings donated by the wealthy old families of the city. Ms. Cherry gave me a sour look, sniffed, and told me quickly what to do, but I knew she wasn't happy that I had been palmed off on her and she let me know she didn't like it.

Another young woman started the same day, a tall, beautiful, light-skinned African-American who came from an upper middle-class family. Her father owned a funeral home and she had expensive clothes and straight hair. We both loved books and we liked to talk to each other in the stacks. She knew Ms. Cherry hated us both, but this girl, her name was Anthea, was more articulate and confident than I was. I was incredibly shy and tongue-tied, but she'd answer Ms. Cherry back or give her a look that would shut her up immediately and then Ms. Cherry would scowl at me and find something wrong with what I'd done and yell and tears would fill my eyes. "Never let her see you cry," Anthea said. "It just makes her happy." Anthea told me that Ms. Cherry, who came from one of the old families of Virginia, thought she should step off the sidewalk when she went by—the way blacks did in the South when a white person walked toward them.

Despite Ms. Cherry, I liked the job, carrying books up into the stacks on the translucent, thick glass stairs, five floors of stacks lined with books and I'd rush up the stairs and shelve the books so I could read, for five or ten min-utes, one of the poetry books—Amy Lowell, Edna St. Vincent Millay, Elinor Wylie, e.e. cummings, light cascading through the stacks, through the trans-parent floors, and onto the poems that soared inside of me, the words seem-ing to take wing against everything gray and ordinary in my life.

One day Ms. Cherry accused me of stealing a book of Shakespeare's because it was missing from where it belonged, and suddenly, all my outrage at the way she treated me, the disdainful way she always spoke to me, rose up, and shy mouse of a girl, I turned on her, my eyes flashing fire. My voice rose so everyone in the library heard, "I do not steal books and don't ever accuse me of doing something like that again!" my shoulders flung back, my eyes say-ing if she didn't take it back I'd slug her. She said, "I'm sorry. I'm sorry. Of course you didn't. I don't know what I was thinking," and Anthea, standing behind us, flashed me a huge victory grin.

GROWING UP ITALIAN
IN PATERSON, NEW JERSEY
Maria Mazziotti Gillan

When I was a little girl,
I thought everyone was Italian,
and that was good. We visited
our aunts and uncles,
and they visited us.
The Italian language smooth
and sweet in my mouth.

In kindergarten, English words fell on me,
thick and sharp as hail. I grew silent,
the Italian word balanced on the edge
of my tongue and the English word, lost
during the first moment
of every question.

It did not take me long to learn
that olive-skinned people were greasy
and dirty. Poor children were even dirtier.
To be olive-skinned and poor was to be dirtiest of all.

Almost every day
Mr. Landgraf called Joey
a "spaghetti bender:"
I knew that was bad.
I tried to hide
by folding my hands neatly
on my desk and
being a good girl.

Judy, one of the girls in my class,
had honey-blonde hair and blue eyes.
All the boys liked her. Her parents and
grandparents were born in America.
They owned a local tavern.
When Judy's mother went downtown
she brought back coloring books and candy.
When my mother went downtown, she brought back
one small brown bag with a towel or a sheet in it.

The first day I wore my sister's hand-me-down coat,
Isabelle said, "That coat looks familiar. Don't
I recognize that coat?" I looked at the ground.

When the other children brought presents
for the teacher at Christmas, embroidered silk
handkerchiefs and "Evening in Paris" perfume,
I brought dishcloths made into a doll.

I read all the magazines that told me
why blondes have more fun,
described girls whose favorite color was blue.
I hoped for a miracle that would turn my dark skin light,
that would make me pale and blonde and beautiful.

So I looked for a man
with blond hair and blue eyes
who would blend right in,
and who'd give me blond, blue-eyed children
who would blend right in
and a name that could blend right in
and I would be melted down
to a shape and a color
that would blend right in,
till one day, I guess I was forty by then,
I woke up cursing
all those who taught me
to hate my dark, foreign self,

Growing Up Italian in Paterson, New Jersey

and I said, "Here I am—
with my olive-toned skin
and my Italian parents,
and my old poverty,
real as a scar on my forehead,"

and all the toys we couldn't buy
and all the words I didn't say,
all the downcast eyes
and folded hands
and remarks I didn't make
rise up in me and explode.

onto paper like firecrackers
                                like meteors
and I celebrate
my Italian American self,
rooted in this, my country, where
all those black/brown/red/yellow
olive-skinned people
soon will raise their voices
and sing this new anthem:

Here I am
      and I'm strong
      and my skin is warm in the sun
      and my dark hair shines,

and today, I take back my name
and wave it in their faces
like a bright red flag.

PART TWO

Blending In

SCENTS
Maria Laurino

Growing up in Short Hills, New Jersey, a suburb that produced debutantes just as Detroit manufactured steel, I learned as a child that the shrill whistle sounding every hour at the station signaled more than an approaching train: the town's dividing line was drawn at the railroad, and we were on the wrong side of the tracks. While many of my friends lived in sprawling ranch houses with stone patios and outdoor pools, our little split-level house in a new development had a modest lawn that blended into the same-sized property of our neighbors, who were mostly small businessmen, middle managers, and teachers. As my neighborhood pal would remind me, we lived in "the ghetto of Short Hills."

Perhaps any child who is poor among the rich learns to kowtow to the needs of the wealthy, and in doing so carries a deep sense of shame over her own inadequacies. The child intuits the sense of privilege that the rich share, and knows she'll be rewarded by indulging them, commenting on how lovely their house is, oohing and aahing at the wall of mirrors in the bathroom, enthusiastically accepting the gracious invitation to swim in their pool. Her role is to be a constant reminder, like a grandfather clock that chimes reassuringly, of just how much they have.

But people pride themselves on degrees of wealth, so I never forgot that the real "ghetto" was in a section of Millburn, the neighboring town where my father had grown up, that housed an enclave of Italian Americans. Because Short Hills was part of Millburn township, the poor kids and young gents went to school together (the public school was so good that there was not the usual channeling of the elite to private schools). In both junior high and high school, there were mainly middle-, upper-middle-, and upper-class teens. Latinos and African Americans were still excluded back then so the only people of color in my high school were the children of the housekeeper at the local Catholic church. That left the largest dark ethnic group: the lower-middle-class Italians from Millburn, and the only kids labeled with an ethnic slur.

Scents

In high school, the Italian American boys were known as the "Ginzo Gang"; they were greasers with beat-up cars that first chugged, then soared, thanks to their work at the local gas station, owned by the father of one of them. Olive-skinned and muscular, they were sexy in their crudeness; and their faint gasoline scent and oiled-down hair defined the image of Italian Americans in our school. The young women who hung out with them had little separate identity other than as the girlfriends of the Ginzos.

The Ginzos were my rearview mirror, a reflection of the near past that I wished to move beyond. They were an acknowledgment of my heritage, a recognition that the small sum of money my mother had inherited from her parents, used as the down payment on our house in a neighborhood a mile away, allowed me to escape from their world. But who was I fooling? My grandfather, who started a small construction company, earned his money by digging the earth; sweat and dirt were part of me, an oath of fealty to my family's peasant past. Yet I preferred to bury the memories of his labor, which provided us with some material comforts but not enough to rid me of the label of the "smelly Italian girl."

In the interval between the accusation of being smelly and an unspoken admission of my guilt, a denial of my ethnic self emerged. Unprepared to confront my fears, I responded like a criminal who'd do anything to get the charges dropped. If the cause of being called smelly were my Italian roots, then I would pretend not to be Italian.

At first I rejected the smells of my southern European heritage. Gone were the tastes and aromas of my youth: the sweet scent of tomato sauce simmering on the stove, soothing as a cup of tea on a rainy night; the paper-thin slices of prosciutto, salty and smooth on the tongue; and my own madeleine, oil-laden frying peppers, light green in color with long, curvaceous bodies that effort-lessly glide down the throat and conjure up memories of summer day trips to Asbury Park, where we ate ham, swiss, and fried pepper sandwiches prepared by my mother. Instead, I began to savor the old flavors of eastern Europe, new to my tongue: pickled herring and cured fish, sour and smoky, and the brisket I was served when I ate holiday meals with my new friend from gym class.

Decades later, when I told my Jewish husband that in high school I tried to assimilate by imitating his culture, he laughed. But in the uninformed world of the adolescent, narrow assumptions get made about the scheme of things. At the time, I didn't understand that the Jewish girls who zealously booked plastic surgery appointments with Howard Diamond, the Manhat-tan doctor famous for creating identical pug noses in Short Hills and Great Neck, Long Island, were undergoing a similar identity struggle.

Stripped of familiar smells, next I wanted to eliminate the extra baggage of vowels, those instant markers of ethnicity.

"Mom, why did you name me Maria?" went my familiar dinner table question.

"Hon, why did we choose Maria?" she'd say, deferring to my father. He had wanted to name me Denise, after a Belgian child who greeted his troop during World War II and remained etched in his memory.

"Mama's name was Maria," my mom would add, interrupting her own question and recognizing that she was the keeper of tradition, the holder of the deciding vote. "Your father's mother was Maria, and I loved the actress Maria Montez."

Her last explanation was the consolation prize, the frayed ticket to the American scene that she had won and wished to hand to me. Naming me after a beautiful, vapid actress (Spanish, no less) would have revealed an unseen side of my mother, one that had rebelled against the expectation of having to show respect. A momentary fantasy, a chimera. I'm certain that I was named after my mother's mother.

But I would adopt the Montez interpretation. That both my grandmothers were named Maria bore little relevance at the time; a grade B movie actress, however, at least sounded glamorous.

"Why didn't you change our last name to Laurin?" I continued my teenage whine. During these end-of-the-day efforts to sanitize myself, washing off an *o* seemed a clean, decisive stroke.

Only years later did I begin the precarious work of trying to replace the layers of ethnicity I had stripped away in order to dissociate myself from the smelly Italians. The alien surroundings of college fostered a nostalgia for familiar tastes, and allowed me to appreciate the foods I had grown up with, although not everyone shared my enthusiasm. Once my freshman roommate approached me, her face a picture of compassion and concern, as I entered our tiny dorm room. How was my weak stomach? she asked. Momentarily befuddled, I soon realized that she had confused the pungent aroma of the provolone I had recently eaten with that of vomit, and believed that I had thrown up in our room.

By my early twenties, I learned more about the girl at the cafeteria table who talked about the smelly Italians. According to the local grapevine, her parents were getting divorced because her father had been making seasonal trips to Italy to visit his secret mistress and their two children. Now I realize that she probably was never invited on her father's frequent sojourns, and the thoughtless remark was the defense of an insecure child, rejected by a man too busy sniffing the earthy scents of Italians to spend much time with her.

✌

Today I have a new fear about smell; I fear that I lack a defining odor. I feel removed from my own sense of smell and the images it could conjure. I feel a languorous appreciation for everyday scents, like my pots of dried lavender, whose wildflower fragrance has faded to a docile sachet, as its deep purple buds grew pale with streaks of beige, a graceful bow to domesticity and old age. I refuse to linger by the coffeepot and sniff my carefully chosen beans, or inhale their smoky end, first ground, then muddied and scorched by a hot rain; instead, I quickly dump the grounds and wash the pot in soapy water, just as I will rush to lather the summer heat off my body. No smell, no mess. Life is measured, careful, far removed from the chaos of dirt and its primitive pleasures, and the smelly label of my youth.

Clean, but without texture; scrubbed of the salty drops that tell our singular stories. I fear that after years of trying to rid myself of the perceived stench of my ethnic group and its musty basement class status, I sanitized my own voice, washed it away.

Certain incidents in life—like being told during gym class that you smell—become emotional markers, and around these events a series of reactions are set into motion: giving up pizza for pickled herring can take years to undo. I have recently come to notice how much time I spend scenting my body, covering it with colognes, milks, and creams, giving it a pleasant but artificial character, or voice, you could say. At first I was unaware that I had become perfume-obsessed, as people can often be unaware of their obsessions. But now I think I can link its beginnings to a time and a place.

Initially, I didn't realize the connection between a fragrance fixation and a freelance writing career, but neither did I fully understand that a spray of cologne can provide a narrative for your body in case your own story lacks luster. My aromatic addiction began when I decided not to return (after a brief stint in government) to the newspaper I had worked at for nearly a decade, which was as familiar as family. I was nervous about the decision to freelance, because it not only took away an important piece of identity, but would force me to choose my subjects, instead of writing about what others expected of me. And perhaps even worse, telling people that you are a full-time freelancer sounds more like a euphemism for unemployment than an adult career choice. So I acted a bit like the child who leaves home for the first time: one part wants to go while the other kicks and drags his way down the stairs, clutching the newel post. The final decision to step out the door and not return to my old work home coincided with a surprise birthday gift from my husband, a five-day trip to Paris. A perfect distraction, except that I found myself spending a good part of the time thinking about a particular French cologne.

I would like to chalk it up to coincidence rather than to Freud that I had occasionally been wearing a French cologne with a light lemon scent and a Roman emperor's name, Eau d'Hadrien, which seemed like an elegant version of the Love's Fresh Lemon of my youth. But maybe the alchemy of a new affection for Europe and my old need to hide Italian smells with lemons conjured an odd sensory experience—reluctance, relief!—when I first sniffed this cologne.

I went to a small Left Bank perfumery filled with fluted glass bottles capped in gold and bought my scent, one of my tasks in Paris, because it was cheaper there than back home. The saleswoman handed me the bag and then made an irresistible gesture: she sprayed my body, from my neck to my thighs, with cologne. Her hands flowed gently yet confidently around me, and the idea of being covered in fragrance, not frugally dabbed behind the ears, was so enticing that I went back to the store every day for a purchase and another spray. I had discovered a scented balm to soothe a shaky ego.

"Is this a gift for someone?" she asked upon my return.

"No, it's for me," I happily responded, waiting for the soft mist to drape me like a gossamer veil.

After that trip, I became even more attached to the fragrance, or perhaps the idea of this fragrance. In department stores, I allowed myself one indulgent purchase: hand cream, body lotion, perfumed body cream (my favorite—it's as if I'm covered in lemons and cream), soaps, other colognes to mix with my fragrance to create a new, layered smell—the possibilities seemed endless. I no longer just sprayed behind the ears but covered myself completely in the scent, letting the perfume conquer the blandness of a scrubbed self, an elixir to enliven a diffident voice.

I used to think that my guilt-free desire for an expensive French cologne meant that I was at least coming to terms with the embarrassing bourgeois side of myself, which capitalized on the chic of a European heritage rather than my real-life peasant roots. But now I realize that like the young girl who wanted to deny her heritage, again I was ducking for cover. I never quite unlearned the lesson from gym class long ago, when the voices of my family and my past were silenced as I altered the scents surrounding me. It's easier to shower away a smell, to censor yourself with a scent, than to accept your body's signature, the rawness of odor and sweat.

Scents

The smelly Italian girl no longer exists, if she ever did. In addition to my fragrance, my body is practically hairless, waxed from lip to toe by a Gallic woman who says "Voilà" after finishing each leg and who reminisces about her country, sharing with me that she knows the colorist who knows the colorist who mixes the blond hair dye for Catherine Deneuve (her six strands of separation from true glamour). During the months between waxings, I let my leg hair grow long and I run my fingers through it, still mystified by the abundance of those dark strands that I wish to find beautiful, but that I ultimately decide to remove once again.

I have tried to escape the class boundaries of my youth, but sometimes, in that lonely space between me and the bathwater, I wonder what has become of my own smell, and what it would be like to uncover a voice that could tell the stories of my past.

DADDY, WE CALLED YOU
Maria Mazziotti Gillan

"Daddy" we called you, "Daddy"
when we talked to each other in the street,
pulling on our American faces,
shaping our lives in Paterson slang.

Inside our house, we spoke
a Southern Italian dialect
mixed with English
and we called you "Papa"

but outside again, you became Daddy
and we spoke of you to our friends
as "my father,"
imagining we were speaking
of that "Father Knows Best"
TV character
in his dark business suit,
carrying his briefcase into his house,
retreating to his paneled den,
his big living room and dining room,
his frilly-aproned wife
who greeted him at the door
with a kiss. Such space

and silence in that house.
We lived in one big room—
living room, dining room, kitchen, bedroom,
all in one, dominated by the gray oak dining table
around which we sat, talking and laughing,

Daddy, We Called You

listening to your stories,
your political arguments with your friends,

Papa, how you glowed in company light,
happy when the other immigrants
came to you for help with their taxes
or legal papers.

It was only outside that glowing circle
that I denied you, denied your long hours
as night watchman in Royal Machine Shop.
One night, riding home from a date,
my middle-class, American boyfriend
kissed me at the light; I looked up
and met your eyes as you stood at the corner

near Royal Machine. It was nearly midnight.
January. Cold and windy. You were waiting
for the bus, the streetlight illuminating
your face. I pretended I did not see you,
let my boyfriend pull away, leaving you
on the empty corner waiting for the bus
to take you home. You never mentioned it,
never said that you knew
how often I lied about what you did for a living
or that I was ashamed to have my boyfriend see you,
find out about your second shift work, your broken English.

Today, remembering that moment,
still illuminated in my mind
by the streetlamp's gray light,
I think of my own son
and the distance between us,
greater than miles.

Papa,
silk worker,
janitor,
night watchman,

immigrant Italian,
I honor the years you spent in menial work
slipping down the ladder
as your body failed you

while your mind, so quick and sharp,
longed to escape,
honor the times you got out of bed
after sleeping only an hour,
to take me to school or pick me up;
the warm bakery rolls you bought for me
on the way home from the night shift.

the letters
you wrote
to the editors
of local newspapers.

Papa,
silk worker,
janitor,
night watchman,
immigrant Italian,
better than any "Father Knows Best" father,
bland as white rice,
with your wine press in the cellar,
with the newspapers you collected
out of garbage piles to turn into money
you banked for us,
with your mouse traps,
with your cracked and calloused hands,
with your yellowed teeth.

Papa,
dragging your dead leg
through the factories of Paterson,
I am outside the house now,
shouting your name.

THIRD-GENERATION HAWTHORNE
Jennifer Gillan

In her basement kitchen love was measured in circles—meatballs, anisette cookies, strufoli, pizzas—all served up at the round kitchen table. It didn't matter that it was a fake-wood-grained table or that the plates were cheap, clunky gray ironstone discs. We all packed around grandma's table, our anticipation illuminated by the globe of the fake Tiffany lamp, its flecks of orange, gold, and cherry colored glasses cheerfully presiding over the meal. We hardly noticed that the table was too small or that the cramped chairs pinched our backs. Often, our knees knocked into each other or into one of the tables' hollow legs as we jockeyed for position as Grandma lowered the steaming oval platters onto the table. Meatballs, sweet sausage, braciola, chicken cacciatore, and always some kind of homemade pasta shaped into circles, globes, or tubes. Despite the chaos that then ensued, we still managed an orderly circular passing motion so that each person could sample something from these platters. In the second and third courses our taste buds were swept up in the alternating currents of saltiness and sweetness, first prosciutto and then pears, first provolone and then figs, the final wave an alternation of bitterness and sugariness, the Fernet aperitifs followed by powdered sugar–encrusted anisette balls. A reverent silence followed the arrival of each course, indicating our concentrated savoring of the variety of flavors. The still moments didn't last and soon voices rose and dishes clanked as discussions that had been interrupted were picked up again midstream and as everyone reached across each other to ladle themselves more gravy or to snatch the last of the sausage. At that table, there was no escaping our physical closeness and no desire to do so. At that table we were a united family no matter how quickly after the meal we dispersed and went our separate ways.

In our suburban living room success was measured in rectangles. The room itself was rectangular in shape with the front door and enclosed entryway dividing the room in two. I always liked that room because it seemed larger and grander than the squares in which my friends' families lived in the pre–family room era of the early 1970s. I especially liked the French door, divided as its panes were by strips of chestnut that created the effect of rows of tiny squares of glass and light. The door had a large, old-fashioned brass key that I loved to hold in my hand, attaching some imagined significance to its cold metal and its surprising weight. Facing that keyhole, I would be situated between my two favorite walls of the room, each of which housed stained-glass windows; two vertical rectangles perched at opposite ends of the chestnut mantle of the large brick fire place and one horizontal rectangle presided over the opposite wall, regally positioned at the exact midpoint above eye level and just beneath the crown molding of the ten-foot ceiling. Beneath the matching windows on the other side of the room, a rougher symmetry greeted the eye and harshly disrupted the elegant flow of that room. On each side of the fireplace, my mother had positioned two bookshelves constructed from stained pieces of plain wood resting on stacks of weather-beaten bricks that my father had taken from a refuse pile when the town had demolished the old Hawthorne Municipal Building. Despite the shame these homemade shelves caused me, I did love the collection of books that they contained. Worn classics, meant to be read in isolated reverie, spilled out of the shelves, speaking volumes about the family that lived in this room.

Of this latter room there are many pictures chronicling the changes in our suburban lifestyle. Couches come and go; the TVs get steadily larger and more flamboyant and our hairstyles keep pace. The world outside that room encroaches on it as my brother and I try to reshape it in the terms which success is measured in the other worlds to which we daily travel. With each reshaping, I erect more boundaries between these new worlds to which I travel and the ones from which I sprang. More concerned with angles and edges, with what is around corners than with what surrounds me, I eventually reject the connected world of that kitchen table. When I finally walk out the unlocked foyer door, I think I will never look back. Filled with yearning for that world I carelessly discarded, I now know what all discoverers must eventually learn: the earth is indeed flat; it is our eyes that are round.

❧

These rectangles and circles suggest the geometry of home, offering a theorem that distance divided by time creates more distance. I associate my parents' Hawthorne living room with other rectangles that evoke the entryways and exits of suburban America—credit cards, matching love seats, and TVs.

Third-Generation Hawthorne

The suburb, with its linear, neatly spaced grids, its houses separated by rectangles of grass, was a rectangular world measured in instant gratification, rather than slow accumulation, by graceful, delicate links, rather than deep, gnarled roots.

❧

In the last years of his life my maternal grandfather reminded me of one of those hospital monitors measuring a patient's life breaths by intermittently inflating and deflating; while his cycle did not come near the regularity of the life support machine, it was enough to keep me aware during the hours we visited him of his fragile hold on mortality. He still got very excited about telling stories; he would suck in his breath and his chest would fill with air; in the telling he seemed to soar out of his decrepit body and a younger version of him would float just above us.

He would seem to take off when telling us a wild story about how his father was a newspaperman, or how his mother worked for the village priest and knew everyone's secret confessions, or how the first time he saw my grandmother she was chasing a runaway pig through the village. He would smile broadly at that one: "You should have seen her. She was shiny and rosy like an apple. And, oh, what energy."

The stories were usually mildly entertaining, even if his broken English was always difficult to understand. I think he imagined when telling them that he was making a speech in front of the Societa Cilentano; the tone of his voice and the way that he inserted pauses and arresting eye contact implied that he took these events far more seriously than we ever did. He would open his eyes wide, and pause dramatically before the best parts.

"You see, the woman had the *mal occhio* and she went to my mother instead of confession and this really angered the priest."

His stories were best when he added some juicy detail like that, but sometimes they were just ordinary grandpa-type stories of who was related to whom. Recounting these genealogies and telling family stories meant a lot to him, but to us they were alternatively mildly entertaining or slightly dull. There were other routines that went along with the storytelling and on our more tolerant days, we found those entertaining as well.

"Irina, Irina," Grandpa would shout at the home health aide. "Irina, Irina."

Finally, she'd come dashing in, saying, "What! What?"

"You didn't offer Maria anything."

He would wink at me as if to say, "I just like to have her rush in here and wait on me a little like your grandmother did." Then in a show of mock subtlety he would then nudge his head in the direction of the dining room table. Irina should have known her part in this show by heart, since he staged it every night. Yet, each night she looked around the table as if confused and after a few more melodramatic gestures by Grandpa seemed finally to notice the giant yellow Whitman's Sampler box on the table. She was either gamely playing along or really as slow-witted as my mother said. When she finally located the box, she would make a show of offering it to my mother and me as if she were a very regal hostess and then said, "You should have, Arturo." And, every night, he wrinkled his nose and shooed her away. He never ate processed food, in fact, never ate anything but fresh Italian food until my grandmother died. Not that he appreciated that cooking when he got it.

"Eh, eh, too much sauce; too hot! Eh, what is this meat, no good, no good." I wonder if he regrets those complaints as he is cutting into some of Irina's overcooked beef or enjoying the boiled hotdogs she serves up. Her "specialties" are even worse than the standard fare. I learned that one day at lunch she coaxed me into staying: "Janet, she told me how to make. Is good. Yes? Zucchini pie." I looked down at the casserole and knew Aunt Janet would never make such a gloppy mess. I smiled and said, "Just a small piece," thinking about how hard it was going to be to actually swallow it. I did draw the line at the bloody chicken she offered next, but Grandpa actually had a piece. By some miracle, he didn't get salmonella, but during Irina's stay, Grandpa did lose a lot of weight. Maybe it was from sadness, though. After all, he spent most of his time looking out the window and pining for my grandmother, "It's my time," he would say melodramatically at least once every visit.

He would often remind us, "You know, they wouldn't let me in the room. And I tried to get there, but the ambulance people kept pushing me away. I shouted, 'Angelina, Angelina,' And she yelled, 'Arturo, Arturo.' I grabbed her hand but they pushed past me and I lost my grip. That was the last time I saw her." He scrunched up his nose and crumpled his face a bit, getting that sentimental look he often had. Tears started to stream down his face, "She will wait for me. It is my time too," and he would look pleadingly in my direction for some confirmation. My mother and I would offer fake comfort, "Grandma loves you. She is waiting for you. Maybe she has to just wait for the bread to rise and then she will call you."

He could be a bossy old man and when we'd get angry with him, we'd joke during the car ride home, "She's just taking a well-earned rest. She's tired from sixty years of waiting on him; or she made a deal with Saint Peter, 'Just a few years of peace, that's all I ask'. 'Sure, he misses me now,' she might complain to Saint Anthony, 'but all he'll do when he gets here is play cards with that Rosalina woman.' She'd look around at the other Italian ladies in black dresses, and they'd all nod. To punctuate her point, she'd fold her calloused hands over her apron-covered round belly. Then we'd feel guilty and we'd speculate, "Maybe she is waiting for him. Maybe she will be a young woman chasing that pig again when he arrives. Maybe the wind will blow her hair wildly around her face and her skin will be rosy and her body will be round and supple as it was before it was ravaged by cancer." Maybe Grandpa's romantic visions would be realized and maybe she will come for him soon. Then we were suddenly sad because we knew we wanted him to stay because there was something comforting for us in the ritual of visiting him and listening to his stories every night. But it was selfish of us because he just wanted to go.

He'd ask, "Did God forget me? I have lived too long. Everybody is dead; I am ready to go. I don't know why I am still here. It is time."

Sometimes we'd distract him, by asking him to retell one of the stories. Yet, because we heard them so often, we didn't really listen closely when he did.

I regret the inattention I gave to those stories. Thinking back on them, I have so many questions, "Why did his father ship his wife and family back to Italy? Did he really go to Argentina to work? "Why did he never return?"

These were the kind of negative details my grandfather would never reveal except when they slipped out toward the end of his life. Mostly though the bad parts of the family history remain shrouded in mystery. The history with which we are left is tinged with my grandfather's optimism. He would get all puffed up with excitement telling those stories as if telling them were somehow keeping him alive.

As soon as he finished them and began to deflate once again, I would instantly regret not being more attentive because the deflation was so hard to watch. It was as if he had just used up the last of his life's breath and had brought himself one step closer to death, all in service of a story that I only kept one eye and ear on while the rest of me tried to catch snippets of *Jeopardy, Murder She Wrote,* or whatever stupid show played too loudly on Grandpa's TV. The deflation really was physically noticeable; Grandpa's posture slumped, he turned his head away and stared blankly at the dingy beige shade as he contemplated the emptiness of his present life. He usually sighed and said to my mother, "Eh, Maria," conveying with his weary tone all that he felt that had been lost since the days when he served as the spokesperson for other immigrants in his role as secretary of Societa Cilentano.

❧

As we pulled into their driveway one sultry July night, I noticed that the fireflies had started to congregate in the backyard garden, darting in and out of tomato plants, zigzagging through the bean stalks, high-diving into the row of peppers, arcing back into the evening sky, and circling above the fig tree. The two white metal chairs sat waiting in the backyard of the squat white house. They were slightly askew and looked recently vacated as if their occupants had just remembered a pot boiling on the stove and rushed in to tend to it. The black hearse-like Ford with the sticky vinyl seats was still parked outside and inside peppers were still frying and the sausage sizzling in its own grease.

Before we slammed the tinny door of our blue Beetle, we could feel Grandma moving toward the back door. As we ascended the crazy popsicle-stick steps, she came to the top of the landing and greeted us with her usual, "Ey, so late, so late. What's wrong with you people?" I knew this pushing us away was just playacting, a ritual of misdirection, a way to trick the evil spirits into looking elsewhere for a family whose happiness they could tamper with. I enjoyed these moments, the more so because Grandma's peasant wisdom dictated that we could not fool those spirits forever. They find everyone eventually, she warned. When I got to the top of the steps, I hugged her. She was still round and healthy then; her embrace smelled like freshly baked bread instead of medicine and alcohol wipes. Right behind me, my mother repeated my gesture; yet, as she reached for her mother, Grandma stepped back and surveyed her, "Maria, what is wrong with your hair?"

This criticism was a ritual too, another bit of misdirection, but I saw that my mother could never quite remember that. As she did every night, my mother winced, stung by the familiar words. In response, my mother made a point of praising me in front of Grandma who'd whisper words of caution, "Maria, shh, you should not say such things." "But why, Ma, it's true?" "Eh, everybody already knows. It's not good to say aloud." Sometimes my mother persisted, "It's true and it's my job as her mother to tell her." And, each time Grandma would shake her head and say, "You people so stupid," the standard phrase she used to marvel at the carelessness of 'Mericani like my mother. Italians knew better than to fool with the gods. My mother knew better too, of course, and was hardly a real 'Mericani like my father, but she straddled the two worlds, believing both in the evil eye and in the *Power of Positive Thinking*. She tried to give my older brother and me all the praise and encouragement she didn't get from her mother, but somehow it backfired. Over the years Grandma's criticisms accumulated in my mother's subconscious and collected as a pool of low-self esteem that, despite her best efforts to the contrary, seeped slowly from my mother's skin into mine even as she clasped my hand and looked me in the eye and said, "You are beautiful and smart and wonderful."

It was my Grandmother's misdirection, not this effusive praise that took root. I understood that misdirection, this act of stating or implying the exact opposite of your real feelings in order to avoid detection and prevent sabotage of your plans and generally to mislead your enemies, was like sending out a decoy. The purpose was to distract evil-wishers and redirect any negativity or adversity elsewhere. My grandmother had learned these simple rules from her peasant ancestors: criticize when you want to praise, berate when you want to belie how much you care; yell at sick people when you are scared they won't get well, lose your temper when you are filled with concern. You can see how this strategy is flawed: because the decoy and the loved one are the same person, it is not easy for the person to always separate what is misdirection from what is genuine feeling. My mother never could and was always pained by her mother's criticisms.

My mother and I both learned from Grandma to toughen ourselves in this way for the inevitable criticisms of the world. As my grandmother liked to tell my mother before criticizing her house or her hair, "If I don't tell you, who will?" In this way Grandma used misdirection as a preemptive strike. Hit each other before someone else does it harder or worse yet unexpectedly. Hers was an evasive strategy of deflection and redirection. Grandma's tactic was intended to keep her family and herself cocooned, their inner lives and thoughts safely hidden from the meddling, prying eyes of others. Following this strategy, I set up a protective barrier that has been effective in preventing the possibility of getting hurt, by not allowing anyone close enough to inflict mortal wounds. I found I could use misdirection in all my relationships to preempt pain, to dump before I was dumped.

This was a perversion of Grandma's original strategy; for her, misdirection was just a delaying tactic, because she was willing to accept the inevitable, that evil-wishers would overpower well-wishers and that bad luck and maybe even death would catch up with you.

Grandma did her best to outrun death. She was always whizzing by in a spurt of immigrant energy and invention, making something out of nothing. Usually, it was a meal. Typically, we'd walk into her kitchen and she'd hold up her hands and exclaim, "Ah, you people," and exude a sign meant to indicate the hopelessness of this new generation. After all, my mother would pack us into the VW Bug every day and drive the few blocks over to Grandma's so we could eat Italian food before my mother had to get back home and cook my Irish father his meat and potatoes which all of us refused to eat. Grandma would look at us and shake her head, "I have nothing. What do I have?" It was a ritual she repeated each time we visited even though she always had something special for us. Her food was her offering of the love she refused to express in words. Instead she'd usually greet my mother, her daughter, with "Maria, what's wrong with your hair?" After such a proclamation, usually delivered at the base of the back door steps, she'd turn and breathe in as if to summon the energy to climb the flight to her kitchen. All the way up, she'd repeat her mantra, "I have nothing," a line she'd continue to repeat as she pulled container after container out of her magician's box refrigerator, mixing all the mismatched contents together to make a wondrous meal out of nothing. She performed other miracles as well. Once it was to rebuilding the flight of brick steps at the front of the house. "It's easy," she remarked. "I watched the mason," as if that explained it all. "Just common sense," she continued as she raised the sledgehammer over her head. It landed with a powerful thud against the existing bricks, which dutifully crumbled under her force.

RACE RIOT

Tom Perrotta

The way I heard it, these two black guys crashed the teen dance in the Little League parking lot. One of them had a funny hat, a red sailor's cap pulled down over his eyes. The other was tall and skinny. At first they just hung out near the band, jiving and nodding their heads to the music.

In 1975 Darwin was still an all-white town, a place where blacks were not welcome after dark. It must have taken a certain amount of courage for the two guys just to thread their way through the crowd, knowing they were being watched and whispered about, maybe even pointed at. The focus of the dance shifted with their arrival, until the whole event came to revolve around the mystery of their presence. Did they like the music? Were they looking for trouble?

Nobody really minded until they started bugging Margie and Lorraine. Later Margie said it was no big deal, they just wanted to dance. But she was wearing these incredible cutoffs, and Sammy Rizzo and some of the other football players didn't like the way the black guys were staring at her ass. There would have been trouble right then, but a cop stepped in when it was still a shouting match and sent the brothers home.

I'd left the dance early with Tina, so I didn't see any of this happen. I didn't even hear about it until Tuesday afternoon, when Sammy Rizzo slapped me on the back and asked if I was ready to rumble.

"Rumble?" I said. The word sounded old-fashioned and vaguely goofy to me, like "jitterbug" or "Daddy-o," something the Fonz might say on *Happy Days.*

"Yeah," he said. "Tonight at eight. Better bring a weapon."

I didn't own any weapons except for a Swiss army knife that seemed completely unsuitable for a rumble, so I had to improvise from a selection of garden tools hanging in my parents' tool shed. My choice—a short, three-pronged fork used for weeding—was a big hit at the Little League.

"Jesus Christ," said Sammy. "That looks like something outta James Bond."

"Yeah," Mike Caravello observed. "You could probably rip someone's balls off with that."

We were sitting on picnic tables inside the pavilion, waiting for the baseball game to end. Caravello sat next to me, twisting his class ring around and around his finger. He made a fist and the ring's red jewel jutted up from his hand, a freak knuckle.

"Some nigger's gonna get Class of '74 tattooed on his face," he said, flashing a nasty silver grin. He was way too old to be wearing braces.

A jacked-up Impala squealed into the parking lot behind the first base bleachers. Caravello pounded the tabletop.

"Fuckin' excellent! It's the twins!"

The twins got out of the car and looked around, using their hands for visors. They were both wearing overalls with no shirts underneath, and their muscles were all pumped up from lifting.

"Which one's Danny?" I asked.

"The one with the tire iron," Caravello said.

My chest tightened up. Until that moment, the fight had seemed like a game to me, a new way to kill a night. But the twins were serious brawlers. They hurt people for fun. Caravello called them over so he could introduce me.

"This is Joey T.'s cousin, Buddy," he said. "He's gonna be frosh QB next year." The twins nodded. They had shoulder-length hair and identical blank faces, like a genetic tag team. I couldn't imagine playing football with people their size.

Danny scratched his head with the tip of the tire iron.

"Joey comin' tonight?"

"He can't," I explained. "He's eighteen now. If he gets busted, they won't let him be a cop."

Danny's brother, Paul, asked to see my weeding implement. Its three prongs were bent and sharpened, forming a sort of metal claw.

"Wow," he said. "You could tear somebody's eyes out with this."

The twins made fourteen of us. Our ranks, I noticed, were pretty much split: half normal guys, half psychos. The normal guys—I considered myself one—were just trying to defend our hangout. The psychos were looking for a good time.

The Rat Man, Sean Fallon, was busy picking his teeth with the rusty tip of his switchblade. I couldn't even look at him without getting the creeps. He got his nickname from his habit of biting people in fights. A few months before, for no good reason, he had bitten off Ray Malone's nipple in the middle of what was supposed to be a friendly wrestling match. A cop had to drive the nipple to the hospital so the doctors could surgically reattach it to Ray's chest. I heard that he carried it into the emergency room in a small white envelope. Norman LaVerne sat next to the Rat Man, frowning and shaking his head. Years ago, when he'd lived in another town, people said that Norman had buried a cat from the neck down and run over its head with a lawn mower. Normally I crossed the street when I saw him coming. But tonight we were on the same side.

"TWO, FOUR, SIX, EIGHT, WHO DO WE APPRECIATE?"

Baseball hats, purple and red, flew into the sky and fluttered down. The players and spectators slowly drifted out of the park. I could feel the tension gather. We stopped talking and fixed our eyes on the paths that led through the woods to the Washington Avenue section of Cranwood, where the blacks lived.

At five to eight, two cop cars drove into the park from separate entrances and converged on the pavilion. Jim Bruno got out of the lead car. He was the greatest running back our town had ever produced; people still called him the Bulldozer. I remembered going to games with my father and watching him plow through the defense, play after play, dragging tacklers for yards before going down. He had a mustache now, and the beginnings of a donut gut.

"Fight won't happen," he announced.

Nobody moved.

"You want me to put it in sign language?"

He looked at the ground and spat neatly between his polished shoes.

The Camaro was brand-new, gleaming white, with a plush red interior and a wicked eight-track system. Caravello's parents had given it to him as a graduation present even though he hadn't graduated. In September he would begin his fifth year of high school. Technically, he was still a sophomore. We cruised down North Avenue, Deep Purple blasting from our open windows. I liked Caravello when he let me ride in his car. The rest of the time I had my doubts about him. He didn't have any friends his own age, and I resented his success with the girls who hung out with us at the park. I especially hated the way he turned on you when a girl showed up. He had this trick of turning his class ring so the jewel faced out from his palm, and then clapping you on the head with it.

Caravello turned down the music as we passed the lumberyard.

"Fuckin' quarterback," he said. "Every cheerleader in the world will want to suck your cock."

"Not quite," I said.

He waved me off. "You don't know shit. Those football parties are wild."

I thought about the stories I'd heard. "Is it true about Margie Waldman?"

Caravello grinned. I could see the rubber bands inside his mouth, white with spittle. "What'd you hear about Margie Waldman?"

"You know. That she did it with the whole starting team after the Thanksgiving game."

"Not the whole team," he said. "Just the defense."

We stopped at a red light in front of the perforating company. Two huge fans blew factory exhaust straight into the car. Outside, swing shifters in rumpled green clothes sat against the red brick building and ate their lunches. They chewed slowly and gazed at us without interest.

"Stupid assholes," Caravello said. When the light turned green, he laid a patch.

Just before we reached downtown Elizabeth, Caravello pulled a V-turn and headed home. Beyond the smokestacks and water towers, the last streaks of color were dissolving in the sky. Instead of continuing straight into town, we turned left at Jim's Tavern and made the quick right onto Washington Avenue.

"What are we doing here?" I asked.

"If the niggers won't come to us, we'll have to go to them."

We drove slowly down the street. The houses we passed were no different from those on my own block, but the idea of black people living in them made them seem unfamiliar. Five minutes from home, and I felt like I'd crossed the border into another country. Caravello cut the headlights and pulled over behind the Cherry Street school. He left the engine running.

"There they are," he said.

A bunch of black guys—you could tell from the speed and grace of their game that they were in high school—were running full court on the lot behind the school. It was a weird spectacle at that time of night. Only the two baskets were lit up, one by a spotlight attached to the school, the other, more dimly, by a nearby streetlight. Center court was a patch of darkness.

It was a game of fast breaks. The players would be visible for an instant around one basket, and then they'd scatter abruptly into the shadows, only to emerge seconds later at the other end of the court, already off the ground, arms stretching for a ball we couldn't see.

I was so caught up in the main game that I didn't notice the kid at first. He was about my own age, and he was playing a game of his own. When the real game exploded into light at one end of the court, he'd suddenly appear at the other, driving to the hoop past imaginary opponents, pulling down his own rebounds, always vanishing just before the stampede caught him from behind.

Caravello pummeled the steering wheel and started pressing on the horn, shouting curses into the night. For a second, I thought the car itself was screaming.

"Fuckin' assholes! Chickenshit niggers! Buncha pussies!"

The game stopped. The players near the school and the kid at the far basket turned in our direction. A couple of the bigger guys started toward us, but their movements were confused, hesitant. I yanked Caravello's hand off the steering wheel. The silence came as a jolt.

"Come on," I said. "Let's get outta here."

∾

The car climbed into the rich hills of West Plains, past stone mansions and big white houses with four or five cars in the double driveways. The air smelled sweet and green.

"Let's get some pussy," Caravello said.

"I have to be home by nine-thirty."

He frowned. "Can't get pussy until ten or so."

"I know. I can't believe my parents still pull this curfew shit on me."

"You think that's bad? My sister's sixteen and my old man still won't let her out of the house on weekends. She just locks herself in her room and cries all the time."

"Jeez."

Caravello took his hand off the wheel and delivered a sharp backhand to my chest. "Ever get any?"

" Any what? "

"Pussy, asshole." He mimicked me. "Duh, any what?"

"Not yet," I said.

"You went with Tina the other night, right?"

"Yeah."

"Are you telling me you didn't get in her pants?"

"Nope."

"Why the fuck not?"

"She wouldn't let me."

Caravello pushed me hard into the passenger door.

"Don't be stupid, Buddy. They all say no, but they don't mean it. It's just something they have to say, so you don't think they're sluts."

"They must mean it sometimes," I said.

Caravello shook his head.

"You better grow up," he told me.

I stared out the window for a while. We drove past Echo Lake. Even at night, you could see that the water was brown and shiny.

McDonald's was on Grand Avenue across from the paper mill. It felt good pulling into the parking lot in the Camaro. Usually I just sat inside the restaurant with friends, sharing fries and writing my name in salt on the tabletop, dreaming of the day when I would have a car.

"Wait for me," I told Caravello. "I gotta take a whiz."

Although the parking lot was packed with cars and kids, the restaurant was nearly empty. My Uncle Ralph was the only customer inside. He sat with his back to me at a table near the window. The dwarf we called Kareem was mopping the floor around my uncle's feet.

The restroom was disgusting. It smelled like somebody had just puked in there. I held my breath and pissed as fast as I could. I flushed the urinal as a favor to Kareem, then went to say hi to my uncle. When I came up behind him he was grinding a cigarette into the overflowing ashtray as though he held a grudge against it. I touched his shoulder.

"Uncle Ralph."

"Buddy, how's it going?" The *National Enquirer* was spread out in front of him like a tablecloth.

"Fine," I said. "What's in the news?"

"Look at this." He pointed with his yellowed fingertip to a headline that read, "Biggest Public Toilet in the Universe!"

"It says here that the Russian astronauts are dumping their excrement directly into outer space. Can you believe it? All these turds just floating around up there?"

"Don't our guys do it too?" I asked.

"No, sir. We cart ours home."

"It's really cold up there," I pointed out. "It probably just freezes right up."

"That's not the point," he said.

Kareem looked up suddenly from the floor and fixed the paper cap on his big head.

"The point is to have some respect," he said. His voice was surprisingly deep.

"Amen," said Uncle Ralph.

"Well," I said. "I better get going."

"You sure?" Uncle Ralph asked. "Can I buy you a cup of coffee or something?"

"No thanks. Gotta run."

When I got outside, the car was gone. I figured Caravello had ditched me, and I couldn't really blame him. What could he possibly get out of hanging out with someone who had to be home by nine-thirty? But then the horn honked and I saw him waiting for me on the exit side of the lot, grinning with his metallic teeth. I jogged over to the car feeling like a celebrity.

I opened the passenger door. Tina was in my seat.

"Look who I found," said Caravello.

I started to squeeze into the back seat but Caravello said, "No way. Nobody rides nigger in my car. Tina can sit on your lap."

She sat all the way up by my knees and held onto the dashboard. She waved out the window as we started moving. I turned my head and saw Jane and Donna leaning against a car talking to three blond guys I didn't recognize.

"Those guys are dickheads," Caravello said.

Tina lit a cigarette as we accelerated on Grand.

The breeze blew wisps of her hair into my face. I wanted to touch her, but I didn't know where we stood.

"How was the shore?" I asked.

She blew smoke out the window. "Great. Like my tan?" She pulled her shirt away from her shoulder to reveal a tan line as thin and pale as a piece of spaghetti, then twisted her head to look at me. "You know that old guy in McDonald's?"

"Yeah. He's my uncle."

"It's kinda creepy," she said. "It's like he lives in there."

"You have to know him," I said. "His wife died of cancer."

In my mind, I saw Uncle Ralph at the funeral, kissing the flower he dropped in Aunt Dot's grave, my father grabbing him as he stumbled.

"Hey Buddy," Caravello said. "You wanna go home now?" He looked at Tina. "It's past Buddy's bedtime."

"Shut up, Mike," I said.

"Well, it's after nine-thirty."

"Fuck that. I go home when I want to."

Caravello shrugged. "Hey Tina, you go down the shore a lot, don't you?"

"Yeah. We have a summer house in Point Pleasant."

"You got a boyfriend down there?" She blew a series of quivering smoke rings at the rearview mirror.

"Sort of."

"Is he a lifeguard?"

"No."

"How old is he?"

"Seventeen."

"Do you go all the way?" She flicked her cigarette out the window.

"You are so queer, Caravello."

For some reason, Tina leaned all the way back, as though I wasn't there. I sank down into the bucket seat beneath her weight. She and Caravello started arguing about the radio station, but I was too absorbed in her body to pay attention. I rested my forehead against the ridge of her spine. She smelled like maple syrup, just the way she had on Friday night.

Tina shifted in my lap. "Am I all right?" she asked.

"You're fine," I told her.

Tina went to Catholic school out of town. When she started showing up at the park that spring, she never talked to me and I couldn't tell if she was stuck-up or shy. Now, even after what had happened between us, I still didn't know if she liked me or not.

I closed my eyes and remembered watching her dance. She was wearing a football jersey that hung down past her shorts, number 24. I couldn't take my eyes off the numbers. It was a warm night, but I was wearing an air force shirt that had belonged to my father. I'd recently found four of them inside a trunk in our attic. They were musty from twenty years in storage, but I imagined I could smell faraway places in them, the Philippines, Korea, Japan. During a break in the music, Tina came up to me and tucked a finger in one of my epaulets.

"I love your shirt," she said, her voice sweet with Boone's Farm.

I brushed my fingers against the soft mesh of her jersey.

"I like yours too."

"I'm a little drunk," she whispered.

The band started up again. They were a bunch of gas station attendants who thought they were the Doobie Brothers. Tina grabbed my wrist and pulled.

"Come on and dance."

"I'll watch," I said.

And later, when Tina asked me if I could walk her home, I felt like I was in a dream, it happened so easily.

She lived across town, up in the hills. On the way, we held hands but didn't talk. The world was as still as a photograph. Near her house we took a shortcut through a patch of woods. It was way past my curfew, but we leaned against a tree and started making out. I slid my hand up her shirt in the back and tried to unhook her bra, but I couldn't find anything remotely resembling a hook. After a few minutes of fumbling, I dropped my hands to my sides and collapsed against her, baffled. She reached inside the jersey.

"It snaps in front," she whispered.

I put my hands where hers had been. We stopped kissing and just looked at each other. After a while I pulled up the jersey and burrowed my head beneath the numbers.

Her father was a dentist, and she lived in a big white house, the kind families live in on television. We kissed good night under a porchlight swarming with moths.

"You want to come in?" she asked. "My parents aren't home."

"Sorry," I said. "I have to go."

She tilted her head; her expression was serious, oddly adult.

"Buddy," she said. "Is this just one of those things?"

"One of what things?"

"You know," she said. "One of those things."

"Yeah," I said. "I guess so."

As soon as she shut the door I started running; my sneakers slapped a steady beat on the sidewalk. The clock in the drugstore window said it was after eleven-thirty, the latest I'd ever been out by myself.

I was panting for air by the time I pushed open the front door. Except for the flickering of the TV, the house was dark. My mother was lying on the couch in her bathrobe, a bunch of balled-up Kleenexes scattered on the carpet below. I waited for her to say something, but she just blew her nose.

I yelped. Caravello had clobbered me on the head with his ring.

"Go on." he commanded. "Tell Tina how scared you were when we went looking for niggers."

"I wasn't scared. You're the one who freaked."

"He shit his pants," Caravello told Tina. "You shoulda seen it."

The weeding implement was on the floor by my feet. I imagined raking it across his face.

"Don't lie," I said.

"You wanna go back?" he sneered. "Or is it past your bedtime?"

"I don't care."

He looked at Tina. "What about you?" She shrugged.

When we got back to Cherry Street, only the kid was left. He was shooting free throws at a basket near the school. You got the feeling he'd still be there when the sun came up. Tina giggled.

"Let's take his ball," Caravello said.

He whispered the plan. I didn't object, even though I had to do the dirty work. Caravello and Tina were supposed to distract the kid while I snuck up from behind.

I slid out from under Tina and shut the door. The car drove off, and I felt alone and vulnerable, hiding behind a tree near the curb. My head still smarted from Caravello's ring. I had to stamp my feet to get the blood flowing in my legs.

For one rotten moment, I was sure that Caravello had abandoned me, but just then the Camaro swung around the corner and stopped in the street on the other side of the school yard, directly across from me. Caravello honked the horn. His voice carried through the night with awful clarity.

"Hey Tyrone," he shouted. "Is that you?"

The kid stopped shooting. He turned toward the voice with the ball held loosely in the crook of his arm, the way you might hold a book walking home from school. I was surprised to see him wearing long pants on such a muggy night.

He heard my footsteps and whirled around when I was just a few steps away from him. When I saw his frightened face, I screamed. The sound that erupted from my throat was shrill and startled. His eyes got bigger when he heard it.

I drove my shoulder hard into his stomach and took him right off his feet—a perfect open-field tackle. He made just one sound, a gasp of amazement, before his head bounced heavily on the pavement.

The ball was rolling slowly toward the out-of-bounds line. I scooped it up and sprinted for the Camaro. As I ran, I couldn't shake the feeling that I held his head in my hand, clutched tight to my body.

Back in town, we pulled over to the side of the road. Now I was sitting in Tina's lap.

Caravello slapped me five. He was laughing so hard he could barely catch his breath.

"Did you hear that motherfucker scream?" he asked.

"He couldn't help it," I said.

We passed the basketball around as though it were some strange new object, something we'd never seen before. Its surface was worn completely smooth from overuse; it must have been slippery and difficult to play with. Tina stared at the ball for a long time, like someone gazing into the future.

"Spalding," she said finally. "I better go," I said.

"You want to come swimming at my house?" Tina asked. "My parents aren't home."

"No thanks. I'm late as it is."

"I'll go," Caravello said. "I could use a dip."

Tina poked me in the back. "You sure?"

"Yeah," I said. "It's past my bedtime."

Caravello laughed. I hated him then, in a way that made me feel dumb and helpless.

"Buddy's all right," he announced.

When Caravello dropped me off, I rushed across the lawn without looking back. I didn't want to watch them drive away together. The car peeled out just as I opened the front door.

My parents were both reclining on the couch, heads on opposite ends, legs tangled in the middle. They looked like some giant, two-headed monster of unhappiness.

"Do you know what time it is?" my father asked.

My mother answered for me. "It's twenty after ten. Where were you?"

"Little League, McDonald's, all over. I saw Uncle Ralph in McDonald's. He's worried about the Russians going to the bathroom in outer space."

"Don't change the subject," my father said. "Who's the hotshot that drove you home?"

"No one. I walked."

"Don't lie to us," my mother said sadly.

"Stay out of older kids' cars," my father said. "I'm warning you."

"We heard something about a race riot," my mother said. "We were worried about you."

My parents had recently bought a police radio, so they knew everything that went on in town.

"There wasn't any race riot," I said.

"Where'd you get that basketball?" my father asked.

I'd forgotten that I was holding the ball. I'd also forgotten about the garden tool, which I'd left on the floor of the Camaro. I imagined Tina using it to scratch Caravello's back.

"I found it," I said.

I glared at them, and they frowned back. Somehow I thought that everything that had happened was their fault, not mine. I bounced the ball once on the linoleum hall floor. The sound it made was hard and hollow. I wanted to say something in my own defense, to explain or apologize, but my head felt as empty as the ball in my hand, a round container of air.

DORISSA
Daniela Gioseffi

Grandma Lucia gave my father—her lame Donatuccio—the grace of empathy to live in another's skin and feel as they do. People at his funeral felt they'd had the most special bond with him. Me, too. Grandpa Donato told me before he died that I was the poetry of his life—a daughter he was proud of. He was always teaching me the romance of everything, dramatizing photosynthesis, or making our kitchen table come alive with molecules or spinning electrons, explaining the components of matter. Growing glass crystals on a clothesline for my older sister. Thrilling us with all he knew of science and history. Quoting, Dante, Shakespeare, Einstein. . . .

I remember when I stayed with Grandma Lucia in her cold water flat in Newark, while my father went to the plant where he was Chief Chemist and my mother went to the factory to sew. Grandma Lucia braided my hair so neatly, tight strand by strand, finely combed, to make sure I had no lice, common in the public schools of Newark then. What would she think of me, her favorite son's child, in prison as a political revolutionary?

As a five-year-old with blond curls, I walked through the Black ghetto, next to the Italian one, on my way to Avon Avenue School in Newark, where Uncle Salvatore still teaches eighth grade. His wife, my Aunt Elisabetta, died in childbirth, trying to have a son, at forty-four, against doctor's orders, though she had five healthy daughters.

"Here's your king," Aunt Elisabetta sighed, handing Uncle Salvatore a baby boy with her last breath. . . .

Even as we cried, we laughed at Grandpa Donato's funeral, mixing comedy with grief. Aunt Eleanora told the story of how Grandma Josie, his "Gracie Allen" Grandpa Donato called her, swatted a fly in the middle of his forehead, "splat!" as he posed majestically on the screen porch one summer night reciting Lincoln's Gettysburg address to impress me—a five-year-old—with the fact that I'd been born on the greatest American president's birthday. "Abraham Lincoln came from the poor like me!" he said. He could recite all the names of the American presidents in a row. He was so proud of his knowledge of American history—the way it was taught in the public schools then—with gloss over the cruel usury of minorities and cruelty to immigrant laborers—as if hordes of Native Americans were not slaughtered and their land stolen, or millions of imported as cheap labor or slaves. We laughed at that swat on his cerebral head—long ago as he lay cold—his face mirroring the dead, a calm Etruscan smile waxing his lips. He was naive about America in many ways.

I remember myself in a pink dress and Mary Jane shoes, patent black leather and white socks, with blond rag curls on my way to kindergarten—through the Newark ghetto—to "grand" crackers, some strange American food, and milk. They tasted so good. We never had graham crackers at home, and sometimes, no milk, though my father's inventions are still earning millions in corporate wealth. He supported his whole big family on thirty-five dollars a week during the depression—including his mother and father. Thirty-five dollars a week earned at G.E., now a big Pentagon contractor, builder of the Mark XII warhead—though my father invented chemistry for light bulbs then. Sometimes, I had the American child's usual favorite lunch—peanut butter and jelly sandwiches on white Wonder Bread inside my tin lunchbox, which I guarded every day with a broken umbrella—rain or shine—from Black boys who tried to steal its treasures. They had no lunch at all. I was afraid to befriend those kids.

"You'll get cooties 'n your hair, Nigger-lover!" I was told for my friendship with Silvy, a Black girl full of quick adult wisdom and wit. She kept the hungry Black boys away while we shared my lunch in a corner of the school yard.

"You mess wiv us, Andrew Jackson, an' um tellin' ywah *mama* on you!" Silvy stood firm with her hands on her hips, and they stalked away. With her cooperation, we ate my hydrogenated "peanut butter 'n' jelly" on white Wonder Bread full of BHA, and laughed about grown-ups, teachers, dumb books, boys' peeters. . . . Years later, Silvy and I marched in Alabama in the days of Selma's freedom riders. Now, Silvy's a civil rights casualty. Shot down like my sweet Yanos, for civil disobedience. My long civil disobedience record keeps me under suspicion.

"What do you know about Yanos Dupres-Nagy?" These relentless FBI interrogators keep asking me.

"Shirley Temple, ywah dirty underpants is showin'!" I can still hear Silvy's childish voice of thirty-five years ago in my head—the first day we met in kindergarten in Newark at Avon Avenue Public School—before the race riots there.

We all laughed and cried at her funeral, too. Now, unless we stop him, Mr. White Wonder Death's white heat is ready to squirt from his sleek missiles and burn us all to bright blooming "kingdom come," instant quick sizzle of human blood!

STRIKE ONE
SEASIDE HEIGHTS, NEW JERSEY
Annie Rachele Lanzillotto

for Rachel Lanzillotto,
and Rhoda Shapiro should she read this

My first cancer

I got diagnosed
at Seaside Heights
by a boardwalk portrait artist
named Rhoda Shapiro.

I was with my pitcher
in a two-week rental on the Jersey shore,
refining signals, throwing
strikes curves wild pitch knuckleballs pitch-outs and sinkers
seventy-five throws twice a day I caught
two hundred times popping up from a squat
barefoot in the sand
throw down to second nab the steal,
the play at the plate, swiping a caught ball
at imaginary runners sliding home.
Each day turned me more blonde more fit more
tan; ready to jump into college action
as a freshman recruit for the softball team.

My last fifty
I designated for a gift
for my mother a great present
not crap, not a silk-screened Elvis mirror,
not a tee-shirt air-brushed with paradise,
not one of the millions of stuffed E.T. dolls

prevalent that summer—summer before I was to leave for college,
summer before A.I.D.S. and Sony walkmans were named,
isolation bought and paid for. No,
I wanted a forever
keepsake, some thing my Mother could look at
while I was away at school.

I took one last walk alone
to the batting range
down the boardwalk
passed the portrait artists who for two weeks had been flashing
drawings of Marilyn Monroe and John Travolta at me, shouting,
"It won't take long."
My mother would love it. Why not a portrait?
The Ivy League was all about portraits in stately rooms.
I walked toward one of the artists
sitting under a Bella Abzug style yellow sun
hat arena around her.
"Plenty of detail for fifty bucks" she guaranteed.

Her arm moved at a rapid speed
from a three-tiered case of pastels
like the pitching machine
automatically
elbow hitching
her hand chose reds and yellows
as her eyes landed firmly upon different parts of me.
She asked questions about my life.
I felt appraised.
I couldn't see her hand,
the sketch pad and easel tall between us.
I answered smoothly, versed from the many college applications
I'd filled out all year. Then she was finished,
she turned the portrait toward me abruptly, and said,
"Good luck with your future."

More feminine, more gorgeous, more feathered
hair more blonde, eyes a deeper blue, and the glow
a white thin halo surrounding the whole image.

My pitcher laughed saying it looked nothing like me but I
could see the resemblance, the cultural idealization of me,
an iconic combination of the monalisa magnetism of John Travolta draw-
     ing you in,
and the full bursting lipped ripe beauty of Marilyn Monroe enticing you to
     take a bite,
and that's just what this point in my life was all about,
college applications blonde and blue-eyed,
energetic recommendations with a virgin's glow
personal statements charged with a pulse.

I handed the scroll to my mother magisterially thanking her
for everything up to this point in my life.
She unrolled it and grabbed my neck
turning her attention from the portrait to me,
"What's this lump on your neck?"
Her hand landed on what Rhoda Shapiro had drawn
but I had not noticed, red and yellow,
with the accuracy of a sonogram,
a diagnosis, a misshapen neck, a lump like a stop sign
amidst a blonde waterfall.

"How'd your Mom like the portrait?" my pitcher called to ask.
"She didn't really say," I said, "she took one look
and said she's sending me straightaway to the doctor tomorrow.
Something about a biopsy. Maybe I should have gotten her the Elvis mirror?"

LYNDHURST MEMORIES
Ed Smith

I grew up in the American suburban culture of Lyndhurst and Clifton, New Jersey, in the 1960s. When people asked me, I said, "I'm Italian." Most of my friends were Italian too. We called ourselves Italian, then, and not Italian American, though that's what we meant. Some of my friends called me Eddie Spaghetti, but they'd tease me, "Hey, Smith, that ain't Italian." Although it was true that I was only half Italian, I never mentioned that my Dad's father was from Germany.

Of course, I did all the standard 1960s American things—played guitar in a garage band, wrote songs, and went to William Paterson College—but the whole time I was growing up, I remember Nonna's house in Lyndhurst where my aunts and uncles all spoke Italian. My five first cousins and I would wrestle on the floor in the living room while the adults assembled in the kitchen. That house at 506 Laurel Avenue was always filled with coffee, cookies, spaghetti, meatballs, bread, and peppers. Even now, I can close my eyes and smell the aroma of delicious food that always permeated that house. I can still smell Grandpa's favorite breakfast of scrambled eggs, peppers, potatoes, and Italian bread. No Wonder Bread was allowed in Nonna's house.

Nonna always told us about when she first came to America from Italy to live with her Uncle Rocco and Aunt Lucia. "There was only one light in that house," she told us. "I wanted to go back to Potenza. I thought I'd die in that apartment where it was always so dark." She didn't leave; instead, she got a job as a seamstress in a factory and had another job stuffing cherries in a bottle. "I wasn't happy," she tells us, "until I met your grandfather."

On summer afternoons, Nonna would give me money to go to the corner store to buy ice cream for myself and my cousin Joey. One day, I think I was about ten or twelve years old, I bought my cousin an ice cream and myself a pen. Nonna couldn't understand that I wanted my own pen. She kept saying, "Here, take my pen," but I insisted I wanted my own pen shaped like a cigarette. "Ok," she said, and gave me another dime to buy an ice cream. She, who treasured her memories of the Italy of her girlhood, loved her half Italian grandson, but could never fully understand his American desires.

QUENCH A PLANT'S THIRST

Edvige Giunta

White roses and red
guard the doorstep of my apartment
in Jersey City, gloomy,
discontent.

I stick my finger in the soil.
Check their thirst, Mother says,
on this cloudy late June afternoon,
hours before my thirty-ninth birthday.

The green hose crawls
and my beloved quenches the roses'
early summer cravings.

My eyes, ears, full
of him, naked legs, arms,
sweat, water on chest—

then

the shape of my father,
tireless gardener,
soothing, old, fresh.

Talìa l'arbuliddra ch'bbriviraiu,
mischineddri, ss'i 'rifriscaru!

Sicilian words rush to
eager roots, miraculous
event of capillary action.

Quench a Plant's Thirst

Oh the tenderness of Father's voice,
his touch on roses, lilies, zucchini,
grapes, fig trees in the orchard
in disarray my brother clears
for my American daughter
who believes you dig
lemons out of the dirt.

ST. THERESE

Edvige Giunta

on Washington Street,
balancing bags of miracles:
olive oil

& three

green tomatoes that will turn
red in the sunny corner
of her window, *basilicò*
and *puddrisinu* on thick bread

two fresh zucchini she will slice
and fry for dinner tonight

her finger pokes my lover's gleeful belly,
bright light shimmering
on chestnut hair,
red glow of
motorcycle. *Capisc'*?

If you don't speak you die
her words like daisies

this tender encounter
with the Little Flower who lives
in the projects

Hoboken, NJ
recently hip town

St. Therese

in long, shabby pants,
nightgown down to her knees

her body a flag, a mantle,
a faded coat

NEVERTHELESS, IT MOVES

Susanne Antonetta

The brain looks as if it ought to be a map. Cul-de-sacs and straight-aways. All that mazy motion. It's a misleading map, because if you followed its spongiform surface it would circle you randomly around, not even ending where you began. Dante described hell's torments as occurring in folds. This when everyone knew just what brain looked like: a dish to eat on toast and a fat spat out in battle as Dante, a soldier, knew. I don't think the torment of memory is that we have it but that it lies on such inaccessible roads and what we think we know we can never trust.

I'm so afraid I'm mentally ill.

I practice my memories. I feel I have to. We Cassills engage so instinctively in rewriting ourselves.

There are the blank years of my life. No one, including my parents, will talk about or acknowledge them. No one wants me to talk about them. I am a wrong turn. And from year to year my family changes the pattern of their forgetting: so a few years ago my parents began to say I'd finished high school, though I dropped out as a sophomore. But I like memory; there's something precious about these walks through the wasted landscapes only I can see.

I imagine everyone else in my family taking their own walks through their own frozen spaces, but no one's talking.

My grandmother set this pattern, a woman whose lifework was creating herself and who needed to invent and reinvent the family that reflected her. She made herself up wholesale, a class-switching Englishwoman, a restless traveler, a Christian Scientist, and a genius at spinning her own narratives, a talent that began with the narrative of her impregnable immortal body.

My grandmother traded in her mortal body for gossamer, the Christian Science body-as-illusion. Docetism: the belief that the body has no material existence. She lived and preened as a rich woman with no money. She believed she'd founded a dynastic succession of great men. She came to the United States as a greengrocer's daughter and became blueblooded, a lover of the crown with Oxbridge accent and Shakespeare on her lips.

She used to say: "You make your own world, you know."

"You know, he never blotted a line, Shakespeare," she also said, which isn't true of him but was of her.

"Shakespeare was a man who understood the human heart," she said, adding, "the man left his wife the second best bed."

What she had us remove from our world: my years of drug use, my cousin Mark's psychotic breakdowns, my psychotic breakdowns, my second cousin Mary who moved in with a boyfriend, my mother's Uncle Frederick who died at the hands of his mother, my mother's aunt who died at the hands of her mother-in-law. We only believe in nice normal deaths.

Of my cousin Helen, my parents said they have nothing against divorce but she should have asked the family whether she could have one. Then they forgot her.

We forget my father and my uncle's Catholicism and my aunt's Greek Orthodoxy. We forget that my grandfather came from the West Indies and call him British. We forget our multiracial family. We forget manic Aunt Rene pronounced Rennie who thought her daughter was the Virgin. We forget our thrown-together shore cottages lie on polluted land licked by polluted water. When we reminisce about the gooseberries, droll fruit the color of seasickness, we forget we picked them walking along a chain-link fence guarding a nuclear power plant.

We forget our séances and table possessed by a spirit named Simon. We forget our long stretches of unemployment and delirium.

Or perhaps I'm wrong about all this.

I discovered Frederick, my grandfather's younger brother, by accident in Barbados though he died in the United States. It turned out my mother and her siblings all knew about him. A sulky ghost bloated on neglect. Now he has this much identity: poor Frederick.

"Tell people you and your brother are Episcopalian," my mother always said, though she's a former Christian Scientist and my father's Catholic. She told me to tell people we had summer houses and were half British and my father had a desk job. Which we had and we were on a technicality and he did.

As far back as I can remember, when I've learned a fact about the family, like poor Frederick's story, I rehearse it to myself. I say to myself what I've heard and I repeat it over and over, maybe write it down. I'm terrified of forgetting. I know if I ask about Frederick again I'll hear a different version of the truth, that I've been offered a shape for the past that'll never come my way again. I know too what I memorize may be false but I'm resolved that my reality should at least be the first one I hear about.

My brother has no memories before the age of ten. My family doesn't speak of me much. It makes me wonder if I still exist or if I too have slipped off. Or my brother was invented to replace me.

My mother, the oldest Cassill child, looks exactly like my Aunt Kathleen, the youngest: same sharp features and beige wavy hair and oblong jaw. My husband used to confuse them. Between them lie another sister and a brother. We share birthdays.

My mother and father called us *Chrisuse! Chrisuse!*

My family has many redundancies.

For creating such an Etch-A-Sketch family, my grandfather and grandmother were extraordinarily suited. In many ways they never meshed but in this way they did: my grandfather provided the vacuum, the absences, and my grandmother the fantasy, fillings for his gaps. Almost everything in the world disgusted my grandfather where my grandmother had her own world that delighted her to no end.

"It's a good address, Fanwood," she said a lot of the town where she lived, though it's a drone of a suburb, boxy and boring as a Monopoly set, a commuter town like thousands in New Jersey. Her previous town, Westfield, had also been a good address.

"Dear Mrs. Swenson" did my grandmother's hair and other dear misters and missuses supplied her needs for meat and groceries and new plumbing, people who seemed so intimate yet so fleet in their duties you'd have thought they materialized from a servants' wing.

"And how is your lady mother?" my grandmother asked when I visited. At meals she said things like, "I believe I shall dilly-dally with some brussels sprouts. Should you like to dilly-dally with some brussels sprouts?"

She managed to make such statements sound, if not natural, at least like she wasn't surprised to hear herself. I described her accent as Oxbridge but that's somewhat inaccurate as the truth is I've never heard another accent like it and doubt it exists or ever did in any real place.

"Who do you think you are," she grinned. "That's who you are, you know."

At the shore she padded over the slanted, ancient green linoleum discolored by rust. She always seemed to be looking for a little girl, to send out for rose hips or wild strawberries or hot water.

She laughed, "Louie does so like roughing it."

It was my grandmother's conceit to call our place Holly Park. Most people used the name Bayville. The fantasy—tony people leaning their work-frazzled faces to the breeze—jumped from the developer's head into hers. Our house (with its heatless pea-green sagging) wasn't really part of the Holly Park subdivision. Anyway there wasn't a Holly Park. It jumped out a Wall Street window in 1929.

My grandmother had copies of masterpieces by Rembrandt on her wall, each illuminated like a museum piece by its own oblong light. Like all the Cassills she kept her rooms dark. I remember her heavy parlor with the indistinct shapes of her offspring scattered around, above them the well-lit faces of her copies in their lozenges of light. I remember especially Rembrandt's *Head of a Child*.

"Do you see the strokes, Susie? A poet with the brush."

She loved cats and said of hers, "Dusty is a gentleman cat, you see he always leaves a bit in his bowl. He doesn't gobble up like a ruffian."

She found and cooked things in the middle of New Jersey like mutton chops and mint sauce. Several times at Christmas she made a plum pudding and brought it to the table in flames, a fat torch burning blue with a wide halo, a burning bush springing from her middle.

Once we arrived at her house for dinner and found the table bijouxed with cloth napkins—the timelessly elegant triangle fold—a tablecloth, candles in silver holders, and a TV dinner set squarely at each place setting.

"I do so think Swanson is lovely," my grandmother said. My mother humbly tucked into her food. My father said, "Jeez." My brother and I sighed in ecstasy.

My grandfather Louis sold insurance; I don't think he graduated from high school. My grandmother had worked as a nurse in World War I, which means someone trained her by giving her a wad of bandages and shoving her at a patient. She didn't have much education either but quoted her Shakespeare and played scratchy recordings of Caruso. She lived at her good address and raised lady mothers and objected violently to my father and my uncle Joe as in-laws, because my uncle had only a seventh-grade education and my father's father, fourth grade. Their families were immigrants, Catholics, poor. My grandmother's children resisted her in choice of spouses though in my mother's case she went on to make my father ashamed of all the things that had made him a good contrarian choice. She refused to eat Italian food, cooking it because my father insisted, and then sitting at the table eating cold peas in mayonnaise.

PART THREE

Crossing Bridges

HUNGRY DOG
Agnes Rossi

We were scrawny, scrappy, not very pretty. We weren't the sort of girls boys in our high school flipped over. Up at the Hungry Dog it was a different story. Everybody loved us there. We went to work in short shorts, tank tops, and Dr. Scholl's sandals that were supposed to make our calves shapely.

Our customers were all men, truck drivers and guys who worked on the assembly line at the Ford plant. We'd look up and see a group of Ford workers in navy blue coveralls waiting for their chance to cross Route 17. When it came, they'd run all together. Eva said they reminded her of a baseball team heading out to the field. She'd nudge me, say, "Here they come."

The Dog stood in the shadow of Stag Hill. Jackson Whites lived there. They were a group of mulattoes who kept to themselves. We heard stories about inbreeding and truant officers being shot at with rock salt. The Jackson Whites who came into the Dog had kinky reddish hair and nervous eyes, paid with crumpled dollar bills and lots of change. It was 1975. We lived in a New Jersey town that was devoid of history—nobody's parents, even, had grown up in Montvale—and there we were selling hot dogs to the descendants of slaves who had been freed by Andrew Jackson.

Our friends worked in supermarkets and fast-food places with names everybody knew. My parents would have preferred if we'd found jobs like those but were glad we were working at all. I don't remember either one of them ever setting foot inside the Dog. When my mother had to drive us up there, she'd stop the car at the edge of the parking lot.

Eva and I couldn't believe our good fortune. Just fifteen minutes from our suburban home we'd stumbled on this pocket of tough guys in their twenties and thirties. The boys in our high school didn't thrill us. They were too much like us: sheltered, amorphous, soft. We all seemed to be standing around waiting for our lives to begin. Our customers at the Dog had declared themselves. The world had worked on them. They had calloused hands, heavy beards. Their blue jeans were darkened with grime from the road or the factory.

Hungry Dog

For a while we were in love with all of them. The way they rubbed their eyes after taking a first long swallow of coffee, the bandannas so many of them tied across their foreheads. One would chastise another for saying cocksucker or motherfucker in front of us. A truck driver would come in dusty and bleary-eyed, go right to the men's room, emerge with his hair damp and freshly combed, the top of his T-shirt wet. He'd sit down, smile, say, hey girls.

Then Bobby, a Vietnam vet with tattoos on his forearms, started bringing Eva jewelry from the Southwest, tough biker-girl stuff, a coiled snake with bright green eyes, a turquoise thunderbolt. She kept it all in a zippered compartment of her purse so my mother wouldn't see it. As we drove up to the Dog, she'd put it on piece by piece.

Eva began leaving the Dog to be with Bobby. As soon as he pulled in, she'd climb up into his truck with an agility I hadn't seen before. When she got back, hours later, she'd look pleasantly mussed, her dark eyes shining.

I liked being at the Dog without Eva. I'd lean against the counter and we—six or seven guys and I—would watch familiar sitcoms on the small black and white. I had watched those same shows with my girlfriends, even at home with my parents. Around eight o'clock we'd turn off the TV and drivers from Tennessee and Mississippi would argue with auto workers from Newark about which radio station we should listen to, country western or a black one that was all the way at the end of the dial. I liked being in the middle of that, knowing that Eva was out there in the night like a scout, riding around in Bobby's truck, wearing all her jewelry.

As was bound to happen, the headiness of close quarters, southern accents, second looks that shot straight through me coalesced into a crush on one man, Mike. He was neither a truck driver nor a Ford worker. I didn't know what he did except that he drove a battered station wagon, one of those cars you see in parking lots, a tool chest on wheels. The backseat was permanently down to make room for ladders and push brooms. Crushed styrofoam cups and empty cigarette packs were sprinkled over everything like croutons on a salad.

Mike was in his late twenties, tall and lean, had a black man's moustache and beard. I think of him whenever I see a picture of Malcolm X. He had a sinewy intensity and sharp wit, didn't say much, hovered around the outskirts of conversations making occasional wry comments. I believed he and I were smarter than the others, made sure he knew I got his jokes.

Mike's skin was white like a Jackson White's, but I wasn't convinced he was one. Unlike them, he always came in alone. They were hicks, said dang and reckon, and he seemed worldly. Then one night a couple of them came in and, as usual, ordered their hot dogs to go. When they left, Kyle, a loud, stupid guy nobody much liked, started bad-mouthing them, calling them J.W.'s, saying they all had blood disease because of incest.

Mike got up, walked over to Kyle, and just stared at him. Kyle's voice trailed off. He withered in his seat. Mike looked ready to swing. A couple of guys stood up in that call-to-action way men will when a fight is about to start. Mike turned and walked out slowly. He stood in the parking lot and I could see his shoulders rising and falling as he took deep breaths.

He started coming in every night. I was nervous around him because I'd spent so much time thinking about us. In my head our affair was progressing nicely. I'd anticipate his laugh seconds before it came and congratulate myself on knowing him so well. I interpreted everything he said to me as clear evidence of his attraction and began taking longer and longer to get ready for work. I'd emerge from the bathroom at home, eyes made up, hair blown straight, reeking of the Charlie I'd put on all my pulse points.

One night I was working alone. Bobby was on the road and Eva had begged off, said she didn't feel like being around people. The sadness in her voice hinted at the downside of all this, the treachery of love. Mike sat at the counter spiking his Cokes with rum he poured from a flat pint bottle and smiled at me in a way that seemed purposeful and sly. I could feel his eyes on me when his back was turned. The smell of his rum found its way to me through cigarette smoke and the salty steam of hot dogs. I wanted only to keep whatever was going on between us alive and knew I was doing all right.

Then I put an onion on the cutting board to slice. The knives had just been sharpened. I cut my finger, blood flowed. Mike saw it happen and straightened in his seat to get a better look. His eyes, my blood. It was a peculiar and intimate moment, like when you drop something and a stranger kneels to pick it up. He came behind the counter, soaked a clear rag in cold water, wrapped it around my finger, squeezed hard. The bleeding wouldn't stop, so I couldn't work. Mike took over for me, told people he was an emergency replacement and they should keep their orders simple. I had never seen such grace.

We closed at ten o' clock. Mike did what I told him to do, put the condiments away, turned off the steam table. He didn't seem fluid and relaxed the way he had earlier. His movements were taut and deliberate now.

Flirting with this man was one thing. It was something else entirely to be alone with him in a gravel parking lot on a summer night. The air smelled of exhaust from the highway and wet leaves from the mountain. My finger throbbed and I squeezed it, felt fresh blood seep into the napkin.

He leaned against the bumper of his station wagon, put his hand on my back, pulled me toward him, said, "You're just a little thing."

We kissed and a tremor went through me, a scalding sense that all there was was me. Now he'd find out I wasn't who I'd pretended to be. I'd kissed boys in the corners of basements and backyards but there'd always been other people around, some of them kissing too, girls smirking at each other over boys' shoulders. Mike's seriousness and plain desire were new. The kiss went on and on and I began to feel the pull of something genuine, something as simple and true as the ground under my feet. I could smell the Dog on us, the sour smell of coffee and fried onions that was in our hair, on our clothes. I put my arms around his neck. When I tilted my head, his followed. I was filled with a sense that my family, friends, school were all behind me. I was marching on without encumbrance. I thought of Eva climbing into Bobby's truck and felt party to that sort of momentum.

Then Mike slid his hand under my shirt and I froze. I had no breasts to speak of, a slight swelling was all, and the way my arms were raised minimized even that. I was sure he was accustomed to breasts with some heft. I stiffened, pulled back, was solidly in the middle of my own life again. Embarrassment revived fear and I knew I wouldn't go any further.

Mike looked at me for a moment, then smiled and crossed his arms. "Go on home," he said. "You need to get in your mother's car now and go home." I did exactly that, drove with my bandaged finger sticking straight out. As I pulled into the driveway, I reached down to turn off the radio but in fact turned it on. It had been off the whole way and I hadn't noticed.

I hoped Eva would be awake so I could tell her I'd kissed Mike. She wasn't. I turned on the light in our room and still she didn't wake up. I took the spiral notebook I used as a diary out of my underwear drawer, looked around for a pen, spotted Eva's purse on the dresser. I opened the zippered compartment, scooped out the jewelry, put it all on. Looking at myself in the mirror, I brought my hand to my face so the snake bracelet would show. Eva stirred and I whispered her name. She nestled deeper in her covers, licking her lips and dreaming, I was sure, of the tattooed forearms of her Vietnam vet.

LETTER FROM NEW JERSEY
Diane di Prima

The sun is out here, but I am freezing from the air
conditioning & I can't really sit outside yet because
all the patio furniture is dripping wet I guess it
rained during the night as well as we had this big
thunderstorm last evening lots of lightning but the
thunder wasn't all that loud & the rain came down
but not a whole lot. Aside from freezing I am also
hungry but whereas yesterday morning was clear
sailing w / three croissants & three bagels out on the
counter & coffee beans findable in the freezer today
there is one hard bagel on the counter & nothing
else but Triscuits & the loose coffee beans are all
used up & we are looking (when we look) at a solid
pack cubic thingie of beans in shrink wrap from
Costco that says Starbucks & I haven't the least idea
how to get into the package or indeed what to do w /
the spilling beans shd I get that far. I woke at a
quarter to six & have of course showered, done
mantra, writ morning pages, read some more of
Mexico City Blues for the panel discussion. I
continue to be baffled by Jack this time: his
Buddhism where it's lip service where it's real,
how much he actually "got" it & where
nothingness / void turns into another salvation
device. Stuff we never thought abt back then but I
can see where he continues to trap himself. My
sister-in-law Jan shd be up soon—she has tennis at
ten—she will no doubt be disappointed a bit the
coffee isn't made she & brother Frankie both got
used to me doing it that last time I was here & she

looked for it yesterday I noticed. They like how I get
up much earlier than them. I have just finished the
Carr's Whole Wheat Crackers I bought along for
the plane. Wish they had real Italian bread in this
place maybe some sausage. If that night-bird sang
again last night I didn't hear it. But at sundown a
rabbit was calmly eating the grass under one of the
big trees, didn't bother to stop or look up for us at
all. Like last fall the deer here eating in and around
the kids' bicycles.

ON THE BEACHES OF WILDWOOD, NEW JERSEY

Mary Ann Mannino

My mother loved me
one week a year
on the beaches of
Wildwood, New Jersey.
We would laugh
jumping the waves.
"Don't go out too far."
We would walk the
boardwalk from dusk
until eleven
stopping to eat Taylor pork roll,
cotton candy, chocolate chip ice cream,
and my mama
would buy one dozen
crullers to eat when we
returned to our room with
astrology magazines
to read our futures.
I remember those
rooms in those hotels,
scatter pins and doilies
demitasse cups and games of chance.
I won a doll once
in a yellow satin dress.
I named her Judy
for my friend. I remember
the scale where I got weighed
our first day and our last
to see if I had managed the feat
of gaining five pounds in that week.

On the Beaches of Wildwood, New Jersey

One week a year
my mother wasn't
in a hurry wasn't
ironing her uniform
sleeping on the couch
too tired to . . .
One week a year we
had money enough
for movies every night
and breakfasts in
fancy restaurants and
miniature golf
and time
to laugh and read
our futures
in the stars.

JUNE WEDNESDAYS

Mary Ann Mannino

June Wednesdays when I was eight or nine, my poppa would lock the door of his barbershop, fill the maroon Plymouth with Esso extra and drive us from Philadelphia to Wildwood, NJ, for a day at the shore. As he drove, he puffed on his *El Producto* cigar and pointed out horses or cows as if they were miracles—and they were to a southern Italian living in a city—as we bounced along the back roads that wrapped around family farms where grandmoms and children offered home-grown asparagus and strawberries under wooden canopies. About halfway there, my mom would pass out sandwiches of roasted peppers and garlic on round Kaiser rolls, and the three of us would munch our way through Tuckahoe, Mays Landing, and Cape May Court House. Sometimes we'd turn a corner and suddenly a patch of river or back bay would lay before us like a surprise package and I'd lose my appetite at the wonderful bitter smell of salt and sea.

Once there, poppa would find a deserted road where, in the car, we changed into our bathing suits to save the cost of a bathhouse. Then we'd rush across the sand to the sea and the icy chill of that first splash of summer. My parents liked to "ride the waves." They would sort of lie down in waist-deep water—neither they nor I could swim—and with their faces down and arms stretched out they would float to shore. My father would laugh if the water went over his bald head, got into his eyes or up his nose. Even my cautious mother, who worried about jellyfish bites, sunburn, drowning, polio, and kidnappers, could not resist laughing aloud when the waves caught her by surprise and tickled her back. Sometimes in water that was waist high for me, they would each hold one of my hands and when the breakers came in, as a team, they would lift me up high above the rough water.

On those June Wednesdays the losses of a country, houses, parents, and sons, the urgencies of bills, chronic illness, and painful relationships were padlocked in the barbershop and we were three children building sand castles and riding New Jersey's waves.

SUBURBAN BACKYARDS
June Avignone

Two months after my mother died I suggested to my big sister Gail that we throw my father a retirement party at our house in Hillsdale, the house we grew up in and had come back to after college, the house that I still love for being so full in my mind even now, as I remember how insidiously empty it felt then without her.

It felt so empty that my father's retirement as an officer with the New York Triborough Bridge and Tunnel Authority, the place that passed as home for the past twenty-seven years of his life, went pretty much unnoticed. Unnoticed is not the right word exactly. It went noticed. By him. But in a way that first became uneasily apparent to me the last day in the hospital room.

He called to tell me at my first publishing job in New York—an established children's book company that, like many publishing firms, was in the deathly process of commercializing the long-time quality out of itself.

I thought I heard right. So I wandered, by rote, as if going to lunch again to yet another new, upbeat little place, towards the ladies room. I wandered past other people's cubicles and filing cabinets, past the waning hardback division that once won prizes for taking children seriously. Eventually into porcelain and mirrors where I stood smearing Revlon's Dark Chocolate lip gloss—the kind that came in a white little pot—rambling to the glass for I don't know how long about which subway line to take. That's what Liz asked me when she came in: how long did I plan to keep that up? Followed by, what's the matter? Then she, an editor for something in the magazine division, took me to the street and put me in a cab headed uptown.

My mother had been transferred from a hospital in Jersey to Columbia Presbyterian for high doses of futile treatments she said would not work and like always, my mother was right. She had told my father in hushed tones at night that she would rather stay at home and read her Bible. She believed in Jesus and, unlike many believers I've run into since who spout the words, she simply lived it. In a way that still haunts me. Simply is not the right word exactly. Still, I think I helped talk her into the transfer, in the name of actual hope.

∽

It was a cloudy day, the kind obnoxiously edged in gray, not raining or really likely to, but full of a translucent anxiety because of it. Bombing up Broadway toward the Bronx reminded me of the day we moved from White Plains Road to Jersey when I was five. Away from the bricks and pavements where women talked in lawn chairs they faced at the building in rows—the same way they faced their beach chairs toward the ocean at Jones Beach—screaming after their children running after Mr. Softee's bells. Then the whispers came. I hid under the first floor stairwell and cried when the moving vans came. They found me.

That day I found myself transplanted. There were lawns and clouds in open space and an eventual sunset that stretched beyond the grayness of the day, over and beyond the tracks where serious-looking men in suits bobbed up and down and away in trains behind our new beige bi-level house. My mother's sister bought another bi-level, the color of the shamrock in Lucky Charms, directly behind us.

There was no fence or hedge dividing the backyard. Sisters who cared enough to move, who bought houses on purpose on adjacent streets that share the same big backyard, who have children who grew up with one another down the hallway, wouldn't do a stupid thing like that.

My grandfather, a retired gardener with the Bronx Parks system, stopped watching his friends play bocce in the park for a while to come over to plant grass seed and fat round shrubs and fruit trees, bringing with him all the piles of cow manure in the world. But the piles went eventually. And there was no traffic, no winding stairwells lined with bright red doors, no people walking around, no store with the bread with the hard crust.

So he left and took my grandmother back with him. My sister and I cried together in the bathtub when my mother nervously broke the news to us that they were moving back, our big tears splashing into Mr. Bubbles, not that his reasons weren't understandable to us. There were no kids, either, at first. They appeared by the dozens later on, by themselves, and kept our minds off the seemingly endless miles of newfound quiet and space.

This day in the cab was different. I tried hard with the deliberate concentration learned with age, despite the messages found in good children's books, to ignore the blocks of clouds pushing their way next to me in the back seat, squeezing in at my head, and, in this suspended state, told the cabbie what had happened. He had jet black eyes and bushy eyebrows the size and shape of medium-sized sparrows, eyes that stared suspiciously back at me now and then through his mirror in between running red lights, but I don't think he believed me. I wasn't crying. After that, I don't remember much, except standing outside her door and what I saw.

∾

It was like this.

His back was toward me. And those same clouds squeezing me in on the ride up had literally come through the window of the white room, collided with the white walls and window sills and shades that faced her bed and the white sheets against her, whiter still, me at the door, his shoulders shaking before her. Everything directly before him was a fogged white-gray.

Then from his back where his shoulders shook over her body, where his head was lowered below his shoulder line, the white stopped. All you could see of him was blue. He was wearing the uniform I thought as a child was somehow pasted on to him. All you could see of him and behind him—from where I stood by the door staring in at the two-toned fog wondering hard at what it was exactly that I was seeing and still not knowing—was absolutely blue.

Things stayed that way for a long time.

∾

The party went very well, even if things didn't turn out exactly as planned.

My father's retirement—marking an end to the years of overtime and double shifts in the name of a future of planned relaxation with my mother—was official the week she died. To put it mildly, he correlated the two heavily for months if not years to come, with a glance or indirect comment. Not so much with words, really, though he took to writing poetry. He showed it to me. Or he left it around for me to read. Or he left it around and I just read it.

My father never wrote much before that, that I knew of. He wrote two things to the community newspaper which were published, after we moved from the house near the tracks, because of the noise, to another house in Hillsdale across from woods, because of the magnolia trees. One piece was about how neighbors help other neighbors by keeping their property up, how the example spreads a spirit. The other one was about how a blue jay attacked his head across the street while he was rescuing its baby from the heavy pursuit of a hungry tomcat.

But the most memorable and sustained blocks of time I spent with my father growing up weren't talking about reading or writing but, rather, spent watching movies on the small black and white television on his bedroom dresser. He would sleep only a few hours between shifts. The television would be on. A television that flickered gray-blue light in the darkness, with words like "I wish you were a wishing well so I could throw you in," belting out from it. Still, I felt safe in the darkness.

"Junie, this was a good one, 1942, Bogart's a bad guy in it," he would call out to my room across from his, half asleep. I would stop reading and come and sit in the gold armchair near their bed. Movies, he would mumble to me in the dark, which he would shine shoes for in the Bronx, and run to the theatre as soon as he'd get a dime. My father would mumble trivia to me, dates, "Al Jenkins . . . he was also in . . . ," always during the important parts, it seemed.

Now he was retired, and had waking hours to be spent doing things outside of working and sleeping. They had done what they said they would do. They delivered us from evil, safe from the crime of the Bronx neighborhood where they spent their lives poor, but until the whispers grew fierce, not in fear. They had once been able to keep our red door open on hot summer nights. Something better for us.

So they came out on a bus together looking for homes. They got off one day in Hillsdale because it was as far as he could see traveling back and forth to New York seven days a week to work. My mother had not gone to La-Guardia School of the Arts, like teachers highly recommended. My father left school and joined the Navy at seventeen. After high school, my sister and I went to good universities in New York City and studied the arts. We were to be given the opportunity to go into professions we could care about. And they were to enjoy themselves now.

But he could not forgive himself. The fogs were able to thrive and loom around the house, around her kitchen, around her trees, even around the television, and for what? Malls. A house they had to stop living to get. A lily-white community under beautiful magnolias he had rarely seen in daylight. We should give a party, Gail, I told her, I screamed from the kitchen window to her in the backyard one day where she was talking to a Born Again who had wandered into her life one day to talk about himself. Normally she may have noticed the intensity behind the tone of my suggestion as not being totally normal, as possessing complications. But there was nothing normal about this situation to me, to her. She agreed.

We knew nothing of his friends at the Triborough Bridge and Tunnel Authority. We heard of strange occurrences, a man's jaw falling off in a car accident and my father holding it there until help came. Of people almost jumping off the bridge and being talked down. Of people just jumping off the bridge. Of weird and cruel customers who thought his arm was an extension of the toll booth. "There's a sick society behind those wheels," he would say to my mother, he still says to us at times. We knew he played poker on what he called blows. We'd know he won by the way he snickered stacking quarters on the kitchen counter before he would go upstairs to sleep. We knew one of the names of the men on the bridge he played cards with, only one, a man, a friend he spoke of by name. Ned.

Turned out to be Nedd when I called asking for him. His last name. Nedd had a calm voice. He told me he would take care of everything there, that he would tell all the guys, that they would car pool it out, that they would bring some steaks for the barbecue if we would get the beer.

The day came. My sister was to keep my father at my aunt's house. My mother's sister, my Aunt Anna, who never stopped missing the Bronx, who now lived down the block and not across the yard—kept him in the house while we were getting ready. "Rick, you can't go!" she screamed when he tried to leave, the story goes. "The girls are cleaning the house." Normally he may have noticed the intensity behind the tone of her suggestion, at our dire need to clean, but there was nothing normal about this time. So he stayed, without suspicion, the story goes.

I was putting beers in the refrigerator when the cars drove up. I had one when I saw them.

With a few exceptions—like my aunt and her family and some friends from the old neighborhood in the Bronx, like the Connachios—everyone was black out there. In fact, it is safe to say that there were more black men in our backyard that day then there had been in Hillsdale before.

So I couldn't think straight. I had wondered so long what he was trying to rescue us from, unconsciously accepting the answers offered by university "leftists" pompous enough to think they could know his intentions, fending off the racist reasons presented as justifiable by those on the right—and so just came to hate the town and the open space and magnolia trees, spaces I had secretly come to love. Hate justified by what it had done to our family as of late. Now this.

But as the day passed under the summer sun and the steaks were barbecued, the fogs died a bit. Particularly the blue one. There were no uniforms to be found on the men in our backyard that day.

It was sunny under the trees. They played a little cards. There was laughter. My father laughed in our backyard that day.

Time Sublime
Americo Raymond Avignone

A second, moment, an hour a day—
　　seven day song.
A year, meteorite, a blink of an eye
Oh! Time sublime.

To think, happiness honored,
　　to unwind.
To find one's self, a century in precious truth,
Borrowed time is our root!

What we accomplish in such a span,
Amazing even to God and His plan.

Enjoy your moment as you can.
Waste time not, it's given once,
　　No return,
Oh! Time sublime.

JERSEY TOMATO WARS

Mary Ann Castronovo Fusco

The first salvos in the annual Tomato War at my parents' house resound early each August.

"*Ancora pumarori?*" ("*More* tomatoes?!") shoots my mother as my father empties the fire-colored contents of his garden basket onto the table in her cellar sewing room.

Here, Dad's vine-ripened *pumarori*—Sicilian dialect for "tomatoes"—are carefully set out to age until they're deemed the perfect shade of scarlet to boil and puree. Just about the same shade of red that slowly tinges my mother's fair Sicilian complexion whenever she surveys the latest fruits of my father's formidable gardening skills. "*Ancora pumarori?*"

When Dad hears Mom's lament, he fires back with the same ammunition he's been using for almost forty years—that is, for as long as he's been planting Jersey tomatoes: "*Basta! L'anno che viene, niente pumarori!*" ("Enough! Next year, no tomatoes!")

At this, my mother merely rolls her eyes. Just as she'd rather die before letting a commercially bottled sauce—no matter what upscale restaurant or celebrity name was on the label—pass her lips, she knows there's no way on earth that my father could ever resist putting in row upon row of tomatoes.

Each spring he shops at his favorite nurseries with the same attention most American males devote to stereo equipment. Supersonics and Big Boys, cherry tomatoes and plum tomatoes all find their way into his garden. And no matter how many tomatoes he plants, if a friend offers a few more, he never refuses. When local politicians hoping to garner his vote in the next election come to the door with free tomato plants, he always accepts.

If tomato vines sprout unexpectedly from seeds scattered the year before, my father will water them, weed them, fertilize them, and stake them, until the stragglers are groaning with plump red fruit—even if they do so smack in the middle of his carnations or roses. By midsummer, it's hard to distinguish any line of demarcation between the original tomato patches he'd laid out in neat formation the previous spring and the dozens of upstart plants that invariably infiltrate his ranks weeks later.

No, my father's vegetable garden isn't the prettiest. But from July to October, for its modest size it has got to be one of the meanest, greenest, most productive gardens in the Garden State.

So there you have the seeds of my parents' summertime discontent, not to mention pride and joy. For from August through November, their home-grown tomatoes accompany 'most every lunch and dinner—at their house and at everyone else's in the family. Even total strangers soon learn they can score a few kilos of tomatoes over my parents' corner fence in exchange for a compliment to the garden.

And when life tosses my folks too many tomatoes, they make sauce, an exquisite taste of summer no matter what the calendar says. Thanks to the canning my mother has taken up in recent years to keep up with my father's ever-increasing yields, the fresh tomato sauce season at their house stretches from summer to the following spring—when Dad, blissfully oblivious to the fact that he's in his eighties, dutifully tills the earth to get it ready to accept the next crop of tomato recruits.

No matter how heated the Tomato War gets in my parents' kitchen, however, not a single tomato has ever been thrown—or worse, thrown away. Both sides in this long-simmering skirmish agree on one thing: A home-grown Jersey tomato would be a terrible thing to waste.

I CHECK OTHER

Carla Guerriero

when the box says white
I check other

I AM NOT WHITE

I AM

    neopolitan tenor melodramatic
    grandpa pressing grapes
    a gold horn pinned to baby's undershirt
    and bread placed jesus-side up

I AM

    mourning clothes earthblack
    the white-white witness of wedding sheets
    a black madonna growing paler
    and daddy growing basil in the backyard

I am the gift of first communion beads,
feast day pastry memories,
and much more

I am midwife knowledge and fourteen miles from africa

born of muslim passing
    christian passing
    spaniard passing
    arab passing
    gypsy,
        passing.

Carla Guerriero

I am immigrant pollen riding a cold wind
and
sunday-fresh pasta on a red cloth on the washing machine
and
TOO MUCH COLOR TO CONTAIN IN A SMALL WHITE BOX

I CHECK OTHER

MIRACLE BABY
A BOY NAMED PHYLLIS
Frank DeCaro

It's safe to say, in my case, that it was not easy being a fetus.

On an April morning after a night of dancing the peabody with Booby Natale at the annual Bowling Banquet at Nestor's Inn—an oasis of sausage-and-pepper steam-tray swank in Singac, New Jersey—my mother, Marian Teresa LaRegina DeCaro, checked into Mount Sinai Hospital in Manhattan to have a large tumor removed. It was 1962; she was forty-three and believed she was unable to have children. When the surgeon, Dr. Salo Boltuch, extracted the melon-sized growth (they're *always* melon-sized) he found me behind it, desperate for attention. As memory serves, I looked up at the gentle-handed jamoke in the football-player-sized scrubs, waved hello, and said "Where the *hell* have you been?" I'd been there almost three months, waiting to be discovered.

I've always joked about being Marian and Frank DeCaro, Sr.'s, fourth miscarriage, and that morning I could very well have ended up in a bag marked MEDICAL WASTE in a dumpster somewhere on 101st Street. Instead, a little more than six months later, I ended up in New Jersey. My arrival turned an Italian Catholic working-class couple into a threesome just in time for their eleventh wedding anniversary.

I made my debut at eight A.M. on Election Day via routine cesarean, which my mother was told would make for a more beautiful baby, one not so squashed. But my father didn't find out I'd been born until five hours later, even though he'd been in the hospital waiting room all morning. "Ooh, I forgot to tell Frank," Dr. Boltuch said, when my father's sister Angie called to find out how things went. He'd goofed again, but it didn't matter. Angie would break the news to my father.

She always knew everything first, anyway.

A woman with jet-black Priscilla Presley-as-Italian-widow hair and a penchant for leopard print, Angie was home that morning in New Jersey making spritz cookies and padding around the linoleum barefoot with wet toenails and paper toweling between each red-lacquered digit so they wouldn't smudge. She had my father paged at Sinai, and when he finally came to the phone, pressing the receiver anxiously to his ear, she said: "It's a boy! Now bring that Miracle Baby home!" That's what my ever-dramatic, ever-outspoken godmother—the woman I most took after—called me: the Miracle Baby. But, as far as I can tell, the only thing truly miraculous about my birth was the location.

Thanks to my mother's honeydew of a tumor, I am a native New Yorker. It says so on my passport. But I didn't grow up "riding the subway, running with people, up in Harlem, down on Broadway" the way that disco song would have you believe. I grew up riding in a white Chrysler Newport, running with people who wouldn't have gone to Harlem if their lives depended on it. And as for Broadway—well, we were strictly theater party, let's-go-see-*A Chorus Line*-on-a-bus, and rear mezzanine at that. We were Jersey people, Marian, Frank Senior, and me, products of the aluminum-sided, lawn-sprinklered, what-exit? wilds of suburbia, genuine dyed-in-the-mall articles. Purple furniture you weren't allowed to sit on, four-foot above-ground swimming pool in the backyard, artificial Christmas tree, Ragu on Ronzoni . . . we had it all, and a two-car garage to boot.

New Jersey was all my parents knew. My bald-headed teddy-bear-cute father and my pear-shaped bundle of Aqua-Net mother were born and raised only a few minutes' drive from the house where I grew up. That's where they still live, and, like all parents of only children, maintain their son's bedroom as a shrine. My father and I even went to the same high school, the class of '40 and the class of '80. But, for me, my hometown of Little Falls was the place from which I most wanted to escape, once I saw that there was more to life than the Little Falls Lanes bowling alley, the Valley Spa luncheonette, and Sunday school at Holy Angels. I left as soon as I could—at seventeen, already an out-of-the-closet homosexual with one serious relationship under my Pierre Cardin, New Wave–skinny belt. But like everyone else who grew up there, I have a lifetime membership. New Jersey is like Catholicism and certain branches of Jack La Lanne—they never let you go.

I suppose there are worse things than growing up in a town that counts among its chief industries the manufacture of latex condoms. (It makes having safer sex feel like Old Home Week.) But Little Falls wasn't exactly the land of milk and hospitality for a young gay boy or, for that matter, anyone who felt different. A jumble of bi-levels and ranch houses—swing sets in backyards, Chevys out front—Little Falls was actually very cute as small towns go.

It was only twenty-five minutes and a world away from Manhattan. I like to think of the eighteen miles between my childhood home and my adult apartment in the gay mecca of Chelsea as aesthetic distance. Kaleidoscopic diversity wasn't valued in Little Falls. Change was bad. In fact, to be anything but ordinary was a mistake. But I couldn't help myself. I was *born* gay. It just took sixteen years for me to figure it out. Unfortunately, the other children in the neighborhood realized my destiny a lot sooner.

Like a lot of major homosexuals-to-be, I spent much of my childhood being haunted by a handful of kids who made sissy-torture their life's work. They were enthusiastically malicious, stripping me (and every other different kid) of the self-esteem we might have had. But they didn't succeed completely. All they did was fuel my desire for escapism and, ultimately, escape.

When Little Falls proved inhospitable, I created my own world to play in. With my friend Heidi, who would turn out to be my first girlfriend, I let television and books and make-believe make up for all that was lacking, beyond the manicured front lawns, in the patchwork houses of our little town on the not-so-mighty Passaic River. Precocious together, we pretended as a way to smooth over the misfitting of our lives in suburbia, excelling at school and keeping each other supremely amused.

We learned what there was to learn in Little Falls in three elementary schools imaginatively called School #1, School #2, and School #3. There was one in each of the town's three neighborhoods—Great Notch, Singac, and Little Falls. We had a half-dozen churches sprinkled here and there, including ours, Holy Angels, where the pastor, a dashing Franciscan with a hint of a brogue, would call me handsome one week and then deliver a sermon on the evils of homosexuality and masturbation the next.

There was the high school, Passaic Valley, home of the Hornets. It was the place where I was most miserable and, for a few shining moments, happier than I'd ever been. There was an Entenmann's outlet that advertised in the church bulletin and where they knew repeat customers like my family by name; and a Shop Rite supermarket so big the managers handed out maps after its last remodeling. Everyone from Passaic Valley worked there at one time or another. For fun, there was a sleigh-riding hill at the top of Third Avenue, and, at the bottom of First, a park with a giant Army tank up on blocks that we loved to climb on and play Vietnam War. On Main Street in the center of town, there was the Oxford Barber Shop, where Tommy Fazio would always call me Little Bucky—Frank Senior was Big Bucky—and then scare me with the noisy hand vacuum he used to suck the hair off. Across the street was Tony's Pizza, where if you held your slice with the point down, the grease would pour off by the bucketful. Next door was Stanton's Drugs, where Aunt Angie would deliver a plate of cherry winks wrapped in aluminum foil once every couple of weeks in the belief that well-fed druggists offered better service, and, near that, the Little Falls Savings and Loan, which we called Jack's Bank because our neighbor was the president.

In Singac, not far from where my mother and Booby cut that prenatal rug, there was a ceramics studio, where in the 1970s Heidi and I painted zodiac plaques, listened to "Rock the Boat" on an old FM radio, and got high on spray fixative. And then there was Prospect Street—and our house, which was white with ivory-colored brick trim, black shutters, and a bright red door.

My live-in grandmother, Anna LaRegina, a four-foot-tall Italian woman who smelled like Chiclets and lavender perfume, was always sitting on the porch steps in WAC shoes, a floral-print muumuu, and a permanent tan, drinking Pabst Blue Ribbon and reading *The Love Machine*. With upper arms that hung like parade-float bunting, the constitution of a battleship, and the salty vocabulary of a sailor on shore leave, she was as much a fixture as the Blessed Virgin Mary statue that stood in front of the place in a bathtub-shaped plaster grotto.

My mother, her daughter, was born in Paterson in 1919 and grew up in Totowa borough. My grandfather, Carney LaRegina, was a fabric finisher in a dye house; Grandma, the former Anna Andiorio, was a winder in the mills that gave Paterson the name Silk City. Marian had a brother named Victor, fourteen months her senior, who had a hairy chest and a growl of a voice. Everyone called him Papa Vic. When my mother asked her brother to teach her to drive, he drove his car to the top of the steepest hill in the neighborhood, put it in park, got out, took his dog with him, and said "Go ahead. Drive." Fifty years later, my mother would still complain, "Can you believe he took his dog with him?"

Vic wasn't any good at school, but Marian was worse. The one time she knew the answer to a teacher's question, she had laryngitis.

"Put your arm down, Queenie, you can't talk anyway," her English teacher, Mr. Charney, said. He called her that because *La Regina* is Italian for "the queen." Marian, though, was more the exotic princess type with brown hair and dark, almond-shaped eyes that earned her the childhood nickname Chink. Her looks made her popular with the fellows and she never wanted for a boyfriend. As teens, Marian and her friends formed the TNT Club, which stood for Totowa's Nutsy Twerps. They once had a party for twenty people, and fed everyone for only $3. That was the one story we heard about them and we heard it a lot. But pictures of the TNT Club—faded black and whites of clean-cut kids of immigrant parents, mugging for the camera—make it look like they had fun growing up.

In her clique, Marian was always considered the fancy one. And, compared to the white-socks-with-suits crowd we called our relatives, she *was* fancy. After dropping out of high school, she used her unemployment checks to pay for beauty school. She became a beautician, eventually owning several salons and developing a weakness for faux Pucci-print dresses, auburn hair dye, and black convertibles with red leather interiors.

"Your mother always acted like she was rich," cousin Jeannie, the Florida divorcée and Virginia Graham look-alike, would say. "She used to intimidate the hell out of all of us." My mother said that's why my father married her. "He thought I had money. I fooled him."

My father was born in 1922 in Great Notch. Neither one of his parents, Santo DeCaro and Mary Luzzi, could read or write. Santo, or Sam as they called him, was a spool carrier in the Beattie Carpet Mills not far from the center of town; then he went to work in a quarry until he developed emphysema. Mary, who raised three children, was a reeler at the carpet mill. None of the kids on that side of the family were very good students, either. But compared to his sister and brother, my father was the family scholar.

At least he showed up to class.

Allen Ginsberg's father was my father's English teacher at Paterson Central High School. Frank Senior used to take a bus there, because there was no high school in Little Falls until his senior year, when Passaic Valley High School opened. He began playing baseball that year, 1940, and wanted to be a professional but never made it. Before that he was a pin boy at the Little Falls Lanes. In 1942, as he was going on twenty, he was drafted and shipped off to Fort Dix, then to various training camps in Texas and Indiana. He spent eighteen months overseas in the 610th Tank Destroyer Battalion. On VE Day, he was in Czechoslovakia. "It was just another day," he'd say. One day wasn't like every other day, however. He received a letter from his sister Angie that, as he says, "shook the shit out of me." His mother had died of a cerebral hemorrhage at age forty-nine. The Red Cross refused to let him go home for services. "That turned me off the Red Cross for good," he would always say. In February 1951, Marian and Frank were introduced by Jean Cosloy, one of my mother's customers at Marianne's, the beauty shop Marian co-owned in Paterson. She told my mother that she knew an eligible bachelor who worked for Curtiss-Wright, which made propellers, and asked if it would be okay if he called her. She said yes, and he did. On their first date, my father wore a gray suit, a charcoal overcoat, and a matching fedora, and picked up Marian LaRegina in a gunmetal-gray '46 Plymouth. Up until then, Frank had been dating a woman named Isabel, whose memory my parents would still debate forty-five years later.

"She was homely," my mother would say.

"Get the hell out of here, she was pretty!" my father would counter.

"She was fat!" Marian would maintain.

"She was a little heavy," my father would admit. "But she had a pretty face!"

It didn't matter what she was, because once my parents met, Isabel was history. Marian and Frank went to the movies a lot, to dinners at Nestor's, and to an occasional hockey game in New York City. They were both good Italian Catholic kids, so they smooched a lot, but never got laid. They didn't believe in sex before marriage. To hear my father tell it many years later, my mother didn't believe in sex *after* marriage, either. "I married a nun," he'd say. "None today, none last night . . ." It was one of his running jokes.

On November 25, 1951, nine months after they met, Marian and Frank were married at St. James Roman Catholic Church in Totowa by the Reverend Francis J. Reilley. She wore a blush satin gown with a Queen Anne collar and a lace-paneled full skirt with a nine-foot train, and carried an orchid and a satin-covered prayer book in her hands as she made her way down the aisle. Aunt Angie was matron of honor in a strapless gown of American Beauty taffeta with a velvet bodice and a matching cocktail jacket. Papa Vic was best man. The bridesmaids wore emerald-green taffeta. The reception was for two hundred people at a nearby hall called Morningside. There was a buffet, which cost them $2.75 a head, and everyone was happy, eating and dancing a fox-trot, a peabody, and as the affair wore on, a tarantella, which was my grandmother's specialty. As gifts, some people gave $3 in an envelope, others $5 and $10. The guy who managed my father's baseball team gave the new couple $25, which was so extravagant, they couldn't believe it. No one had that kind of money to give away so freely.

Marian and Frank went on a road trip to Washington, D.C., for their honeymoon and then, with my grandmother Anna, moved into a white ranch house on Lincoln Avenue in Pompton Plains. For a decade, they lived there, all three, more or less together. They always wanted to make it four and, despite my father's jokes about no sex after marriage, tried desperately. But Marian and Frank remained childless. Until Little Frankie—"Franconino," as Stepgrandma Carmela, who didn't speak English, called me—entered their lives that November in 1962. Before my first birthday, we moved to Prospect Street in Little Falls—three Italians and the future boy named Phyllis.

Then the fun *really* began.

CLASS QUARTET
Janet Zandy

I was born into the working class, a fact I hid from my knowing self for almost thirty years. I can see now how that fact has marked my life, determined my choices, stirred my wrath, tied my tongue, and opened my mind.

I am seven years old. I am in my aunt's apartment in Union City, New Jersey. It is four blocks from the tiny apartment I know of as home. We have a porch. This apartment has a stoop. It is attached to another building exactly like it. Today I might call them brownstones; I'm not sure. It doesn't matter. It is five miles from Manhattan, but might as well be five thousand. The shadows of the skyscrapers are just that, shadows. This is not Manhattan; this is urban Jersey.

I am in this apartment for a family gathering, maybe a child's birthday party. There is food, seltzer, rum cake. My grandfather sits at one end of a table, a bottle of Four Roses, a pack of Luckies, and a silver lighter in front of him. His fingers are long, hard. His arms exposed below his white rolled-up shirt are thin without being fragile. Tattoos blue the olive skin. There is noise, laughter. I walk through the front rooms, railroad rooms.

The bedrooms are crowded with dressers, the beds covered with coats. The odor of urine is heavy in the air. I deny it. We are a family and we are together. The uncles are waiting for the race results on the radio. The aunts talk about food and wait on the men. I cannot breathe.

I go into the bathroom, which in memory is surprisingly large. It is lovely there. White and cool. A band of penguin wallpaper travels around the room. It is old and stained, but lively. The tub and toilet are white, smooth, round. I cannot resist. I stroke the rim of the tub. I go to the only window. I push hard to get it open. I look out. On every side I see red brick, solid, hard. I see light in the center. I am confused; is it coming from the top or the bottom? I look down. I see a narrow patch of grass, some trash, but no light. I twist and bend my neck to look up to find the light, to see the sky, to breathe the air. I cannot see without sticking my head out the window. I am tempted.

They call, "Who's in there? Come out. What's wrong?" I want to feel the light in the center of the airshaft. But, I can't get out. I give up. I unlock the door. "Nuthin's wrong, Momma."

Enclosure.

I am seventeen years old and a freshman in a state teachers college. I am a scholarship girl. The tuition costs one hundred and fifty dollars a year and my parents cannot afford it. I do not think this is unusual. I am at a Dean's Tea in honor of Dean's List students. I won A's but I do not know what a Tea is. I tell no one my secret. The table is long, the tablecloth is starched, unstained, crisply white. Silver pots are lined up in one corner, cups and saucers, silver spoons, napkins in another. There are too many silver pots. I am confused. Which is water? Which is tea? Which is coffee? Is there coffee at a Tea? Which is cream? Which is which? A lady with blue eyes and hair the color of country clouds smiles and offers me a cup. I murmur, "thank you," and spill its contents.

Exposure.

I am twenty-eight years old and eleven weeks pregnant. I lie in a hospital bed in Passaic, New Jersey, bleeding more blood than I have ever seen in my life. My mother and husband wait outside the dark room. It is 3:00 A.M., and I know I am in this bed alone. I still think I am pregnant. I think that the fetus has not slipped out, gotten caught on a blood clot, and been flushed down the toilet.

A male doctor has been called; he arrives, reluctantly, because of the time. He will save my baby. He examines me. He hurts me with his hands. I scream at him to stop. "You are too rough. Too rough. Get away from me." He responds with a question: "Are you married?"

"What?" "What has that got to do with anything? Leave me alone."

I feel like a force inside me will break open my skin and out will come babies. A voice in an unfamiliar recess of my mind coolly observes: "So, this is what it is. He has presumed something about you and acted accordingly. What? What is he seeing? A whore? A prostitute? Some broad trying to abort herself? A foreigner? A woman punished?" I want to scream out in my best school teacher voice: "I am a married, middle-class woman, a teacher, and a taxpayer!" The doctor returns. He is flushed, annoyed with my behavior. I want to please him, the good daughter genuflecting before male authority. I want to look acceptable, to be accepted. I resist the good daughter. For a while. He insists on a D & C. He tells me the baby's gone. "It was probably deformed anyway." I don't know anything about D & C's. I don't know whether my baby is inside me or not anymore. I just want to leave—this bed, this hospital, this town, this state.

The bleeding speeds up; my blood pressure drops. A nurse's aide strokes my hand and whispers to me, "you have no choice." I sign the permission form for the D & C. I am wheeled into the operating room, fitted into the stirrups. The mask of anesthesia covers my mouth. I cannot speak. Before the blackness, I observe my coldness. Layer after layer of sterile hospital bedding refuses to warm me. The coldness penetrates deeper and deeper.

Knowledge.

I am forty years old at an academic conference of English professors. I join the crowd hurrying from meeting room to meeting room to learn about the human experience and great literature. I am wearing a suit and passing as an academic. My illegitimacy is a knot in my throat. I am a part-time professor, a long-time adjunct. No institution pays my way to this conference. I have come to see if I am smart enough to be here.

I hear a paper about an obscure Danish novelist. The speaker admits to the dilemma of praising a novel that justifies racialism. Racialism? "What's the difference between racialism and racism?" I ask. Dumb question, I see on their faces. "Racialism is a Briticism, a perfectly good English term, suggesting that one race is, well, better at doing certain things than another race. In this case, racialism means the Northern, nordic people are more capable, more industrious, than the Southern, darker people." "Oh," I blurt out in a voice deliberately unbleached of its working-class color, "is that why we are in these rooms giving papers and other people are in our hotel rooms cleaning toilets?" Another participant shouts at me, blue eyes, red: "That's social; that's not literary!"

Ignorance.

Interstate Commerce, New York & New Jersey Bound

MOVING TO WOOD-RIDGE

Bill Ervolino

In 1990, I discovered that the further you live from your Italian parents, the more food they bring when they visit. At the time, they were living in West Babylon, Long Island, and I was in a rented two-bedroom apartment in East Rutherford, New Jersey. It was almost three years before they would accept my invitation to come for dinner, and it was a nightmare from start to finish.

"We're going to need directions," my mother said, in one of the 264 telephone conversations leading up to that visit.

"No problem," I told her. "Why don't you put Dad on?"

"No," she insisted. "Give them to *me*."

"Isn't Dad driving?" I asked.

"Yes," she told me. "But I am your father's *eyes*."

"Oh."

I asked if his nose and ears were coming, too, so I would know how many steaks to buy.

My directions had to begin from their driveway ("Go to the corner and make a left . . ."), and they had to be so explicit that it took me more than forty-five minutes to recite them.

"Then," I continued, "you get on the George Washington Bridge . . ."

"Hold on," my mother said, scribbling down her notes. "Do we take it north, south, east or west?"

"Ma, it's a bridge!" I screamed. "You take it to the side *you aren't on*." Despite the painstaking care I took in putting the directions together, they *still* managed to get lost. This was because, at one point, my mother saw an exit for East Rutherford, and assumed I had made a mistake. They spent the next twenty minutes trying to find their way *out* of the Giants Stadium parking lot.

As comedian Joy Behar once observed, "Italians do not travel well. These are not the Vikings we're talking about . . ."

Italians also do not travel *light*. I knew this from my childhood visits to Jones Beach. In the parking lot, I would see these cute little blond families pop out of their station wagons carrying sunglasses, sun tan lotion, and towels. *That was it.*

My family wasn't like that. For starters, my mother would cook for three days: potatoes and eggs, peppers and eggs, eggplant parmigiana, there was no end to it. We had a big silver cooler that weighed about 600 pounds, a thermos that weighed another 40 pounds, two dozen rolls, twelve loaves of Italian bread, peaches, plums, nectarines, cherries, assorted condiments, nuts, nutcrackers, forks, spoons, knives, napkins, towels, sheets, blankets, pillows, pillowcases, suntan lotion, floats, inner tubes, iodine, bandages, a complete change of clothes for each one of us, books, newspapers, magazines, two aluminum patio chairs, a chaise lounge, our own umbrella, pails, shovels . . .

It would have been easier to go to the beach, dig up the sand, and bring it home.

By early afternoon I was so embarrassed, I couldn't take it anymore. "I'm having a *horrible* time," I'd tell my mother. "Everybody is *looking* at us!"

"Why would they look at us?" she said. "Come with me to the water fountain so I can wash the pots."

For their first visit to my apartment they brought enough food (not to mention pots, pans, and everything else) to feed an army, even though I had invited *them* for dinner.

"But I wanted to make you steaks," I said, "with vegetables and couscous. Have you ever had couscous?"

"What is it called?" my mother asked, eying the box suspiciously.

"Couscous, and it's really good," I told her. "It's Moroccan pasta."

"I don't think so," she said, wrinkling her nose. "It probably has bugs in it."

In 1997, I had decided to buy my first house and asked my parents to drive out to New Jersey to take a look at it, and give me their blessing. They arrived shortly before noon, and the first thing my mother did when they entered my apartment was open a bag full of food, so my father could have lunch. She even brought plates, utensils, and napkins.

The house, in nearby Wood-Ridge, was small but charming, with a nice-sized backyard and deck—perfect for entertaining. "Once I'm settled in," I said, "you're coming for dinner. And I'm cooking. You are not bringing *anything.*"

By this time, my parents were in their seventies, and their first visit to my new home was with my brother Donald, his wife Joyce, and their one-year-old daughter Talia. It was a beautiful summer day, and I ran out to the curb when my brother's car pulled up.

"You made it!" I yelled, pulling Talia into my arms. "Welcome to my new home!"

"Why is it so hot here?" my father said. "It was so much cooler on Long Island."

"Oh, don't mind your father," my mother said. "He's turning into such an old grouch. Donald, open the trunk."

My brother quickly opened the trunk, which was filled with bags and boxes.

"What *is* all this?" I screamed. "I made so much food!"

"Bread," my mother said. "Don't tell me you don't need Italian bread. Where are you going to get good Italian bread like this in New Jersey?"

I began counting. "I don't believe you! Fifteen loaves of Italian bread? For six people? Are you out of your mind?"

"This is good bread," she screamed. "What you don't use, you freeze."

Then came the boxes.

"Why did you bring cake?" I groaned. "I told you not to bring cake. I have fresh fruit for dessert."

"It's not cake," my mother said. "It's Danish. We can't have lunch yet. It's too early. So make some coffee and we'll have some Danish. You like Danish. And I got two boxes. What you don't use, you freeze."

Then came a *third* box.

"I told you not to bring cake!" I yelled.

"It's not cake. It's pastry. Miniature cannoli . . . everything you like. What you don't use, you freeze."

Then a *fourth* box.

"Now what?" I said.

"This is cake," she told me.

Also in the trunk was an enormous package of toilet paper: twenty-four rolls wrapped in plastic. Since he retired, my father had become *obsessed* with buying large amounts of anything—as long as it was on sale.

"Here," he said, handing it to me himself. "You use toilet paper, don't you?"

"No, Dad," I said. "I live in the trees now, with the monkey people."

We adjourned to the backyard, where I tried my best to keep them entertained, occupied, and happy.

"The yard looks so beautiful," my sister-in-law said.

"Doesn't it?" my mother added. "The flowers look great . . . don't they, Emilio?"

"*It's hot as hell back here,*" my father screamed, wiping his face with a napkin. "*Why is New Jersey so damned hot?*"

Shortly after one o'clock, we had lunch and everything came out perfectly. I'd made a bruschetta, sausage and peppers, and a nice, healthy rice and veggie stir-fry.

"Everything is so delicious," my sister-in-law said.

"I'll say," my mother added, "and the rice and vegetables was such a good idea! Wasn't it, Emilio?"

"If it gets any hotter," my father said, fanning himself with a plate, "I'm hanging myself."

We talked. Had coffee. Ate dessert. And, all in all, it was a terrific day.

"I'm so glad we came," my mother said, as I helped them back to the car.

My father slumped into the front passenger seat, and by the time my brother and I had loaded up the trunk with Talia's toys, Dad was fast asleep. Within seconds, my brother had turned on the air-conditioning and pointed all of the jets at my father's face.

"Now, he'll sleep all the way home," my mother said, from the back seat. "I'm sorry. He's been like this for months now. He's useless in the heat."

"Not a problem," I said, kissing her goodbye.

What you don't use, you freeze.

PIZZA

Michele Linfante

Characters

GRACE INNOCENTI: A woman of thirty.
PIZZA LADY: A pizza deliverer.
LENA INNOCENTI: Grace's mother.
SADIE PETRILLO: An older lady and crony of Lena's.
BONSEY: A punk in the original fifties style.
PERLA THE EXOTIC: A Latin nightclub performer.

Setting

The play is set in Grace's San Francisco apartment in the present, with flashbacks to a pizzeria in Paterson, New Jersey, in the fifties and sixties.

The apartment, which occupies one-third of the set, stage right, is realistic, whereas the pizzeria, which takes up the remainder of the playing area, is more suggestive and dreamlike.

The apartment is created by two walls with an entrance to the extreme stage right. On the upstage wall are houseplants, a case full of books, a cassette recorder, assorted objets d'art. A faded Oriental carpet is on the floor and some tasteful, handpicked wall hangings serve as decoration. A homey armchair sits in front of the bookcase and a low coffee table holds the telephone. The room is studious and comfortable.

The pizzeria walls, abutting those of the apartment, are suggested by a skeletal structure of metal bars strung with small, colored Christmas-tree lights. A larger-than-life, cartoon-style pinball machine and juke box are along the upstage wall. A shelf above the pinball machine is covered with baseball trophies. Left of the juke box is a curtained doorway to the kitchen. The metal framing angles away from this door to create the storefront. The large window holds a bright, neon "PIZZA" sign, which faces the street.

191

Pizza

Downstage from the window the metal framing creates the open door to the street. Below the "PIZZA" sign is a counter which holds all the trappings of a fifties' pizzeria: telephone, pizza trays, chrome napkin dispenser, large pepper shaker, etc. In the center of the pizzeria space is a table flanked by three chrome-legged chairs.

While the pizzeria remains in blackout the lights come up on Grace who is sitting alone in her apartment. She's dressed in layers of clothes including a robe and slippers. In the opening moments she's holding a pad and pencil and is anxiously mulling something over. She finally puts down the pad and dials a phone number, long distance.

GRACE: Hello, Richard. This is Grace. I've been thinking . . . well maybe it's not such a good idea to send Ma all by herself on the plane. I mean, she's a sick woman, you know. Yeah, I know you know. But the idea of sending her with a note pinned on her dress is kind of callous, don't you think? It's a long way. Can't you arrange a business trip or something and bring her yourself? . . . Or maybe you can convince Daddy to take a plane and he could come too. . . . Yeah, I know he needs a rest. How's he doing, anyway? That's good . . . Yeah, well make sure she brings the note from the doctor about her medicine, and remember to pack some warm clothes. It's not that sunny here, you know. And tell Daddy not to pack any dented cans or anything, I've got plenty of food . . . I guess that's it. Er, are you sure there's-nothing else I need to know, because I might unplug the phone and then you won't be able to reach me for a While. . . . Uh-huh, well I guess that's all, then. All right, Richard, good night.

As she is saying good night the doorbell rings. Grace goes to answer the door and there is a pizza lady there holding a pizza. She's dressed in black trousers and a short-sleeved white shirt. She's wearing a cap with a winged pizza emblem and on her back is the same emblem in an oversized applique with a considerable wingspan, giving her an almost angelic appearance when she turns around.

PIZZA LADY: Here's your pizza. It's $6.50.
GRACE: Oh sure. (*She goes to get the money.*) You know, I don't know what came over me tonight. I haven't ordered a pizza in years.
PIZZA LADY: Well, the moon must be in pizza tonight 'cause we sure got plenty of orders.

GRACE: (*Nervous smile.*) Maybe that's it. I thought maybe it's because I'm a little nervous. I'm one of those people who eat when they're nervous. I also eat when I'm not nervous. I eat when I'm depressed. I eat when I'm happy ...

PIZZA LADY: Can't complain. Keeps us in business.

GRACE: It's awful cold tonight. Are you sure that jacket's warm enough?

PIZZA LADY: I got a truck full of pizzas to keep me warm.

GRACE: (*Finds her money and hands it to the pizza lady.*) Keep the change.

PIZZA LADY: (*Already out the door and offstage.*) Thanks. Good night.

GRACE: (*As she carries the pizza to the coffee table she is giving herself a lecture to calm herself.*) Nothing to be nervous about. I'm a grown-up person of indeterminate youth. My rent is paid. I have no cavities. My mother is coming to stay with me, but I can handle that.

GRACE *puts the pizza box down on the coffee table and arranges the few things beside it in an elaborate gesture of meticulousness and composure. She then goes to the bookcase and activates the tape player and we hear the strains of Erik Satie's "Trois Gymnopédies." She then sits down, composes herself, and opens the pizza box. As she opens the box the telephone in the pizzeria starts ringing and the chorus (composed of* LENA, BONSEY, *and* SADIE*) is singing "Sh Boom." During the opening bars of the song the lights have also come up on the pizza set.* RONSEY *is animatedly playing the pinball machine.* LENA *and* SADIE *are seated at the table playing with a larger-than-life deck of cards.*

CHORUS: Life could be a dream. Life could be a dream.
　　　　Life could be a dream
　　　　　　Sh Boom. Sh Boom.
　　　　If I could take you up to paradise up above.
　　　　　　Sh Boom. Sh Boom.

LENA: (*Calling to* GRACE *over the sounds of the song and the telephone.*) Gracie. Gracie.

GRACE: (*She has gone first to the doorway then to the tape cassette to discover where the music is coming from. She responds to the call inadvertently in the annoyed voice of a twelve-year-old.*) Whaddaya want, Ma?

LENA: Gracie, answer the telephone.

CHORUS: (*Continuing.*) And tell you darling you're the only one that I love. Life ...

Pizza

GRACE *finally suspects the music is coming from the pizza box and slams it shut, freezing the action in the pizzeria. As she opens it again the sounds and actions continue.*

CHORUS: . . . could be a dream, sweetheart. Hello, hello again. Sh Boom and hoping we'll meet again.

LENA: Where is she? (*The phone keeps ringing.* LENA *goes to the counter to answer it and the* song *fades out during her conversation.*) Lena's Pizzeria. Yeah we got some pies left but we can't deliver anywhere tonight. We close in half an hour if you want to come down and pick up your pie. Yeah, that's right. Dominick is here, but the car got stolen. No, we didn't call the police yet. No, my son can't drop the pie off. He's the one that stole the car. (*Hopeful.*) You think so? When does the drive-in get out? (*Whining voice.*) Oh. I don't know. That car is such a junk it wouldn't make it to Hackensack. I'm afraid the engine'll blow up or somethin'. Yeah? Well why don't you call your sister and have your nephew Raymond call me as soon as he gets home. And if you want any more deliveries tell my husband to buy his son a car. All right. Yeah. Good night. (*Calling out the front door.*) Gracie!

GRACE *responds to this last call and enters the scene as a twelve-year-old.*

SADIE: (*Using all her willpower not to peek at* LENA's *hand.*) Lena, come on. Finish this hand.

LENA: (*To* GRACE.) Where were you?

GRACE: Down by the dye house.

LENA: Down by the *river? I told yo*u not to play by the river!

GRACE: Aw, Ma, nobody could drown in the river, there's too much junk in.

LENA: Look at your clothes. They got all holes. What happened to your clothes?

GRACE: I dunno. We were just playin' with this box a' rags. And then we saw our clothes were gettin' all funny. Kind of eaten up.

SADIE: She looks like a swiss cheese.

LENA: It's the *chemicals!* Go wash your hands!

GRACE: I already washed my hands. Doreen took us to her father's store and let us wash. Then she gave us ice cream and let us look at the comic books.

LENA: Why do you play with that girl Doreen?

GRACE: Is Richie back yet?

LENA: No, and I'm worried sick.

GRACE: I brought you a Chunky.

SADIE: Look, Lena. You gonna finish this hand or not? I gotta go before Sam gets home.

LENA: What are you, afraid somebody's gonna steal all your money? Don't go yet. Dominick will walk you home. (*To* GRACE.) Where's your father? (*To* SADIE.) Stay and have some pie. (*Phone rings: She runs to answer it.*) Yeah, this is Lena. We only make one size. A dollar ten. We got a half-and-half pie with anchovies and a combination with peppers and sausage, or peppers and mushrooms or mushrooms and pepperoni . . . or you can get a garlic pie with just tomatoes and garlic or a zombie with everything on it, that's two and a quarter. (*Pause.*) Yeah, well I'm sorry. We're closin' for the night. We only got two pies left and we're gonna eat them. Call back tomorrow.

Toward the end of the phone conversation, GRACE, *who has gone over to the pinball machine, gets into a fight with* BONSEY *which overlaps the last part of* LENA's *conversation.*

BONSEY: Get your elbow off the machine.

GRACE: I didn't do anything.

BONSEY: I was hittin' sixty-five thousand on the fourth ball. That coulda been the week's top . . .

GRACE: Not a chance. Decker got the week's top. Ninety-five thousand.

BONSEY: Who aksed you, pimple brain?

GRACE: Except for Richie. He got ninety-eight thousand but that don't count 'cause he lives here.

BONSEY: You busted my streak.

GRACE: I didn't do nothin'.

BONSEY: Tell your mother to give me another dime.

GRACE: I'll tell her you won last week 'cause you put a matchbook under one a the legs.

BONSEY: Shut your mouth, half pint.

GRACE: Who you callin' a half pint? Ya half wit.

LENA: Shaddup, botha you. Bonsey, you go home now.

BONSEY: Come on, Lena. I was on a streak till a certain adolescent messed it up.

GRACE: You're crazy.

LENA: (*Shouting and shutting them both up.*) No more games tonight!

GRACE: (*To* BONSEY, *sheepish and conspiratorially.*) She's in a bad mood cause Richie's missin'.

Pizza

LENA: Aaaaaa . . . (*She bites her hand in a rage.*)

BONSEY: Awright. I'm sorry, Lena. I'm goin'. I'm goin'.

LENA: (*To* GRACE.) What do you fight with that moron for?

GRACE: (*Quiet and angry, wronged.*) I wasn't doin' anything.

LENA: (*Going over to* SADIE.) There's men fightin' and dyin' in stupid wars, all over the world and these kids are gonna wind up just like them and there's never gonna be any peace unless people learn how to talk to each other.

SADIE: These kids today are no good.

LENA: I got no more patience. I see them fight and I want to break their heads. (*Phone rings.*) Dominick. Is he still upstairs? (*Phone keeps ringing.*) Gracie, you better get that.

GRACE: (*Answers the phone, singing to the tune of "Bella Ciao."*)

> It comes with sausage and pepperoni,
> And extra cheese if you please,
> On your pizza pie.
> It's hot and tasty
> That's why we're crazy
> About our pizza pies.

(*Lena turns to look at her.*)

> Oh yes we're crazy.
> Our future's hazy.
> But there's one thing for sure
> That our sauce is pure.
> My mother made it.
> Sometimes I hate it.
> And I'd like to run away.*

She hangs up the phone ready to run as LENA *gets up and goes toward her.*

LENA: What did ya do that for?

SADIE: Look, Lena, I gotta go.

LENA: Don't go yet. Dominick will walk you home. (*To* GRACE.) Where's your father? (*To* SADIE.) Stay and have some pie. Gracie, put a pie in the oven with a lot a garlic like Sadie likes.

*© 1980 by Marga Gomez.

196

SADIE: No, I shouldn't stay. I dunno if I want any pizza.

LENA: Come on. You want a little glass of wine.

SADIE: No...Well, maybe just a little glass.

LENA: And a slice of pizza.

SADIE: Well, maybe just a little slice.

LENA: With a lot of garlic.

SADIE: And some anchovies, maybe?

LENA: (*Calling into the kitchen.*) Put some anchovies on the pie, Gracie.

SADIE: And some peppers?

LENA: And some peppers.

SADIE: (*Calling into the kitchen.*) And don't cook it too crispy 'cause I can't eat it so good.

LENA: (*Returning to the table with a glass of wine.*) You know, Sadie, as much as you eat, that's too much work for one tooth. Why don't you take some of that money from under your mattress and buy yourself a set of teeth. (*Phone rings.* GRACIE *appears from the kitchen and answers it.*)

GRACE: City Morgue.

LENA: (*Frantic, thinking it's the city morgue calling about her son.*) What?

GRACE: You kill 'em, we chill 'em.

LENA: (*Shouting at her daughter for fooling her.*) Shut up!

GRACE: Actually this is Lena's Pizzeria. Home of the world famous Zombie Pizza. Oh, hi, Raymond. Yeah, she's here. Ma, it's Ray Donato.

LENA: (*Grabbing the phone.*) Raymond, were you out with Richie tonight? (*Pause.*) Was Gabe with you? ... What about Gene Cherini? ... When was the dance over? And you didn't see any of them? ... You wouldn't lie to me would you, Raymond? (*Curtly.*) Yeah. All right, never mind. Yeah, good-bye.

GRACE: You think we should call up Missing Persons and they could send out a search party?

LENA: *Be quiet!*

SADIE: (*Now she's getting mad.*) This game's no good anymore. You don't want to come and play 'cause I'm winnin'.

LENA: You probably got all my cards memorized by now. Why don't you finish the game yourself?

SADIE: You can't talk to me like that. What are you mad at me for? You think you can buy me off with a piece a pizza.

LENA: (*Coming back to the table, nervous and distracted. Whining.*) I don't wanna finish the game. I can't concentrate. Maybe Gracie wants a finish or we could play three-handed scope.

GRACE: I don't feel like it.

LENA: (*Nervous, as if stalling for time.*) Why doncha tell us your story, then?

SADIE: What story?

LENA: What story? Your one story. The one about the devil. (GRACE *ad-libs a grimacing remark and attempts to go back to her chair but her mother pulls her over.*)

SADIE: Oh . . . in that case, lemme see. Are you sure that pizza's not gettin' too crispy?

GRACE: I just put it in.

SADIE: Jeez, the time I saw the devil. Can you imagine? It was after my first son was born and my mother was still alive, God bless her. My mother was a saint. I still get masses said for her. How she suffered, poor woman. She never liked Sam, you know. He's the one person she called an *imbecile*. (*With an Italian accent.*) She never said that about anybody. She was such a good woman.

LENA: (*Prompting her.*) *Go* ahead. Tell us the part about the devil.

SADIE: I'll get to that part. Where was I?

GRACE: Your mother was callin' Sam an imbecile. (*English pronunciation.*)

LENA: It was after your first son was born.

SADIE: Ohhh. An' I got so sick. And in them days they didn't have any medicines like they do now. An' I swelled up like a gourd and I couldn't get outta bed. An' I couldn't eat to save my life. Er, are you sure that pie won't burn?

GRACE: I put it on the top shelf and turned the oven off.

SADIE: An' there was snow outside higher than the doorway. And the wind was bangin' at the windows.

GRACE: (*Incredulous.*) I never heard the part about the snow before.

LENA: Shhh.

SADIE: An' I had such a fever I got so I couldn't see nothin' even with my eyes open. An' I closed my eyes for a minute and I opened 'em an' that's when I saw him.

GRACE: The devil.

SADIE: Standin' at the foot a the bed no farther away than you are now.

GRACE: What did he look like?

SADIE: He looked like a man who was too handsome to be any good. An' he was wearin' a red suit and his hairy arms were reachin' out to me.

GRACE: How could you tell his arms were hairy if he had a suit on? Did he have a pitchfork?

SADIE: No, I don't remember seein' no pitchfork.

GRACE: What did he do?

SADIE: He told me to come with him. He said "Veni qua," and pointed his hand at me. I said, "No," and he got mad an' he said it again. "Veni qua," an' he looked right at me with his black eyes like a couple a coals an' I tried to reach my throat for my crucifix but my arms wouldn't move. . . . An' then he opened his cape an' he was naked as a red devil.

GRACE: I thought he had a suit on.

LENA: Shhh.

SADIE: An' I said, *"Go* away, devil." An' I closed my eyes and started to pray but I felt myself gettin' pulled by my feet to the foot a the bed an' I musta wet my pants 'cause I felt wet—down there, y'know—an' I heard a sound like spit on a hot stove. And I made the sign a the cross inside my mouth with my burning tongue an' when I opened my eyes I looked right at that devil an' said *"No."* The bed shook but he started movin' away an' the last thing he said to me was, "Tu sei più forte di me . . . you're stronger than me."

GRACE: I never knew the devil spoke Italian.

SADIE: Sure, what do you think?

GRACE: Did the sheets get burned?

SADIE: Black as coal, an' they never did come clean, either.

LENA: Get the pie outta the oven.Gracie.

GRACE *goes to get the pie while* PERLA *enters to the sound of a low wolf whistle from outside. She's in spiked heels and flamboyant clothes.*

SADIE: Speak of the devil.

PERLA: Aren't they a little young to be hangin' around at this hour?

LENA: (*Goes to the door and calls out.*) Bonsey, go home before I call your mother.

PERLA: Are you still open?

LENA: We're closin' up but come in. We were just goin' to have a pie.

PERLA: I thought I'd see if I could get a pizza to take upstairs and maybe rest a minute.

LENA: (*Motioning her to sit down.*) You want a soda? (*Calling back to the kitchen.*) Gracie, bring a couple a sodas, too. (*To* SADIE.) This is the new neighbor from upstairs.

At this moment GRACE *enters with the things from the kitchen and as the action slows down or freezes for a second she acknowledges this new memory, quietly, with a half laugh, as she reminisces.*

GRACE: You too, huh, Perla?

LENA: (*To* PERLA.) What's your stage name again?

PERLA: Perla the Exotic.

LENA: This is Sadie Petrillo from across the street.

PERLA: Pleased to meet you.

SADIE: (*Very close-mouthed and disapproving of* PERLA.) Hello.

LENA: Perla's a dancer. She toured in South America and everything. (SADIE *lets out a whimpering harrumph. To* GRACE.) Did you put the cheese away? (GRACE *nods.*) We gotta put the sauce away too. An' take out the garbage. Where's your father?

GRACE: Last time I saw him he was upstairs calling in the numbers.

LENA: (*Giving* GRACE *a high* sign *with her face behind* PERLA's *back. to be quiet.*) Sta zit. (*Which means "be quiet" in Italian. Then to* PERLA *to make sure that she didn't understand.*) Er ... you don't speak Italian, do you?

PERLA: No. But a lot of people think I look Italian. Do you think so?

LENA: Oh yeah, yeah, you could be. But you're not, huh?

PERLA: No. My father was Spanish, Castilian. My mother is Puerto Rican. (SADIE *lets out another disapproving whimper.*)

LENA: (*Brusquely, to* SADIE.) Well, what are you doin' just sittin' there. Eat your pie.

GRACE: Eugene next door is Spanish.

PERLA: Oh.

GRACE: He never goes out anymore since the time he tried to drown himself in the river. But he had on this bulky jacket that made him float until they fished him out, right, Ma?

LENA: (*Reminded to be anxious again.*) Don't talk about the river. Look what time it is and your brother's not home yet. Go get your father. (GRACE *leaves to go upstairs. To* PERLA.) Have a piece of pie. Go ahead.

PERLA: Well, I was thinking of ordering one.

LENA: Have some of this. It's for us. It's got peppers and garlic. You like garlic?

PERLA: Yeah, sure. Have you got any forks?

LENA: Forks? Eh, sure, if you like. I'll get you one.

PERLA: No. Don't get up. I'll get it. Where are they?

LENA: There are some on the counter back there. (PERLA *gets up and sashays back to the counter.* SADIE *leans over to look at her ass.*)

SADIE: Guarda the culo. (*Loosely translated, "Look at that ass."*) Pizza with a fork like a real American. (*Said with an Italian inflection.*)

LENA: (*To* SADIE *curtly.*) So, what's the matter with your pizza? Is it too crispy, or what?

SADIE: (*Tartly.*) Yeah.

LENA: Then dip it in your wine. Or eat the middle part. It's soft in the middle like the brain of an old woman. (PERLA *returns with a fork and sits down.* GRACE *returns.*)

GRACE: Daddy fell asleep listenin' to the baseball scores. Not only that, but Richie is takin' a shower and the car is parked across the street.

LENA: (*Incredulous.*) No! (GRACE *nods.* LENA *goes to look out the door for the car.*) He musta sneaked upstairs. (*Angry whine.*) Oh, I could kill him. He had me so worried.

SADIE: (*She is starting to grill* PERLA *before* LENA *swoops in.*) Do you let your mother see you dressed like that?

PERLA: My mother knows I'm in show business.

SADIE: You Catholic?

LENA: (*Bustling.*) *You* finished with your wine, Sadie? You finished with your pizza?

SADIE: (Still to PERLA.) You married?

LENA: (*Hustling* SADIE *out.*) Here, I'll wrap up a piece for you to take home with you. Gracie, bring some wax paper for Sadie.

SADIE: (*Putting her sweater on.*) You told me Dominick would walk me home.

LENA: Yeah, well I don' wanna wake him up now or he'll get started with Richie and wake up the whole neighborhood. (*She looks out the door.*) Hey you, Sheik? What are you still waitin' around for? You walk Sadie home and I'll give you some free games on the pinball machine tomorrow.

SADIE: Lena, you wanna gimme another little piece a' pie for my breakfast tomorrow?

LENA: (*She rushes to wrap up another piece of pie from the tray.*) Sure. You want one or you want two?

SADIE: Naw, one's enough . . . er, well, all right. Two. Maybe one with anchovies.

LENA: Yeah, I got it. (*She brings the pizza to* SADIE, *who is still hanging back at the door.*)

SADIE: You sure it's all right to go home with this kid?

LENA: What are you talkin' about? I know these boys like I know my own son. (*Thinking of her son immediately inspires her whining anger again.*) Oh that lousy punk! Wait'll I get my hands on him.

SADIE: All right, I'm goin'. I'll see ya tomorrow. (*She goes out.*)

LENA: Good night, Sadie. (*Calls after her.*) Don't forget to dip it in your milk if it's too crispy.

SADIE: (*Off.*) Go on.

LENA: (*To* PERLA.) You want to hear some music? Put the juke box on, Gracie, and lock the door. (*She comes to sit down.*)

PERLA: You look as tired as I feel.

LENA: Yeah, I'm always tired lately. Anyway, I think I was born tired. My mother used to call me sheep-eyes because I always had such dreamy eyes. An' my husband still jokes about when he used to come and take me out and he'd hear her yell, "He's comin'. Go wake her up."

PERLA: You do have beautiful eyes.

LENA: Oh, you should have seen them when I was a girl and I'd put on makeup, you know. And with my dark hair, it was long then. Once at the World's Fair in New York they gave me a card to take a screen test.

PERLA: No kidding? Well, I can believe it. What did you do?

LENA: I didn't do anything. I was stupid. Backwards. You know. I never called up.

PERLA: Have you still got the card?

LENA: What for?

PERLA: You could still call up. It's never too late.

LENA: (*Titillated, opening up in a big smile.*) Go on.

PERLA: You got to follow all those leads. You never know what somebody can do for you 'til you find out. I've been in a few movies myself, kind of like an extra.

GRACE: You know how to cha-cha?

PERLA: Yes, but that's not the kind of dancing I do in the shows. I do this special act with fancy costumes. Feathers and sequins. They cost plenty, let me tell you. And I sing, too. Would you like to be in show business when you grow up?

LENA: Gracie, do your Jimmy Durante impersonation for Perla.

GRACE: Maaa, I haven't done that since I was little.

LENA: Then do the Sid Caesar, or the Bette Davis. "Peter darling." Go ahead. She does it so good. (GRACE *shakes her head no.*) Come on, Gracie. Do it for Perla. She does stuff like that all the time in front of the mirror on the cigarette machine. Come on, Gracie. You do it so good.

GRACE: (*To* PERLA.) I wrote a poem, if you want to hear it.

PERLA: Why sure.

GRACE: Life is a two-pronged fork
    With space in between.
    Life is a cold butter knife,
       Rather dull
    Life is a napkin ring
    An eternal type thing.

PERLA: (*To* LENA.) She's very bright, huh?

LENA: Yeah, she got skipped once, already. And she draws, too. (*To* GRACE.) Go get the sketch you did of Pinochle with his big mustache. And the comics. (GRACE *goes off.*) My people are all intelligent. Two of my sisters finished high school and they're both teachers. My mother always used to say, "I'd rather be bad than stupid. If you're bad, you can always move to another town. But if you're stupid, people know it as soon as you open your mouth." (GRACE *comes back with various pizza boxes.*)

GRACE: (*Showing* PERLA.) There's comics in this one and this one. This is the little match girl and this one's a story about Niccolina; she's a wicked girl scout who's mean to everybody all the time and she gets hit by a car. See, these are her legs under the car. I've been practicing how to draw cars. This one's an Impala. This is old stuff, the animals in the movie house and the talking peppers. And this is a paper doll I made and these are all her clothes. They don't fit so good now 'cause I got mad one time and ripped her in half and now she's got all this Scotch tape around the waist and she can't really wear two-piece outfits anymore.

PERLA: You're really good. I should have you design some of my costumes sometime.

GRACE: No. I don't know. I don't design clothes anymore really. I'm getting ready to throw all this stuff out.

PERLA: Are you sure? I'm working on this new act and I've got to come up with something really special, you know. (*She is pulling them in to her with her energy.*) It's got to be a costume that when you come out on stage in the nightclub you can hear their eyeballs fall in their glasses. Now it's a challenge to design a good costume when all the clubs really want to show is your body, let's face it. But I got this idea for a number and the costume is going to be important.

LENA: Well, what do you need? Maybe I could think about it too?

GRACE: Yeah, she's good at that stuff.

PERLA: Well, you know Sonja Henie the ice skater, right?

GRACE: I *love* her movies.

LENA: She's got a fat face though, doncha think?

PERLA: Well, it's going to be like a Sonja Henie number, except without the ice.

GRACE: (*Excited.*) Oh, I do that all the time. (*She jumps up and "ice skates" around.*)

LENA: Yeah, that's how I get her to polish the floors when we wax 'em.

PERLA: Then you got the idea perfectly. I want to come out as an ice queen.

I want to look so cold that they will have to put on their fur capes and order hot toddies. And then the number will be so *hot* that the costume will start to melt and by the end of the song they will be fanning themselves and ordering rum coolers.

GRACE: What's a rum cooler?

PERLA: You don't need to know that.

LENA: (*Thinking.*) So you want something like a big ice cube maybe.

GRACE: What's the song going to be like?

PERLA: Here, I'll show you. (*She takes* GRACE's *hand and takes her to the middle of the pizzeria. Then she goes to get* LENA *by the hand.*) You too, Lena. Play these. (*She takes maracas out of her bag.*) And when I tell you, you sing the chorus, it goes "Turn up the heat." You got that?

LENA: (*Sheepishly.*) Oh, I don't know.

PERLA: Come on, you can do it. (*She poses, readying herself for the song. She skates forward.* LENA *and* GRACE *join in and eventually get carried away by the end of the number.*)

> My story is sad.
> But I don't feel so bad.
> Romance was a thrill.
> Now it gives me a chill.
> I'll be icy 'til I meet
> Somebody who can turn up the heat.
>
> CHORUS
> Turn up the heat. Don't let me shiver.
> Turn up the heat.
> When I can quiver, Turn up the heat
> *And* raise my temperature.
>
> You better get lost
> Or you'll turn into frost
> Unless you are sold
> On a passion that's cold.
> I'll be icy 'til I meet
> Somebody who can turn up the heat.

CHORUS . . .*

*"Turn Up The Heat" © 1980 by Marga Gomez.

LENA: Come on, Gracie. Why don't you do one of your impersonations now? Do the Jimmy Durante.

PERLA: Yeah, come on. I'd like to see it. (PERLA *and* LENA *seat themselves and* GRACE *fusses a little and then goes into her act.*)

GRACE: (*As Jimmy Durante.*) I was takin' a bath when the telephone rings . . . And I gets up and I goes to the phone . . .

LENA: I get such a kick out of this one. She looks sort of like him, don't she? She does those funny parts so good.

GRACE *hears what she says and stops, distraught. Then she runs off, back to her chair in the present. The light darkens on the pizza set and* PERLA *walks off.* GRACE *is left breathing hard, remembering this incident.*

GRACE: Don't think I'm ever gonna forget that, Ma.

PERLA: (*Notices* GRACE *has run away.*) Gracie, Gracie, come back.

GRACE *finally gets up and walks back into the scene. She talks in her adult voice.*

LENA: Why did you run away like that? Why did you get so mad?

GRACE: Because you said I was ugly.

LENA: I never said you were ugly. What are you talkin' about?

GRACE: It's when I was doin' Jimmy Durante and you told Perla I looked like him.

LENA: No I didn't. I just meant you did it so good.

GRACE: I am ugly.

LENA: You're not ugly. Don't talk like that. You got nice features.

GRACE: Perla's beautiful and you were beautiful and I'm ugly.

LENA: Who says I was beautiful?

GRACE: You say it all the time. Daddy says it.

LENA: (*Sheepishly.*) I wasn't so beautiful. I just wore a lot of mascara. You shouldn't think so much about beauty. Do you think beauty is every-thing? I got news for you: a lot of beautiful people are unhappy.

GRACE: Yeah, well as long as I'm gonna be unhappy, I'd rather be beautiful and unhappy.

LENA: You got brains. That's more important. And you got a good personality.

GRACE: That's what you always say about people who are ugly. You hate me because I'm not beautiful like you.

LENA: (*Crying.*) Don't talk like that. That's not true.

GRACE: And I hate you. I didn't ask to be born. I'm gonna die and you'll be sorry.

LENA: Don't say that. Never say that.

GRACE: Die, die, die, die. I wish you'd drop dead. (*There's a gasp between them.* GRACE *reverts to her twelve-year-old voice.*) *I didn't mean it, Mommy.*

LENA: I never wanted to hurt you.

GRACE: I'm sorry, ma. I didn't mean it, honest. (*She goes over to* LENA.)

LENA: I'm sorry, Gracie. I didn't mean nothin'. I just meant you did it so good. I love you so much. You gotta believe me. I love you more than anything in the world.

GRACE: I know, ma.

LENA: Put the lights out, Gracie, and put the juke box on. (GRACE *goes to put the lights out.*) Come and sit by me. I like to sit here sometimes with just the light from the juke box on and the sign light from outside. It's *cozy.* (*Opening strains of "In the Still of the Night" can be heard faintly.*)

GRACE: Richie wants me to massage his arm. He's gotta pitch tomorrow.

LENA: Keep me company a minute. (GRACE *goes over to her.*) Gracie, let's have a Halloween party here. We can turn the lights out like this and have a stuffed dummy over in the corner. We'll make it scary. I kind of like that. To scare people, you know. Even when you and Richie were in the baby carriage I used to make those big scary eyes at you. You think that's normal?

GRACE: Probably not.

LENA: Is the oven off, Gracie? (GRACE *nods.*) We better go upstairs or I'll never get you up for school in the morning.

GRACE: (*Going into a subtle performance.*) Oh yeah, that reminds me, Ma. You know I had this funny dream that I was hit by a truck right down by the playground on the way to school.

LENA: (*Scared; the anxious voice again.*) What are you saying? You're kiddin' me.

GRACE: No, I just remembered. I think it was a Wonder Bread truck.

LENA: Don't go to school tomorrow! I'll write you a note.

GRACE: I really ought to go. I got that editorial due for the paper.

LENA: You can take it in on Monday.

GRACE: Well, if you say so. I think I feel a little sick anyway. You think I got a fever? Feel my face. (LENA *feels* GRACE's *face with her face.*)

LENA: I don't know. You feel a little warm. But you were back by the oven.

GRACE: Maybe you can make me some tea and toast tomorrow and some

Lipton soup and I'll take my blankets and go lie on the couch in the living room . . . and you can help me write my editorial.

LENA: I thought you said you wrote it.

GRACE: It's almost done. I got the idea . . . And we can watch the afternoon movie on Channel 5. It's a Fred Astaire movie.

LENA: I don't like Fred Astaire. He's got no sex appeal.

GRACE: Then we can play cards, and I'll draw your picture. Or we can play Modern Art.

LENA: What's that one?

GRACE: Tessa and me invented it. I'll show you. (GRACE *wraps herself around* LENA *in a bizarre pose, then shouts.*) Modern art!

LENA: (*Laughs, but acts annoyed and tough.*) You're chokin' me. (*They poke at each other playfully.*)

GRACE: Gimme a kiss. Oh, let's play the kissing game and see if I can catch you. (LENA *shakes her head slowly from side to side and* GRACE *moves her head until she zooms in and plants a kiss: this is a game that they are obviously familiar with.*) You're gettin' too slow. See if you can get me.

She starts shaking her head while LENA *tries to plant a kiss. When they start the kissing game the sound of "In the Still of the Night" drifts in while the lights fade and* LENA *backs out of the scene. As the song fades out* GRACE *slams down the pizza box and dials the phone again.*

GRACE: Hello, is this Suicide Prevention? This is Grace Innocenti. I used to work there, answering the telephones? Oh, you're new. Well I've got this pizza over here that I can't eat and I thought maybe I could bring it over to you. No, it wouldn't be any trouble. . . . You did, huh. . . . Oh, yeah, that's all right. I could always freeze it or something. . . . No, this isn't the kind of mood I feel like sharing with a friend right now. . . . Oh no, I've just been reading too many psychology books. You read them and you start thinking about how messed up your parents were and then you start thinking about how messed up you are and how messed up the world is and you get to feeling how you just want to crawl into somebody's armpit and feel safe, you know. And then you start thinking about all the people you've ever loved and wonder where they all are and you wonder who's going to care if you die and then you get mad and think about dying just to spite everybody that doesn't care, and you start thinking about how nobody needs you. But as soon as you find out somebody needs you you start worrying about your freedom. You know what I mean? . . . (*Repeating what the other person has said.*) You hear what I'm saying, huh? (*Sharply.*) *Of* course you hear what I'm saying, your phone's working, isn't it? Anyway, I just thought you might like some pizza. I better let you get back to your phones. Good night.

During the last two lines the doorbell rings and it's the PIZZA LADY *with another pizza.*

PIZZA LADY: Here's the pizza you ordered.
GRACE: (*Slightly bewildered.*) Thanks. (*She goes for her money again and brings it back to the* PIZZA LADY.)
PIZZA LADY: You know, it's a good thing you don't like pizza or we're liable to run out tonight.
GRACE: (*Smiles weakly.*) Yeah. Look, I'm sorry to make you come all this way again.
PIZZA LADY: It's all in the line of duty. (GRACE *pays her.*) Thanks. (*She exits.*)
GRACE: (*Calling after her.*) Be sure to lock your car door. (*Then, coming back into the room, she talks to the pizza box in a whining tone.*) What did I say that for? (*As she carries the pizza box over to the table she talks to herself in the voice of an Indian guru.*) Nostalgia is a dangerous thing. Too much mooning over the past, like too much mooning over the future, may not leave enough time for living in the present. (*She sets the pizza box down delicately and then speaks in a normal but dreamy voice to herself as she goes to open the second pizza box.*) One must, however, acknowledge certain modes of receptivity where the slightest provocation . . . a melody, a scent, the look of your own aging hand, a wad of tissue in your pocket . . . brings on the deluge.

The lights come on in the pizza set while LENA *summons* GRACE. *This is a quick and delicate change.*

LENA: (*Quietly.*) Gracie.
GRACE: (*From her apartment.*) What, Ma?
LENA: Something's wrong with me, Gracie. I can't remember how to make the dough. (*A bowl is on the pizzeria table in front of her as if she were standing over the dough.*) I don't remember what to do. My mind is trying to tell me but it doesn't work. (*There is crying in her voice*)
GRACE: (*Slowly enters the scene as a fifteen-year-old.*) Don't cry, Ma. Maybe you're just nervous or something.

LENA: No, it's not that. That's what Dr. Pellicone says. He thinks I'm just nervous, but it's more than that. Something's happening to me, Gracie. I don't know what it is.

GRACE: Well, maybe we ought to take you to another doctor.

LENA: You think maybe I had a stroke? Is this what happens when you have a stroke?

GRACE: I don't know, Ma.

LENA: They think I just complain. Nobody understands. Nobody believes me. Your father doesn't believe me. Take me to the hospital, Gracie. Something's wrong with me.

GRACE: I took you to the hospital last week. They said they couldn't take you, that you had to go through a doctor. They can't tell what's wrong.

LENA: Take me to the state hospital, Gracie. I think I'm losing my mind, Gracie.

GRACE: (*Nervous, trying to cope.*) Come on, Ma, you just forgot how to make the dough. It can't be that hard. I'll help you. You showed me before.

LENA: I got this terrible feeling I can't explain. I don't understand. I'm scared.

GRACE: Don't be scared, Ma.

LENA: Take me to the state hospital, Gracie. We'll get Katy's son from across the street to drive us. I've got five dollars in the underwear drawer.

GRACE: Ma, I don't want to go to the hospital again. They're shitty. They ask you all these questions and then they say they can't do anything for you. Anyway, you can't be so bad if you remember you got five dollars in the underwear drawer, right?

LENA: No, something's wrong, Gracie. You gotta believe me.

GRACE: I believe you, Ma.

LENA: Promise me you'll take me to the state hospital, Gracie. Make them do something for me.

GRACE: I promise, Ma. We'll take you to a specialist.

LENA: I can't make the pizza anymore. I never feel good anymore. Who's going to make the dough?

GRACE: I'll help you, Ma. (*As she says this she starts backing out of the scene toward her apartment.*)

LENA: I can't clean the house anymore. I get this lousy nervous stomach all the time, I can't do anything right anymore. (*The lights eventually fade to a blackout on* LENA *by the end of their exchange.*)

GRACE: Don't cry, Ma.

LENA: Do something for me, Gracie.

The lights are up on GRACE *standing behind her chair. She is shaken, not wanting to cry, trying to look tough. She crosses her arms in front of her and looks down at the culprit pizza box.*

GRACE: For six lousy dollars you'd think they'd at least sell you a pizza that makes you forget. (*To the pizza box.*) People pay to forget. Who wants to remember anything anymore? Who wants to feel anything anymore? What do you think, I'm a chump? (*She has sat down nervously and is giving sidelong glances to the pizza box as a real enemy. Petulant and trying to sound tough.*) A person could starve trying to get a bite to eat around here.

She goes through an elaborate strategy of trying to sneak a piece of pizza out of the box. As if stealing something, she has sneaked her hand into the pizza box and sneaked out a piece of pizza. As she raises it to her lips we hear the strains of the first lines of "Mama," a sappy Italian-American song that Connie Francis used to sing. A look of comic despair and defeat crosses over her face through this first bar of music and as she opens the box to replace the slice of pizza the second "Mama" swells out.

The lights come up on the pizza set, but the lighting is different to indicate a change in the place. The colored lights are dark on the outlined pinball machine and juke box, leaving just the bare construction showing. There is a large James Dean poster over the pinball machine, a cloth over the table, a colored spread over the counter to give the place a look of abandonment, of a closed resort, besides indicating that it is GRACE*'s living space now. There is a typewriter on the table. Some books and cardboard packing boxes are scattered about.*

LENA *is standing, leaning on the table. She is stooped, aged; one arm is bent and her leg drags. She's wearing a soiled housecoat, slippers, and stockings drooping around her ankles. She has a handkerchief or a wad of paper towel in one hand that she twists nervously during the scene. It is obvious that she is sick and has deteriorated from the first scene. She has a certain bright-eyed, tic-like animation because of the medication she takes.*

LENA: Gracie, where are you? You in the bathroom? Don't squeeze your face. What are you doin'? Where are you?

GRACE: (*Entering the scene as a twenty-year-old.*) Ma, you know you're not supposed to come down the stairs by yourself.

LENA: You wanna come upstairs. Daddy bought some cold cuts.

GRACE: Not right now, I'm busy.

LENA: What are you doin'?

GRACE: I'm getting some of my things together.

LENA: "Animal Kingdom" is on.

GRACE: Yeah, so what?

LENA: Put it on and watch it with me.

GRACE: I don't want to watch "Animal Kingdom."

LENA: You know I like to watch it when the animals fight. You think that's normal?

GRACE: (*As if in disgust with the human race.*) Probably.

LENA: I like the way you got it fixed up here now, Gracie. Like Picasso.

GRACE: What do you know about Picasso?

LENA: I know. He's a painter, right? What do you think I'm stupid? (*She has been walking around, crotchety and childlike at the same time, looking at things like a visitor.*)

GRACE: All right, ma.`I want you to sit down here, okay? So you don't fall down. I want to talk to you. (*She guides* LENA *to a chair.*) Did you take your medicine?

LENA: Yeah, but it don't make me feel so good anymore, this new medicine.

GRACE: Well, I was reading about it. It's all experimental, you know. They don't know that much about it. It's important that you don't take too much or you get these weird side effects.

LENA: I got to take the medicine, Gracie, or else I can't do nothin'.

GRACE: I know, I know.

LENA: Daddy got some rolls, too.

GRACE: All right, all right. I'll come up and eat later. I want to talk to you first.

LENA: Put the television on, Gracie.

GRACE: (*Getting a little angry.*) Not now, Ma. In a little while. I want to have a talk with you, Ma.

LENA: What's the matter? Somethin's the matter.

GRACE: Nothing's the matter, Ma.

LENA: Gracie, you wanna make me a sandwich?

GRACE: That's one of the things I like about you, Ma. Your dedication to the à la carte school of philosophy. "I eat therefore I am."

LENA: Yeah, go on. What do you want to talk about?

GRACE: My friend Jay found me an apartment in New York.

LENA: What are you talkin' about?

GRACE: I found this great rent-controlled apartment and I'm gonna move to New York.

LENA: *You're crazy.* What do you want to move to New York for?

GRACE: Lots of reasons. I got my friends there . . . and, and there's lots of museums and lots of theaters and . . .

LENA: Lots of murders.

GRACE: Yeah, well I don't plan on getting murdered.

LENA: You're crazy, Gracie. All the relatives used to live in New York. We all left. Now you want to go back and live in New York. It's stupid, stupid.

GRACE: (*Petulant, angry.*) It's not stupid. Living in *this* dying, polluted city is stupid. Living in this dying neighborhood with its boarded-up, broken-down corner stores and its broken-down pizzeria is stupid.

A light comes in on SADIE *in a corner of the set. She's an apparition. Only* GRACE *sees her.*

SADIE: A girl ought to stay home and take care of her mother.

GRACE: You shut up. You're dead already.

SADIE: The devil's gonna get you.

GRACE: He should be so lucky.

LENA: (*Who hasn't acknowledged this interchange.*) Don't go, Gracie. Stay here. You don't have to pay any rent.

GRACE: Ma, I gotta live my own life. I need to . . . gather my rosebuds, sow my wild oats.

SADIE: What's she gonna do? Go live on a farm?

GRACE: I can't stay here living in a closed-up pizzeria, reading old magazines, writing letters to dead authors.

LENA: But you got it fixed up so nice.

GRACE: I want to *do* something with my life. (*Quieter, half-assured.*) *I* want to be a beatnik.

LENA: What do they do?

GRACE: (*Shrugging her shoulders.*) Nothin' . . . (*Brusque and defensive.*) I don't know. They write, they paint. They make love.

SADIE: She's gonna get in trouble and then she'll come back.

LENA: What do you want to move to New York for? It's so expensive. It's so much trouble.

GRACE: Give me a break, Ma. Nobody sticks around here. Even Perla moved back to New York.

SADIE: At least she got married. She's respectable.

GRACE: (*To* SADIE.) She's bored.

LENA: There are no jobs. What are you gonna do? You can't find a job.

GRACE: I'll do something. Anything. You think I can't live on my own.

SADIE: She thinks she's better than everybody here in the neighborhood.

GRACE: (*To* SADIE.) Just different.

LENA: You can stay here. You don't have to pay any rent.

GRACE: Look, Ma. Nobody said anything when Richie left us, right?

SADIE: That's different. He's a man.

LENA: He's got his own family.

GRACE: He got married and got his ass outta the ghetto and nobody made a fuss. He wasn't around when your brains started leakin' and we didn't know what was happening. It was me you used to talk to, right? Well my brain is leakin', Ma. I've got to get out of here.

LENA: (*Whining voice.*) You won't come back. You just want to be with your friends. You'll never come back.

GRACE: Ma, it's only thirty minutes away. I can come back a lot. Or you can come and see me.

LENA: (*Still whining.*) Oh, it's so much trouble. You got to take the bus and the train.

GRACE: (*Blowing up.*) Jeezus. Life is too much trouble, right? Let's face it. I'll go turn on the gas on the pizza oven right now and we can stick our heads in it. Is that what you want?

LENA: (*Angry, sullen.*) *All* right. Go on, go on, go on.

GRACE: I'll come and see you a lot. I'll take the bus. . . .

LENA: Yeah, sure, sure.

GRACE: Jeez, Ma. You could be happy for me.

LENA: (*Still sullen and sarcastic.*) Sure, go ahead. I'm happy.

GRACE: You don't look happy. Why don't you try and get happy about it?

LENA: (*Curt and standoffish.*) I don't feel good. I feel lousy. I never feel happy. I feel lousy.

GRACE: (*Trying to get through to her mother, who is sitting there rigid and angry.*) If you just think about it and try to accept it . . .

LENA: (*Angry and sharp.*) *I* don't think about nothin'. I feel lousy, that's what I think about. I think about nothin'. I feel lousy. (*More quietly.*) I'm gonna die. (*She whines on the last line and rocks back and forth in a series of short moans.*)

GRACE: (*Blows up and swats her mother impetuously on the head.*) I'm gonna die. Everybody's gonna die!

LENA: Go on, hit me. Like your father. Like your brother. Everybody hits me. (*The juke box starts playing "Mama" again;* GRACE *goes over and kicks it. It stops and* SADIE *disappears, too.*)

GRACE: (*Trying to get through to her mother, holding her shoulders.*) Ma, you're not gonna die from the Parkinson's disease. Especially now that you're taking the medicine. You just got to help yourself.

LENA: Go on. You sound like your father.

GRACE: You're just afraid to die because you never lived enough, Ma. I got to go out and live, Ma. I gotta find out about things. Why didn't you tell me anything, about anything? About girls. About boys. About getting married or having babies. Or being normal.

LENA: I never knew much.

GRACE: I can't stay here like this, Ma. Afraid to leave the pizzeria. Being I sickly all the time. Never leaving the family, like the girl next door. Like the whole family next door.

LENA: (Whining cry.) I want you to go, Gracie. I know it's no good for you here. I only care about you. I don't want you to be like me. I want you to go and have a good time. I want you to be happy.

GRACE: I want you to be happy.

GRACE *and* LENA *repeat this phrase, each in her own inflection, simultaneously as* GRACE *backs away. Lights fade on* LENA. *We eventually hear only* GRACE's *voice as she returns to her set.*

GRACE: I want you to be happy. I want you to be happy. I want you to be happy. . . . Is everybody happy? That's what I want to know. Because it seems I can't be happy unless everybody's happy. (*Looking over to pizza set.*) I know you're not happy. But it's you who got sick. I didn't make you sick. Why are you making me sick? You're making me sick, Ma. I'm supposed to have it together by now. I had to leave you. Can't you see that? I couldn't hang around trying to keep you alive with every breath I take. I still do it. I keep everybody alive with every breath I take. (*The doorbell rings. She thinks it's another pizza delivery.*) Oh no. Cancel my order. No more pizzas tonight.

The bell still rings incessantly until GRACE *gets up to answer it. As she moves to the door* LENA *enters from the kitchen door in the pizzeria and crosses over into* GRACE's *apartment. She's an apparition of a younger* LENA, *more youthful and graceful than we have seen her in preceding scenes. Her hairstyle may be different and she is dressed in heels and a stylish, classic coat suggestive of a twenties' style. Her opening lines startle* GRACE, *who's standing at the open doorway.*

LENA: Hello, Gracie.

GRACE: (Stunned.) Ma?

LENA: What a nice place you got. Real cozy. (*She turns to* GRACE, *who is still dumbfounded at the doorway.*) Gracie. You should close your mouth or you might catch a fly.

GRACE: (Starts to look suspiciously at LENA while she closes the door.) All right, who are you?

LENA: I'm your mother.

GRACE: YOU are *not* my mother.

LENA: I surprised you, didn't I?

GRACE: This is crazy. Come on, who are you? What is this?

LENA: I'm telling you. I'm your mother, Lena. You were thinking about me and waiting for me, weren't you? Who, then?

GRACE: How come you're not drooling?

LENA: (*Indignantly.*) I don't feel like it.

GRACE: You're not moaning. You're supposed to moan. You're sick. You feel lousy. There should be food stains on your clothes. I don't know who you are, but you are *not* my mother. *What did you do with my mother?*

LENA: Look at me, Gracie. It's me. You want to see the mole on my neck? Remember how you used to want to bite it off?

GRACE: (*Grilling her suspiciously.*) Where were you born?

LENA: The Bronx.

GRACE: How many miscarriages did you have?

LENA: Two.

GRACE: Who won the World Series in 1955?

LENA: (*Sharply.*) How do I know? The Dodgers probably lost is my guess.

GRACE: Where do you keep your money?

LENA: Well I used to keep it in the underwear drawer but I got it all with me now. I thought maybe we could go shopping.

GRACE: (*Shouting, beside herself.*) What are you talking about? We haven't gone shopping in twenty years.

LENA: (*Calmly.*) That's why I thought it would be time for something new.

GRACE: (*Whining cry.*) Where's my mother?

LENA: Gracie. You shouldn't get so upset. I hate to *see* you agitated like this. What are you making a big deal about? You wanted me to be different all these years, didn't you? You're the one that always used to say anybody can be anything they want to be. If you don't peg people a certain way anything is possible. Right? Isn't that what you always say?

GRACE: Yeah . . . but *this isn't possible.* You're not like my mother.

LENA: *How* do you know what I'm like? Besides, I'm not all that different, I'm just more like I was before you knew me. Isn't that what you always wondered about? Who I used to be? Who I could have been? Well, here I am. And maybe tonight we could go dancing?

GRACE: *Dancing?*

LENA: Yeah, I love to dance. Before I knew you I used to like to go to Roseland Ballroom. You got someplace like that out here?

GRACE: But you're sick. You moan all the time.

LENA: Jeez, I wish you wouldn't be so morbid. I came all this way to see you and I went to all this trouble so you could see me looking good.

GRACE: (*Still stunned but wanting to accept it.*) It's a miracle.

LENA: (*Casually and skeptically.*) Maybe. Whatever you think.

GRACE: (*Dejected, skeptical.*) It's no miracle. (*Hitting on in.*) It's jet lag. That's what it is. It's some kind of cosmic jet lag . . . (*Getting anxious.*) You better go and lie down, Ma. Don't you want to lie down? I'll fix up a bed for you. Don't you want to lie down and watch television?

LENA: No, I don't feel like it.

GRACE: Now look, Ma, I'm gonna make your bed and I want you to lie in it.

LENA: What I might like to do is go out and take a walk, look at the sunset.

GRACE: By yourself?

LENA: And why not?

GRACE: But you never like to take walks or look at sunsets. You've never been alone in your whole life.

LENA: That's not true. Sure, I lived with my family until I got married, but when I was a girl I used to like to take long walks in Crotona Park, right near my house, especially in the winter when the snow made everything so clean and quiet. I used to wear this big brown overcoat that I loved and it was like I could look down from above and see myself standing there against the snow and think, "This isn't just the second-born daughter of the shoemaker, or the pretty one, or the lazy one, or the girl on the end of the line at the candy factory that got all the jokes a little late." I'd think, "There's a part of that girl that nobody knows. That nobody will ever know."

GRACE: (*Stunned and then grumbling.*) Yeah, well this neighborhood is kind of tough. Maybe you'd better not go out by yourself.

LENA: It don't look any worse than the Riverside. I can take care of myself.

GRACE: You might fall down or something. (LENA *is walking around the apartment and* GRACE *is following right behind her with her arms out as if waiting for her to fall down.*)

LENA: (*Turning to her daughter abruptly.*) I feel fine and I'm not gonna fall down.

GRACE: (*Whining voice exactly like her mother's in the first scenes.*) Nooo, I don't know what's going on but you're really old and sick and sooner or later you're going to fall down. (*Last lines are especially wimpy.*)

LENA: Stop it, Gracie. Stop it.

GRACE: (*Same whining voice.*) And I'm going to have to pick you up.

LENA: Yes. But why don't we worry about that when the time comes?

GRACE: (*Sits down.*) What's the matter with you? I'm worried. I'll call this friend of mine. She's a doctor. (*Picks up telephone.*)

LENA: (*Sarcastically, crossing to* GRACE.) Good, ask her if she wants to go for a walk. (*Still behind chair.*) And you should. come too, Gracie. You look a little pasty.

GRACE: (*Slams telephone down.*) What are you so anxious to go for a walk for? You just got here. I've been thinking about you all this time. I've been worried sick.

LENA: What for?

GRACE: Worrying about you. I don't know. I worry about you all the time.

LENA: Well what good does that do? You should worry about yourself. Or better yet, you shouldn't worry at all. And do me a favor, Gracie. Quit thinkin' I want your blood. Just because you're a bleeding heart don't make everybody else a vampire, you know.

GRACE: (*Looking at her mother mildly, quietly, incredulously.*) Who are you anyway?

LENA: Come on, let's not go through that again. Listen, Gracie. I smell pizza. Is that a pizza you got there? Maybe we could have a piece before we go for a walk, huh?

GRACE: You are my ma, aren't you?

LENA: That's what I been tellin' you. You got some with sausage?

They lean down toward the pizza box together.

BLACKOUT

SNOWBALL

Rosette Capotorto

We are the city cousins and they are the country cousins. When they come to our house they run to the window every time the number two train roars by. We never know what they're running to the window for. We're so used to the sound we don't hear the train screech to a stop high up on the tracks.

When we go to their house we sneak under the fence in their backyard and slip through the woods onto the golf course. It's called the Ridgewood Country Club even though it's in Paramus. The golf course is better than a playground. In the winter you can skate on the pond. The pond is good for skating, very smooth and no one else is there. In the summer you can find skunk cabbage and wild scallions. The scallions can be eaten. Sometimes you see a real skunk.

We were playing Indian scouts in the woods around the pond when we saw him. A beautiful white rabbit. Snowball was easy to capture. He offered no resistance. He belonged to all of us because we found him together but he was to live at my cousins' house. In Paramus they had grass and trees and room to build a hutch for Snowball in the backyard. We knew Snowball wouldn't be happy in our apartment in the Bronx. They said we'd see him on Sundays when we went there for dinner.

When we go to my cousins' and it's summer and no school, we beg to stay over. The grown-ups don't seem to be able to make up their minds. They don't say yes and they don't say no. When it's time to go home we hide. We hear them calling and calling, but we pretend not to hear them at all.

"We're leaving without you," they threaten, just the words we want to hear.

We continue to hide until finally, at last, they say yes.

"All right, you win. You can stay. Just come out to say goodbye."

Me and my sister and our cousins are so happy we dance and jump and throw ourselves on the ground.

"A whole week. A whole week," we sing.

We can play with Snowball every day. His nose is the pinkest thing I ever saw. He doesn't do much except eat and poop and make rabbit faces, but he's a great pet.

When my uncle comes home from work, he makes jokes that he doesn't have to mow the lawn all summer with Snowball around. The rabbit does his work for him and is getting nice and fat to boot.

In September we all go back to school. No more vacations in Paramus. No more snooping in the Howard Johnson's motel rooms or spitting at cars from the overpass on Route 17. The leaves change and it gets cold. Weeks pass before we go there again. As soon as we're out of the car we look for Snowball but we can't find him.

"He'll show up," the grown-ups say. "Go and play. We'll help you look later."

We search high and low but find no sign of Snowball. They call us in to eat.

We ask again, "Did Snowball show up?"

"No," they say. "Wash up now. Look at you, you're filthy. All of you. Go. Dinner's ready."

We troop through the kitchen past Grandma who stirs the big pot of gravy on the stove. We all cram into the tiny bathroom together. Each of us wants to be first in the kitchen. If you're first, Grandma gives you a meatball on a fork right from the pot. The hot red gravy and the bite of meat fills your mouth and your stomach and makes you realize how hungry you are.

The tables are set. One for the grownups with a white tablecloth and tall wineglasses. The other a bridge table with a plastic tablecloth and paper cups. We don't mind sitting at our own table. We like to eat fast and run back outside. The grownups eat slowly and talk gossip and politics and drink Grandpa's wine. They wait between courses so they can eat more. The men eat so much they can do nothing after dinner but sit in the living room smoking and unbuckling their belts.

The women clear the table and wash the dishes and make the coffee before calling the men back for dessert. They drink espresso from tiny cups that look funny in the big hands of the men.

After dinner we look for Snowball again. Still, we can't find him. Maybe he ran away. Maybe someone has stolen him. My cousins have a suspect, that kid Bobby from up the street who's been looking at Snowball with a funny eye. We run over to Bobby's house to see if he's kidnapped our rabbit. There's no car in the driveway and no sign of Bobby or of Snowball.

Snowball

When it gets dark, it's time to go. We can't argue because tomorrow is Monday and school. We leave my cousins sad and worried. The next time we go there's still no sign of Snowball. My sister begins to cry.

"Poor Snowball, where can he be?"

Nick, the oldest cousin and a boy, says, "I know what happened to that rabbit of yours."

"What happened, what happened?" we ask in unison.

"Do you really want to know?" Nick asks.

"Yes, we do. Tell us, Nick, tell us," we all say at once.

"Are you sure you want to know? I'm not supposed to tell."

Nick sounds pretty serious. "Are you going to be crybabies about it?" Nick hates crying.

"Come on, tell, tell us," we beg.

"What will you give me?" Nick asks.

His sister, Jo, says, "We're not going to give you anything. That's blackmail. But if you don't say what you know right now we'll know you don't know anything."

He lunges after her, but she runs across the yard in a flash. Jo is the lightest and fastest runner in her school and no one can catch her. Nick doesn't even try.

"Nick doesn't know anything," Jo sings.

Nick is mad now. You can see it in his face. He looks like he might cry, but Nick never cries. He hates crying.

"You want to know what happened to your precious rabbit?" We all grow quiet. "You really want to know? I'll tell you. But just remember. You asked for it." Nick points his finger at each of us in turn. He speaks slowly as if inside a dream.

"You ate him. You ate Snowball in last Sunday's gravy."

We freeze in a long moment of silence as if we are playing a life or death game of Statues.

"I don't believe you," Jo whispers from her hiding place. "You're making it up."

Nick stands his ground. "Go ask Dad. Or Grandma. Go on, ask them." Nick is not fooling. "They were afraid you'd cry and carry on so they didn't want any of you to know. They only told me." Nick turns on his heel, a boy soldier, a GI Joe, and stalks off.

We stand quiet, our mouths open, our eyes stinging, our stomachs heaving.

PASSAIC RIVER CROSSING
Flavia Alaya

In 1966, when I first came to New Jersey to live, I was Italian, not Italian American.

Young, a New Yorker still ambivalent about my family—in whose bosom this whole identity business had started with the spelling of our name—I'd let the time I'd recently spent in Italy make all the difference. Long before me on another crossing, my father, *napoletan* to the heart, to the soul, had come to America as Alaja, the "j" spelling odd but quite Italian. He admitted he'd been misguided to change the j to a y (only, he protested, to make Alaja more pronounceably "American"), but he thought it was too late for him to change again. My two brothers thought otherwise. They'd thrown it up to him in the first place out of some self-conscious East Harlem ethnic thing they were going through. They wanted to declare themselves Italian American, and not . . . well, not something else. They became Alaia. My sister did too.

I balked, father-identified, maybe in an odd way already Italy-identified too, my father having been Italy to me before I'd been there myself. And yet I can remember thinking that *not* to change in this case meant also accepting the change that had already happened, perhaps the very idea of changefulness, of a force that had made choices like his possible. Yes, Alaja was Italian: at least four centuries in Italy had made it so. But like so much that is Italian it was mixed up with other places, other races, you could trace it to somewhere else, and someone had. "Spanish," my father had said, "and who knows, maybe Moorish before that, and before that . . . ?" I imagined the Alaja family a little cell of secret self-makings and remakings under the Inquisition. I could see how a name could capture a history of change like a time capsule or a palimpsest, written on and erased a dozen times.

Maybe all the more reason to admit the snobbery behind the choice my siblings made to avoid being taken for those Puerto Rican upstarts moving into

Italian East Harlem. But was I any better, choosing to blur the boundary they wanted to sharpen, if I didn't quite know why?

∼

My crossing to New Jersey was my own little migration. Not that I didn't still love New York, which I did (and do) almost to perdition, and moving to Ridgefield you could say I never really left it, especially when those once cheap, fast trips across the George Washington Bridge put me just a spits-throw away. But I needed to escape, having between Italy and back made a few choices my father disapproved of. At the same time I had a few good reasons not to escape too far, though I know now that reasons mattered little, loyalty to places, like loyalty to people, being in my bones.

Luckily, Ridgefield was a town it was easy to be Italian in, with nearby Bergen Boulevard, local mecca for pasta and olive oil, only one of several demographic epicenters of Italian America in North Jersey where to this moment food rules. I despised the local Italian American restaurants, where nobody spoke the language and every dish looked like a wading pool of red-sauce in extreme mozzarella meltdown. But my next door neighbor was an Italian chef—*Italian* Italian—and I filched his recipes for pesto and risotto and saltimbocca as often as I could nail him, flying by on the porch.

Who knows just how much re-assimilation I might have resisted had I stayed in eastern Bergen County—on the edge? But I didn't, and maybe Freud is right: one trauma isn't enough to mark you for life, it takes two. My second was in this case another crossing four years later, over the Passaic into Paterson.

There were still lots of Italian Americans in Paterson in 1970, though post the 1968–1969 riots the statistics had almost everybody who wasn't too old or too poor fleeing or already fled. One such transition family set me back a full identity decade. It happened like this: I'm driving home from my *new* Italian food mecca, Corrado's "Family Affair." A big car backs too fast out of a driveway in front of me, crunching my front fender and tumbling my three-year-old Nina into the back well of the car. The driver leaps out, her hands butterflying nervously in the air. Very young. "Sorry, just got my license," she says, and then in mid-sentence panic suddenly jumps back in and speeds off, leaving me dumbfounded.

Nina came out of it fine, but the hit-and-run upset my husband Harry as well as me. With the plate number and a little police help we traced the girl—Italian American, it turned out—to a sprawling new development in Wayne where ex-Patersonians now seemed to live in bland ranch houses as sourly hunkered down as refugee Cubans in Miami. We were greeted by four family members, all of them beefy, sullen, and menacing. No girl. They said if we didn't leave they'd throw us out.

Harry was a forgiving Irish American Italophile if there ever was one. Not me. I thought we'd just seen what *famiglia* really meant to this degenerate bunker culture, their slick new houses trapping all their meanness and xeno-phobia like a smell. Sure, these were the days of the Valachi Papers and Mafia hunts. Even self-secure Italian Americans were having nervous breakdowns. But I still felt ashamed and unforgiving.

Still, there was work to be done in Paterson. We needed to get on with it. We could've worked day and night getting on with it, writing about it, trying to salvage the brilliant stuff here—Carlos Williams and Ginsberg, the Great Falls, the industrial district, art and architecture everywhere to see, to cele-brate, new and old—to keep it alive. I discovered that the bronzes of historic city fathers in front of every old building had, most of them, been made by one man, Gaetano Federici, *scultore*, the "Paterson master," who'd passed on in 1964 leaving easily some forty or more public or semi-public works within two miles of City Hall. I saw them, every one. I counted them.

Harry and I spent the year before he died researching Federici and teasing out the kind of hidden history my father's name had taught me to respect. There was no blinkering it: Federici had worked out of a deep-rooted Italian American community, some of it still here, and yes, some gone to Wayne, but much like me, to escape without leaving. And yet the beauty of it was that it was real in all its complexity, contentious and disunified and northern and southern and dark and fair and weavers and dyers and ironworkers and artisans and stonemasons and working-class and middle-class and professional-class and religious and irreligious and Catholic and anarchist, and all of it mixed up together and all of it as good as gold. And Italian *American*, not just Italian, though Federici had been born in Basilicata. Before the mid-twentieth century some of these networking families had been here three or more generations.

And they'd felt wounds to their identity self-esteem infinitely worse than ours. As a boy in the 1890s Federici had called himself "Fredricks" to dodge the hate dished out to people like him then—*niggers* and *dagoes* and *camorrists* and *anarchists*—real hate, assault, murder, lynchings, and then Palmer raids and deportations and the whole arsenal of legal weapons that cleared the way for the judicial murders of Sacco and Vanzetti. Sometimes it was like seeing my father young all over again, standing on the dock proud as a duke and then finding himself, in America, slowly humiliated to the core. I understood why he might erase his name, even if just a little, even if it did him no good, so as not to erase its history altogether. I could see why my dark Sicilian mother Maria would call herself Mary and try to flatten out her kinky hair.

I'd sometimes wondered whether having grown up on the edge of the largest black community in Westchester had made it easy for me to fit into a black neighborhood in Paterson, until I discovered that the most stable, non-fleeing neighborhoods in Paterson were Italian American, criss-crossed with enclaves of blacks. I'll never forget the tough black girl who stood on my front porch one day and asked me, "You Italian?" and then, "You mixed?"

It's mixed we are in the changefulness of New Jersey, and mixed Italian America was, is, and will be. More and more my neighborhood is becoming Latino now. Striving working-class families are buying up the old houses in the near East Side where I live. Across the street a black family has moved out and a Dominican family moved in. I'm practicing my Spanish on their nine-year-old who comes over sometimes looking to use my computer. And I'm getting pretty good.

LINCOLN TUNNEL
JERSEY BOUND
Salvatore Amico M. Buttaci

Policemen inside their booths flashed by us like paint strokes on the tiled walls of the Lincoln Tunnel. My younger sister Joanie and I counted each one in a game we later on reminisced as "tunnel vision." It kept us busy. Otherwise, we would've gagged on the repulsive fumes that somehow had seeped back inside the tan and white bus we rode from New York City.

"Don't think about the smell," Papa said. "Make believe it's not there." Then he would tap his temple to remind us this was another slice of wisdom safely filed in his brain, ready at a moment's notice to pluck and apply to whatever the occasion demanded. Still, we could tell the fumes were nauseating, even for him and Mama and our older sister Anna, because while we were counting the policemen, the three of them sat twitching noses and screwing up their faces.

We were going to New Jersey. It was the closest we Brooklyn kids ever came to a day in the country. And the day would fly by as all our visits had. Before long we'd be back tonight counting cops on the tan and white until exhaustion pulled our lids down and we slept, heads against the hard window frame bouncing us awake now and then as we moved in and out of the fumed haze of our brief bus ride dreams.

"Why don't we just move to New Jersey?" Joanie asked Papa. I nodded. It made sense.

We would not have to make these excursions all the way from Brooklyn, New York, to Union City, New Jersey, every few weeks. We would already be there. And who would miss Brooklyn anyway. "Can we live next door to Aunt Laura and Uncle Joe?" At seven Joanie was one of those babes out of whose mouths come jewels. Personally I thought she was a bit of a show-off.

I was nearly two years older and nothing I said made Papa and Mama smile the way they were smiling now. Then Joanie outdid herself: "Or live in their house!" she said. Oh, boy, Joanie. Let's go back to counting the booth cops.

Papa knitted his brows. He sat with Mama in the two seats ahead of us. Twisting at the hip, his handsome head of black wavy hair tilted to the side, he looked at us and said, "You don't like Brooklyn?" It sounded like an admonishment. How dare we turn our backs on Brooklyn!

Wasn't that where we lived? Four blocks from our grammar school where those black-habited Dominican sisters at Most Holy Trinity taught us all we knew? Ruled with an iron hand? "Ruled," as in "iron ruler" and "hand," as in "Salvatore, put out your hand." Brooklyn where we lived in too few rooms of a cold-water tenement flat on Graham Avenue. Brooklyn where several blocks away on Johnson Avenue Papa worked nights at LiCausi's Italian Bakery and early mornings walked home with hot Sicilian loaves we called frankfurter bread that Mama served on Saturdays with hot dogs and beans. Not like Brooklyn? Across from us in a seat next to the window Anna was nodding her head as if to say, here it comes now. The story of *Acquaviva Platani*, Papa and Mama's mountain village in Sicily. How he missed those cobblestone streets, the bells that rang in the belfry of the ducal tower, *La Madonna della Luce*, the Catholic church where they were both baptized, attended mass, got married way back in 1932. How Papa could still remember as though it were yesterday when he was a boy of fifteen, valise in hand, turning his back on that village for a ship in Naples that would sail him away from *la bella Sicilia* forever.

But what Papa finally said surprised us. "I think we'll be saying goodbye to Brooklyn." Anna did a triple take. Joanie had no jewels to say. I heard myself ask, "Goodbye?" Then the three of us like kids in a rehearsed school play said in one voice, "For good? Where?" By their smiles we could sense the news was good.

The bus at last drove us free of the tunnel. The afternoon outside was bright again. Though the windows were airtight, we could imagine taking in gulps of fresh New Jersey air. We saw trees. Birds clustered up there in circles around the tallest branches. We were ecstatic.

Up ahead we knew by heart the course of lefts and rights the bus would take. First it would barrel off Route 3 West at the Park Avenue, Union City, exit, scaling the hill onto a sinuous Boulevard East, tossing us in our seats as it snaked passed Weehawken toward Union City where Papa's sister Aunt Laura and her husband Uncle Joe Lanza lived on Forty-eighth Street.

Across the river on our left the New York skyline was a dull gray primer, an unfinished cityscape some painter left for later on. Less than an hour before we had walked Manhattan's skyscrapered streets, but now the big city seemed so distant. Soon we would leave it behind; I liked that it was so far away. We were quitting Brooklyn. I was nine years old but I'd be meeting ten in New Jersey and I hoped we'd never go back. Maybe we'd live in the house of the Lanzas where we could stay up all night, eat handfuls of salted peanuts from a huge blue crystal bowl, watch TV all hours, listen to our parents and our uncle and aunt laugh heartily in their remembrances of *lu paisi*—the village—the cobblestone mountainous town they left behind.

They'd jabber away in that secret Sicilian language about which we kids understood next to nothing. We'd listen for the few words we did know, like *Mangiamu* and *Seditivi*. It was Aunt Laura calling us from the TV room, "Let's eat." And Uncle Joe motioning us to the chairs in the dining room, "Sit down." Racing, we kids would storm the dining room and jockey for the best seats left over after the grownups sat down. I always tried to elbow my way to the chair next to Uncle Joe because he would talk to me and say things that made nine-year-old boys laugh.

Under the table Joanie kicked my leg. I moved my leg away and she kicked the other one. I knew Papa's strict rule that demanded we behave during visits to relatives and friends. Likewise I knew if any of us got in trouble for mischief it would not be Anna or Joanie, but me. Papa would not say a word. He would squint his eyes nearly shut and glare at me. In my best sarcastic voice I would say, "I can't do anything right." Papa would pretend I meant it and he'd say, "Work on it. Think before you do something that's not right so you don't regret it later." So I sat there in my stoic face as Joanie slouched down in her chair, stretching her leg so she could kick me in the shin. Aunt Laura's meatballs were delicious so I did my best to focus on that. Taking Papa's advice, I would "pretend it wasn't there." My shin hurt like the devil, but I smiled and told myself I felt no pain. Joanie was toe-jabbing my shin, but on a higher level I told myself she wasn't. I was not feeling any pain. These meatballs are delicious. These meatballs are delicious. All at once I howled in pain. "Owwww!" Then I leaped from the chair like a boy set on fire. Uncle Joe made a joke about ants in my pants. Aunt Laura smiled and said she hoped it wasn't her meatballs that made me cry out. My father continued to eat but with his eyes he glared at me. Meanwhile, Joanie busied herself winding spaghetti around her fork, not lifting her eyes, pretending she had nothing to do with whatever just happened.

"Pa," I started to explain. He raised his right hand which usually translated into "I don't want to hear it." "Ma." She shook her head the way she did when I disappointed her. I pushed my plate in front of me. I could feel the tears climbing in my throat. "OK, nobody kicked me under the table. I don't have black and blue marks on my shin. This is not Saturday. We're still home in Brooklyn, all right?" With that I stood up and walked away from the table and sat in the parlor staring at the dark TV screen.

"Are we still moving away from Brooklyn, Pa?" Anna asked.

Papa nodded.

"Will I finish eighth grade at Most Holy Trinity?"

"Only if you can finish by next week, Anna." They all laughed because it was March and school held us like prisoners until liberation day in June. "We're moving to God's Country," he said. "This is where you go outside and breathe the fresh air without worrying somebody drives by and knocks you down dead. It's safer here. God looks after New Jersey more than He does Brooklyn. More than any place! We'll live close by here. A few streets. And me, I'll be taking a short bus ride to work." From the other room I tried to imagine my father not walking home from his job at LiCausi's, my father without the folded *Daily News* under his arm, the long white bag of hot bread in his other hand. When they'd finished the meal, Mama, Aunt Laura, Anna, and Joanie cleared the table and headed for the kitchen. Papa and Uncle Joe walked into the living room and sat down. I asked my uncle if I could put on the TV.

"Sure, kid."

"Keep it low," Papa said.

"Keep it loud as you want," said Uncle Joe. And the two of them were at it again! Uncle Joe loved to argue. And he knew my father was the perfect adversary because it was always difficult for Papa to hear something he disagreed with and keep his mouth shut. Now apropos nothing at all, Uncle Joe says to my father, "You know, Truman's no good for this country. That guy sold hats for a living. We need a Republican president." Now Uncle Joe knew darn well my father was a diehard Democrat. He also knew Truman was one too. For that matter, so was Uncle Joe, but he loved to debate. He loved to say things that pumped red blood in my father's face, then say something else to drain it. Papa played right into his hands. He'd rant and rave. "What're you talking about! Truman's a great president." To which Uncle Joe would toss out some more bait like, "He got his job from Roosevelt who got this country in that second war" and Papa would open his mouth wide and bite the hook because nobody but nobody could badmouth FDR and expect Papa to keep silent. It was his duty to defend FDR and Papa was a man of duty. When the two of them played out all the issues Uncle Joe could dream up, he'd smile, tap Papa on the shoulder. "Hey, Mike, I'm just kidding. I like to argue. You know that. Take it easy."

I'd be half-watching Randolph Scott take on an entire Western town in a TV cowboy movie and half-listening to the two of them arguing, thank God, in English. If I had dared, I would've interrupted them and asked what they thought of Duke Snyder of the Brooklyn Dodgers, just to see how my uncle would fan it into one more fire. Instead I left standing up to tough men to Scott and my father and my Uncle Joe.

On the long bus ride back to New York City where we would board a subway train for Montrose Avenue in Brooklyn, I could hardly close my eyes. Thoughts of soon living in God's Country filled my head. I could hardly wait. While my parents and my sisters slept, I peered out into the darkness, at the lit houses along the streets and wondered what our apartment in God's Country would look like. How my new school would be. If my Brooklyn friends Vinnie Accardi, Al Cimino, Jim Hogan, and Ernest Verazzano would forget me.

When the tan and white pulled out of the Lincoln Tunnel into the City of New York we woke up. At our stop we all exited the bus: Papa and Mama and Anna in front of me. Behind us Joanie was laughing and pushing me down the aisle toward the door.

SUMMER JOB
Frank Finale

When I was a boy and waiting in line with my father to enter the Lincoln Tunnel, he'd turn to me and say, "See this tunnel? I helped build it. Those steel rods . . ."

"Where, Dad?"

"Well, you can't see them now. They're in the concrete because they're used to reinforce the wall. I used to bend those steel rods. The foreman said I was one of the best steel rod benders he ever had. It took two men to bend one rod, but I used to do it alone."

"How come you still don't do it?"

"Because when the job was done, they laid off most of the men. But you can tell them," he said rolling down the window to pay the toll, "your father helped build this tunnel."

I hadn't dared to ask who he meant by *them*, but I guess it would be my own children; he told the tunnel story with minor variations every time we drove through it.

When roses and honeysuckle perfume the air and my teacher's manuals are shelved away until September, the anxiety of looking for a summer job blossoms in my mind. Years ago when work was scarce and money scarcer, I took whatever I could get in the summer.

Late one June during the year of a gas crisis, when few jobs were to be had, I picked up work thanks to my older brother. An insurance executive who had connections with builders, he didn't want to hear my mother say one more time, "With your influence and all the people you know, you still can't get your brother a job!" She had a way of bringing this up whenever he had company.

Thus I entered the world of the carpenter's helper, helping to build houses at the Shore. The work was hard, the pay good. When I started I didn't even know how to drive in a nail properly.

The carpenter's son took me aside and showed me how to drive an eight-penny nail into a two-by-four with three swift strokes. With practice I was able to swing a hammer well enough to help frame houses. That summer I picked up a new vocabulary (lintel, jamb, stud, joist . . .), a tan, some muscles, and a raise.

This was a job close to nature even as we were pushing it aside, building houses that pressed farther and farther into the woods, meadows, and wetlands. Somewhere down the road, other developers were doing the same. What would happen when the houses met like railroads connecting east to west, north to south? Where would the deer, foxes, turtles, and possums go?

After lunch on those drowsy summer afternoons, the crew would sprawl on a half-finished porch in the shade of a sassafras tree, make idle conversation about the Mets, watch bumblebees work day lilies and half-listen to cicadas sizzling in the elms. Eventually one of the crew would pack away his lunch, stand up, brush off his pants, and say, "Well, it's that time again." Then a lone hammer would begin to tap, tap, tap joined by another, till the houses resounded with the percussion of hammers. With everyone into the swing of things, I would look back to the porch where we ate lunch. The bumblebees were gone, the cicadas silent.

Every once in a while now when I pass the houses I had worked on, I slow down and say to my sons, "See those houses. I helped build them."

The boys look at each other puzzled, and my wife says, "We know, you told us already. Can't you speed it up a little? People are beginning to stare."

As still another summer and more buildings take the Jersey Shore, I think of those houses long since sold. Houses that have become homes in which children grow up and leave, only to remember their lives spent in those houses. And I feel proud that a part of me is drilled into the framework of those houses. And you can't even see the nails.

PART FOUR

Changing Direction

LIBERATING MEMORY
Janet Zandy

It is Parents' Weekend, a minor ritual in academic institutions. This particular Sunday in early October 1963, my father has to work the weekend shift at his chemical plant and cannot attend. I am disappointed because he is not there, but say nothing. I am a freshman scholarship student and a commuter. I live at home with my parents and sister. My mother and I drive together to Parents' Weekend activities scheduled for parents who have weekends.

We arrive overdressed and feel a discomfort we do not voice. We follow the crowd and sit on the damp steps of an amphitheater carved out of old Watchung Mountain stone. Within a decade much of the mountain will be leveled for parking lots, but today it is a shaded and beautiful outdoor theater. We listen to the welcoming remarks of some college administrator. Neither of us feels welcomed. I see in my mother's face a hidden sadness; I feel a shame I try to deny.

This is not a memory of continuation or development. It is a memory of rupture. The discrepancy between what my mother and I felt and the scene that was played out could not be acknowledged. We had intense feelings but we didn't have the language to identify and affirm them. We could only push the feelings down and go home.

Today, I cope with middle-aged memory blocks. I forget familiar names, repeat stories, blank out whole days. Old, acute shards of memory crowd out the short-term data and demand attention. I remember that Sunday thirty years ago because I cannot forget the consciousness of discontinuity between the two great loves of my childhood: my family and school. I loved school *almost* as much as I loved my parents. But, the more schooling I got, the more separate I felt from them. It is an old working-class story.

We didn't have a telephone until I was eleven years old. Even after the phone was a black fixture, there wasn't a lot of planning or scheduling. Calendars were there to keep track of birthdays, anniversaries, and deaths. Everything else just happened. My childhood was noisy. Company, usually relatives and rarely friends (who needed friends when there were so many relatives?) would stop by, never quite unexpectedly, on the way to other places. Out would come the coffee and cake, and the joking, teasing, and visiting continued until everyone was too tired or too full. When I was in high school and college and needed quiet to study, I would retreat to the basement, working at my old black desk, wrapped in a blanket during the damp, winter months. I was always excused to study.

My parents were conscious of the value of education to their daughters' future. They both had had to quit school after the ninth grade to get a job and give their pay to the family. My mother was the oldest daughter of ten children; my father was one of seven children. This is not counting the siblings who did not reach adulthood. There was a great sense of obligation on my father's side of the family; a great sense of responsibility and pleasure on my mother's side.

My father's Italian family lived in Hoboken, an enclave of first- and second-generation Italians who antagonistically shared the same crowded streets with third-generation Irish. They stubbornly kept Italian traditions of food and religion, but spoke English at home in order to help their children make it in America. I remember one uncle much touted within the family for having a white-collar job and working on Wall Street. He said little and kept his eyes down. The other five brothers were blue collars. My aunt, the only daughter, married late for an Italian girl and died giving birth to her tenth child. My grandmother outlived several children and died at ninety. She was always carefully dressed, manipulative with her children and their spouses, and insistent that her many grandchildren kiss her on the lips. For most of her long adult life she was a widow. Her husband, the grandfather I never met, left one morning for work and never returned home alive. He was a passenger in a car that was struck head on and he was killed instantly. The accident happened on Route 3 near what is now the Meadowlands, a stadium and racetrack, but what was then a thick marshland where crabs with low toxicity were netted by urban fishermen. By the 1950s and 1960s these marshes became one long garbage dump. As kids, my sister and I would roll up the car windows as fast as we could to beat the stench on Route 3. Heading east, it is the road that has the best view of the beautiful New York City skyline—on clear days.

My father hung out with my mother's oldest brother and that's how he got to meet my mother, avoid Hoboken, and spend a lot of time in Jersey

City. My father was very smart, and always acutely felt the absence of what he called "the sheepskin." I remember the story of his stolen education.

When my father was living at home in Hoboken, something happened one day that brought everyone to the street-side windows—perhaps it was a parade, a peddler, or a fight. While everyone's heads were poked out the window and their backs were turned, someone came into the apartment and stole the money that was supposed to be for Carlos's education. I say *story*, because even as a child I had a hard time believing that one.

So much of the goodness and generosity that is as much a part of my childhood as uncertainty and loss stems from my mother's family. My mother's mother died shortly after I was born. Anna was the daughter of a rabbi whose family lived along the German/Austrian border. She was sent to New York City as a child to stay with distant relatives. Whether the decision to send her to America was an act of rescue or oppression is hard to say. She told stories of having to hide in the skin of a cow when soldiers came into her village. No one explained why. She was apparently sent to America to be a servant in the home of wealthier relatives. One day, she was distracted while she was hanging clothes on the roof of the building where she lived. She fell. She recovered from that fall, but while she was recuperating she met Albert, an immigrant from Italy. Perhaps he gave her the first attention she had had in a long time. In one sudden shift, before she was sixteen, she was a mother, a wife, and an orphan. Her Orthodox parents in Europe lit candles, tore their clothes, and sat shivah. She was dead, but not dead. She never learned to read and write, but her children always praised her ability to travel all over New York City and the boroughs by reading the subway lights. Mostly, though, she stayed at home and worked—the daily battle against dirt in crowded spaces, cooking on a wood stove, scrubbing clothes on a washboard, giving birth to fourteen children, feeding the neighborhood "poor souls"—she worked. Many Sunday afternoons of my childhood were spent at the Jewish cemetery where we would place stones on her grave and visit.

Anna's inheritance to her children and grandchildren was a bone-deep knowledge of what it meant to be shut out. The aunts and uncles, brothers and sisters, trusted each other a lot more than they trusted institutions or any promises of the American Dream. They practiced an unpoliticized and unnamed socialism. Whoever had extra that particular week, month, or year shared it with the others. It came in the form of continuous, spirited, gift giving. My mother never shopped for my sister and me without "taking care" of some of the cousins. My uncle just happened to stop at the house after a trip to the butcher. When the aunts baked, the trays of cookies and cakes were for the family, never just their own smaller household. No one asked . . . it was expected that each would recognize the other's need. And it was expected that any stranger who was on the arm of a member of the family would be heartily welcomed. I used to think that the same five-dollar bill was in constant circulation, only enclosed in different happy birthday, anniversary, and get well cards. Until the time came for braces, a car that worked, and a college education, it never occurred to me that my own family did not have much money.

Since they never had to be concerned with monetary accumulation or investment, there was space for play. They were gamblers. The aunts played the numbers. They would call each other and discuss numbers that figured in their dreams. Every once in a while, a number hit—for a few dollars. The uncles played the horses. In the days when there was no such thing as off-track betting, they would take the bus to the Big A, or Belmont, or contact their bookies. I remember one uncle giving me tightly folded pieces of paper to take to a local candy store. The guy behind the counter of this tiny, dirty shop was fat, cigar-chewing, and not particularly delighted to see children. I handed the paper to him. Sometimes I got a Three Musketeers bar for my efforts, most times not. Such was my short career as a runner. On Saturday afternoons my grandfather would demand absolute silence; uncles, aunts, and children would come to a complete stop so that the radio could be turned on and the race results heard. Every now and then a particular set of horses would win, place, and show, but usually there was just a flash of anger, something thrown at the radio, and then everyone would continue where they left off. On those occasions when I accompanied my uncles to the track, I noticed they were less interested in the physical animals and more interested in their scratch sheets. Sometimes they didn't even watch the race. What they loved was the luck . . . the thrill of risk . . . the possibility of momentary freedom from care . . . a chance to take care of the family . . . not the money, but the luck . . . the great promise . . . the charm . . . the dare and the desire . . . the Luck.

My protected, loving childhood and adolescence halted with my father's unexpected death in 1965 at the age of forty-nine. I cannot recover what is not completely lost. He would fit no stereotype of white maleness. Without an education or many models, he figured out a way to defy the worst in his own culture without abandoning it. He used his meager allowance from the paycheck he handed my mother to buy books for his daughters. Even in our tiny dwelling, our privacy was always respected. He shared all the domestic chores, and enjoyed his woodwork and garden. I never heard him utter a racist or sexist epithet. His life should have been longer. If he had had a physically safe work life, it might have been.

I was very slow to make that particular connection. It is too late now to piece together a causal relationship between his work at the chemical plant and the sudden cancer, embolism, and death. Despite the deep tiredness he carried from his shift work, my father seemed strong and healthy. He was hurt, occasionally, but never sick. Now and then, there was an accident at the chemical plant, some spillage, a minor explosion, and he would be sent home, the red burn marks tattooed on his chest. Long defunct, Trubeck Laboratories was once located on Route 17 near where it crosses Route 3. It manufactured expensive perfumes. Instead of Christmas turkeys, the men who worked there got little bottles of Shalimar and White Shoulders. There must have been "family days" since I remember walking inside the plant, holding my hand to my nose to block the acrid smell, noticing the open drums, the pipes, the noise of dripping chemicals. That smell touched everything my father owned or wore. I can smell it still. I often wonder how many of the men who worked at Trubeck Labs—before even the minimal restrictions of OSHA on the chemicals, the toxicity, the penetrating smell—survived.

My father was my intellectual companion and he was gone. I have no memory of my junior year in college but the transcript says I got straight A's. My college studies and my time at home were completely severed. I was so slow. I thought knowledge worth learning was inside the library, the classroom, and my professors' minds, not at home. There was no intellectual space to make sense of my private pain. Women, labor, black, and ethnic studies did not exist; there were no occasions to glimpse shared struggle. We learned the Anglo-American story and were implicitly told that was *the* story.

I graduated from college, found a job teaching high school English, and for two years lived at home with my mother and gave her my pay. I read Martin Buber, Nietzsche, Tillich, Gurdjieff, and Jung—but not Marx—looking for answers. I left for graduate school, protested the Vietnam War—a source of great tension in the family since all my uncles "served" in other wars at other times—married because my mother would disapprove of "living together," and became a mother and a feminist. Before I read the great feminist texts of the 1970s, it was the lived experience of delivering and caring for a child day after day, alone, that made me question knowledge in a profound way. I had bouts of anger, depression, and debilitating migraine headaches. Days and days were locked inside a punishing migraine. I had trouble speaking and could barely answer the telephone.

As an act of self-rescue, I joined community women's study groups and the editorial collective of *New Women's Times,* one of the early U.S. radical women's newspapers. Learning about women within the circle of other women enabled me to find a public voice. I was still angry, but now I understood why—at least partially. As we read *Sisterhood Is Powerful, Of Woman Born,* Mary Daly, Kate Millet, and Redstockings, we, collectively, began to construct the categorical differences of gender. We signed our letters "In Sisterhood" with good faith, as we began to test what "woman" meant in relation to race and class. Perhaps it was 1978 or 1979; we might have been reading a historical novel by a Black woman writer. I blurted out, "Well, slavery is gone; it's much better now." The only African American woman in our study group, whose love for me I have never questioned, replied, "Easy for you to say, Miss Janet." Wilma Campbell reminded me that even though neither one of us may have a lot of money to spend in a downtown department store, it is not likely that the store detective will follow me.

The dream of a common language and the power to connect seemed to dissolve during my infrequent visits home to my mother. My female relatives tell me now that my mother was always "proud" of me. But too many conversations ended in constricted silence. My head was so much in theoretical radical feminism that I could not even see the conditions of my mother's life. And all she could see was the daughter she used to know. My mother worked in a greasy-spoon luncheonette serving heavy lunches to working people. Everyone in town knew Millie and wanted to have their sandwiches made by her. For all the years she worked there, I never once went in, sat down, and had a cup of coffee with her. Connections are easier to make in books. I could not replicate my mother's life—nor would she want me to—but I could find a way to affirm it without sacrificing my intellectual work. And that's when I began to collect and edit working-class women's writings.

For fifteen years I worked as an adjunct teacher of composition and literature in a local community college. At first, the part-time work seemed satisfactory because it enabled me to care for my children during the day and work evenings and weekends. As a child, I had never had a babysitter who was not a relative, and so day care for young children was not part of my inherited family epistemology. I was able to sustain this because my husband was an engineer who earned a middle-class paycheck. My students at the community college were familiar to me in their language, their attitudes about work, their values and relationships. Many of my full-time colleagues mocked these students for their malapropisms, their lack of class. Of course, these students did not lack *class*. Class was obviously inscribed on their fatigued bodies and in their desire for associate degrees that might earn them a little more take-home pay. What they lacked was the power of class definition. They also lacked the wanna-be-patrician, bourgeois sensibilities cultivated and nurtured in the greenhouses of graduate English departments.

At the community college I learned two profound lessons: how it was possible to connect lived working-class experience to the study of literature and how to organize and struggle for change. I developed and taught a course called Working-Class Literature and I organized adjunct faculty.

My usual zigzag movement between experience and theory became more focused. It was 1981/1982 and I was publishing in feminist journals and newspapers, and claiming a public voice. The intellectual ground that was once my formal education was broken up. In the fissures and recesses I began to develop an alternate ground of being that promised location inside the dislocation. Without naming it, I was acting on Foucault's assertion that "knowledge is not just made for understanding; it is made for cutting." In the past, the cutting had been in the power of the owning class to cut down, literally, the lives of working people—but also, I came to realize, in the power of language and the academic elite to cut out working-class studies and sever workers from their own history and culture. It was time to cut in another direction.

I taught working-class literature to working-class students. I realize now that without overt autobiographical references, I was uncovering/recovering the integrity of my own working-class family life to produce curricula, texts, and cultural criticism. Here was a legitimate, powerful alternative to acculturation, nostalgia, or assimilation. I quickly found that the most difficult problem in developing a curriculum of working-class studies is the enormity of the subject. (This is not a problem, of course, for those who do not concede that working-class culture exists.) I organized my course around the interplay of three powerful pronouns: I, they, and we. Who tells the story? Who mediates it? And what is missing? I began with personal narratives, often oral histories, and asked students to do their own autobiographies and interviews along the Studs Terkel *Working* model. We looked at writing of *witness*—the work of the next generation or the informed insider to tell the stories that were not voiced. We read Harriette Arnow's *The Doll-maker* and Maxine Hong Kingston's *China Men,* tracing the long journeys of "DP's"—displaced persons—in the land of broken promises. We looked at Lewis Hine photographs, listened to the music of coal miners, read contemporary poetry by working-class women, and studied episodes of resistance in the film *Salt of the Earth* and recovery in Leslie Marmon Silko's *Ceremony.* I grouped texts, photographs, music, and films in a montage that included differences of gender, race, and ethnicity around questions central to suppressed histories: What kind of work is going on here? Who controls it? Who profits from it? I wanted students to discover not only neglected texts, but also those conditions which thwart and suppress the production of culture. I was allowed to do this because I was a harmless adjunct.

If working-class culture becomes exclusively an object of study, and not a means of study, the larger struggle is lost. My intellectual work gave me political courage. I also knew that I had nothing to lose. When a full-time position finally opened after nine years as an adjunct, I applied, but was not given an interview. I tasted my own invisibility. I did not like the taste. I took Joe Hill's advice and started to organize.

I shared the labor of meetings, phone calls, letters, petitions, questionnaires, research, and talking, talking, talking with another longtime part-timer, Chris Munson, and a sympathetic female union president, Judy Toler, who was never reelected after supporting us. We won our first raise in ten years and representation at the union bargaining table. We made small gains, securing mail boxes, the right to assign our own textbooks, and inclusion in the college directory. I published a front page article in a Rochester newspaper and pushed for voting and meeting privileges in my own department. I became an outspoken critic of academic work exploitation at conferences and meetings. I had not lost my pungent working-class tongue. When I began adjunct teaching in 1972 I earned $875 a course; when I left fifteen years later as an adjunct associate professor, I was earning $400 more a course. I still had no benefits, no retirement, and no guarantee that I would actually teach the course I prepared. When the next full-time opening came up, I was not surprised when I was again not invited to interview for the job.

Opportunities for praxis in class struggle are available behind the academic gate; one does not have to travel to Wigan Pier. But it does mean confronting uncomfortable questions: How does my work rest on the labor of others? How can I use my power to practice democracy in the workplace? The increasing use of adjunct faculty is a piece of a larger labor story; white and blue collars blur in a common history of being overworked and underpaid. To be an adjunct is to be an academic "other," a category for academic managers, a flexible object, a thing. In the dynamic of this work relationship, I caught a tiny glimpse of the reality of my parents' work and that of so many others. I also learned there are alternatives to liberal humanism with its emphasis on individuality and its naive faith in progress. I was cutting my way back home.

CIRCOLO
Michele Linfante

I sit at the table with my new friends
　　the *Circolo Italiano*
Others bring to the table
　　Sicilian pasta with goat cheese, eggplant, and fresh basil,
　　Neopolitan bread with olives and *pinons,*
　　flaky homemade pastries with delicate lemon cream filling
　　Piedmontese folksongs
　　　secret ways to clean the slime off snails
　　　　stories of uncles that grafted peach trees and aunts
　　　　　that grew "lemons as big as your head"
And I feel
　　　　impoverished

The things I have Italian
　　seem like a few thin relics
　　in a small trunk

Distant memories
　　like the taste of my grandfather's roast pork
　　　and the smell of the glue in his shoe shop
The elusive tune of a nursery rhyme that Uncle Tito sang
　　that were always hieroglyphs to me

I gather these few things
　　in a ritual task
And ask them to multiply

I am a person dis-membered
　　And I seek to re-member myself

I flew from my life the day I was out of the womb
　　the pieces of me going in every direction

Michele Linfante

My breath wanting to run from my flesh
My flesh wanting to run from my bones
My cells fighting each other in relentless disease

The words Italian and American have always been hard in my mouth
always flying from each other
and neither of them fit

I saw my mother and father
      deteriorate
long before they headed into death
toxic from unleavened dreams

I felt the sweet Italian taste
  fade from my family
and the bitter Italian taste
   You know that one?
it rose in the throat
The recipe for balance was gone

But my brother has another story
He says that everything was fine
So don't listen to me

Maybe I was born under a dark star
   like a *strega*
and came here singed already
from another time
with a vision too clouded
            or too clear

I sit at the table
  in the *circolo*
    and bask
     in the familiarity

    Even stronger than the way I felt
    when the train first brought me to Italy

Circolo

and I stepped into
        a whole country
      that behaved like my family!

More like the way I feel
when I gather with my own mob
  of artists and witches
  anarchists, weirdos, and queers

I sit at the table and listen
to the stories and the laughter
while bodies and dishes and words
move around me
             in a molecular dance
And the smell of espresso
perfumes
      the deepening night

I sit at the table trying to
  remember myself
The way I always do now
Like a picture coming into focus

My courtesan self seeks my virgin self
My child self seeks my mother self
My Italian self seeks
my American self that's always screaming or wanting to hide
in this country that rents by the hour to lost souls
from everywhere else

My worker ant seeks my cicada self
  that knows how to sing in the summer

All my parts
       seek each other now
The way notes seek each other to make music
The way words seek each other to make language
The way a wound seeks a healing
      to become a light

BALD

Loryn Lipari

I saw my brain collapse on the steps leading into a NJ Transit Bus #88. Maybe it wasn't exactly my brain. Maybe it was just what I thought my brain looked like if it climbed out of my skull. A moist, helpless mass with two eyes that pleaded to be saved.

The bus stopped in front of one of the numbered streets along Kennedy Boulevard and its doors opened. At first there was silence, no movement. Then, indistinguishable howls like those of a wounded animal caught in a trap. A few passengers stretched their necks toward the open doors. A mass seeped itself onto the steps. A stout arm with stumped fingertips reached into the air in the aisle and begged to be grasped. The hooded head could not conceal the Down's syndrome face that pushed my body inside the gap against the window and the seat. I couldn't tell if the woman's legs were lifeless, but when the young suited man who sat in the first seat got up to help her, it seemed that she was crippled. The bus's steps were deep and high. Somehow, she was caught in the middle of them. She moaned and sighed and screamed obscenities in Spanish while the man lifted and pulled her distorted, dwarfed frame up inside the bus. A woman quickly rose from her seat and moved to the other side. I watched the young man to see if he would wipe the hand that had helped her on his pants or hold it away from his body. He didn't. She propped herself up on the seat for the handicapped and elderly. Her feet dangled in the air. She slept until we reached Journal Square.

I said a prayer for both of us.

Sometimes I feel as if God poisoned my blood. I've taken HIV tests and am told the results are negative, but I feel as though I have been spreading my disease. A carrier without symptoms.

Right before my brain surgery, the nurse came to my bed to take blood. The needle's tip hung in my vein as she unscrewed the vial. I searched inside the plastic tube to see if the color was wrong. I expected to see creatures swimming inside the deep, dark red, faces grinning widely, exposing sharpened teeth, long, skinny arms and legs, fattened bellies nourished with my blood.

The blood moved slowly into the cylinder like lava filling an insect's carved path inside a volcano's wall. I couldn't see a disease if one existed, but I silently cautioned the nurse to handle it with care. She filled vial after vial with blood. My fingertips froze and stiffened. My arm felt as if the bones were being loosened and sucked into the vial. A warmth gathered behind my eyes and my breath shortened. I don't know how many vials she filled. She took the extra blood for transfusion during surgery, in case of an emergency. I was relieved to learn that no one else would be getting it. Two aneurysms in my brain have proven to me what I had thought for years: something is seriously wrong with me. I might be contagious.

Thick, putrid odors fill my nose and my mind. I have never had surgery before. The surgeon feels like a child molester as he reaches for the circular saw, and aims it toward my skull, carves, pushing inside me. The aftermath spills outside the flesh; it bleeds and creates a stench that will last long after.

The nurses, the anesthesiologist, the aides, all watch the doctor as he lifts the piece of my skull with sterile, stainless steel tools into the air, under the heated lights of the ER. Its bloodied bottom drips fluid across my chest and onto the paper towel–covered tray. My naked brain unmasks my thoughts in the twists and tucks of each nerve cell. I imagine the doctor cringing as he lifts the organ up with forceps to expose the area behind my left eye. My secrets run and dive into the crevices like cockroaches racing for shelter when the lights turn on in the kitchen.

"*Oh god, she's a drug addict. Look at this, she's a lesbian . . .*"

❧

Nanny died of cancer in the mid 1980s. Bone cancer. The chemotherapy failed to cure her and in the process it managed to suck into its technology her home in the Senior Citizen building in Leonia and the neck-length gray hair from her head. Her condition did not allow her to live alone. She was so ill she barely ate. The treatments clanked radiations into her body just about every other day, but the cancer spread like a forest fire right into her brain. Her last days were filled with imaginary knitting needles that she held tightly in her shriveled hands, looping and linking invisible yarns of yellow, blue, and red.

In her bathroom, the exhaust fan spun unevenly every time she snuck there to smoke a cigarette. There was a pride that pushed her from the kitchen stove to the dining room table every Sunday afternoon to serve trays of food to her family, but kept her from ever wanting anyone to know that she smoked. She crocheted doilies that she mastered and wound as tightly as herself, but hid under the lamps, the ashtrays, the glass candy trays. Never bare for the naked eye to see.

The last time I saw her standing she was crouched at the back screen door of my aunt's kitchen in the same town as the Senior Citizen building. I entered my Aunt Angie's house through the front door. Something that is rare at any of our homes. Front doors are locked and side and back entrances are open. I called out Nanny's name more than once and swerved my way around potted plants and dining room furniture, until I got to the counter that led into the kitchen.

She clasped a cigarette between the fingers of her left hand. Her wig must have been on the hospital bed's corner of what once was the den, but now was Nanny's room. A few strands of hair flew up into the air from her reddened scalp. She paused briefly, debating whether or not she should hide the cigarette or her exposed head. She gave into herself that day, exhausted from fighting a disease that was much stronger than us all. She decided to finish smoking her Parliament; she didn't rush to find her wig. I joined her for a cigarette. We smoke the same brand with the same hand.

I think about the woman she was. I think about her house at the bottom of the hill on 73rd street in North Bergen, one block from Tonelle Avenue. In the 1980s, the drive from my childhood home in Woodcliff Lake to Nanny's house took approximately forty-five minutes. The exit ramp of Route 80 West was lined with broccoli that stretched thin like the head of a balding man. Gaps of mountains and land blotched the view and lessened as we drove east toward North Bergen. By the time we reached Route 46, the trees became buildings, the buildings became factories, and the broccoli became the Pathmark produce section.

The air thickened on Tonelle Avenue. The blue-black smoke expelled from the factory's chimneys into the air darkened the early afternoon. Cars seemed to chain themselves to each other. They hovered over each other and raced around the winding twists and turns of the road, hugging the bottom of North Bergen's hills. I could see Nanny's house stacked side by side with the roofs of her neighbors. I can't say that I ever enjoyed going there to see her, but that may be because my father had instilled the belief in his children, early on, that we would live better. The crowdedness of

Hudson County, the cemented back patios and hardened factory air choked us all.

He wanted something more for his family, the hills of North Bergen enveloping his childhood, a cessation that he tried to end with his generation. He moved our family to northern New Jersey. Upper Bergen County. The old cliché: better schools, better homes, a better chance for his children. The hills in Woodcliff Lake were different. They were mountains and farmland filled with grass and trees. The houses were spread out in edged manicured lawns. Sidewalks did not exist there, nor did street lamps. Fewer people, less need.

∽

I wake from the drug-induced coma not by choice. It feels hollow inside, as if the surgeons removed my entire brain and left only the shell of my skull. My left eye sees nothing but the darkened pressure of the cotton that holds its place with thick, white medical tape across my eyebrow and cheekbone. My head is covered with a light, white gauze cap. I feel the pressure of the IV burn the edge of the vein on the outside of my left hand. When I force it upward to touch my head, the sharp, metal tip pulls against the plastic tube slowing the push of saline solution into my body.

They shaved my head. Tiny points of hair stand at attention on my scalp, not even $\frac{1}{4}$" long. The incision, a carved half circle, starts at the edge of my hairline, in the middle of my forehead, and snakes its way across the left side of my head. It ends in front of my left ear at the hinge of my jaw. Thirty-seven staples hold my scalp and my skull in place. A drainage tube pumps excretions from my brain out of the top of my head toward the back. I carefully touch the incision; pink swollen hills erupt where each staple pushed its way into my skull.

The pain festered behind my left eye, its lid lifeless against the tip of my cheekbone. A day before its collapse, my vision blurred and doubled. I blink, pleading with my pupils to readjust themselves so that I can see. I cover my right eye with the palm of my hand; it smells of neglect, body oils, exhaustion, and stale cigarette smoke. For the last three weeks, ever since that stabbing pain in my left eye buckled my knees and loosened my bowels, slowed my walk, chewed my words, I haven't been the same. And when I covered my eye, one at a time, the structure that should have worked for its focus refused me. I gave up when my left eyelid did.

I know that after having spent over six hours in the emergency room, I expected a doctor to walk briskly toward my bed, chart in hand, and tell me

I was fine, give me a prescription for my insanity, and send me to a good psychotherapist. He didn't. Instead, a neurologist cautiously approaches my bed positioned right in front of the nurse's station. There is no bounce in his step or smile on his face. My prescription is emergency brain surgery at University Hospital in Newark.

Brain Surgery

Take one small metal device.
Insert into brain.
Only one application necessary.
Consult physician twice after initial application.
Send Christmas cards once a year.

I wanted to die right before entering the emergency room of University Hospital early in December of 1999. I hoped that I would not survive my surgery. I just couldn't bear the thought of having to be strong. Pretending I could take it. That I'd make it. For most of my life I prided myself on my intelligence more than my attractiveness. I thought I would never be the same again. The moment the anesthesiologist pierced my vein and asked me to count backwards, I hoped that it would all be over. That I would be over.

Nanny died in 1983 and I wanted her to. I think we all did. Her shriveled frame, bare head, and boned fingers became a silent plea amongst her family. We all had hoped that it would not be long before someone saw fit to take her away. To let her die. She had no control left in her. Even the daily tasks of wiping or bathing herself had been left in the hands of nurses and family. I was embarrassed for her and for my father. Embarrassed to know that no one could help her, not even herself.

My nurses introduce themselves, but their names I do not know until the last days I spend here. My face is expressionless, but the shaking of my hands says more about me. The staff takes the mobile blood pressure machine from my left arm and replaces it with the stationery system attached to the back wall. The IV stays to the right, its drip quickened by the movement.

The wires that pull themselves from the wall behind me chain me to the ICU Unit. A prisoner rather than a patient.

Twenty-two tubes and seven IV's is what my father counted the day they wheeled my frail body out of more than eight hours of surgery. My face was so bloated that my father's skin turned milk-white as he stumbled, until his arm felt the hospital wall behind him and he was able to lean against it.

My family told me that when I came to consciousness I had something to tell them. I claimed, and I don't recall this, that my grandmother had come to me during surgery and told me it was not time.

I climbed a mountain the day I got discharged from the hospital. I crawled for my life for over a month, from a bed in my apartment, from a hospital bed, from a deep-set ceramic tub I took a bath in the last day in the hospital. For three hours I stayed in that bath water trying to wash it all away, carefully patting my wounds from the IVs on my hands and upper right chest. That was the biggest IV: a two-inch tube inserted into my main artery.

I did see my brain collapse on the steps leading onto a NJ Transit Bus #88 and thank God I did. As I return to consciousness with a tube down my throat to breathe, another inside me to urinate, thirty-seven staples pierced inside the flesh of my skull, and a patch over my left eye, I open the mirrored compartment of my hospital table. I pull it closer toward me. Its rubber wheels roll against the tiled floor without sound. My face is drained, but my eye sparkles with life. For the first time ever I realize I am lucky to be alive. This time there are no secrets. I am not ashamed. I am bald.

TODAY YOUR NAME IS MARY
Carole Maso

My grandfather lifts his ax. When it is poised above his head, my father, just a boy, freezes the scene. He is afraid to watch the ax drop, for my grandfather is not chopping wood as one might expect. My father pulls himself from the bed and moves closer to the window. He rubs his eyes just to be sure and then he sees it: his father is cutting down the beautiful tomato plants, grown from seed, hacking them down to the ground. Earlier that season they had put up stakes together for those fragile plants to hold on to.

Is this what my father means when he says there are things it is better to forget? Is this what he is forgetting—his own father out in the garden chopping the tomato plants into pieces, insisting that they are Americans now, not Italians? Did his father announce that there will be no more Italian spoken in his house? No more wine drunk with lunch, as he burned the grapevines? Did he tell his wife there would be no more sad songs from the old country? How much she must have wept, hugging her small son to her breast!

My grandfather takes his ax from the toolshed, and when he lifts it above his head the scene freezes—but only for a moment. He hacks down those sweet tomatoes while the small boy looks on from his bedroom window and the eggplant and the peppers cower in terror.

꩜

"Maria," my grandfather said one day long ago, "today your name is Mary. Today I change my own name from Angelo to Andy. Today we are real Americans."

I am forever grateful that I was not there to witness the scowl that must have appeared on my grandmother's face at this news. It must have been terrible. Of course, she never once called him Andy and the name, unused, faded. And when she refused to answer to Mary, my grandfather sadly returned to Maria, for he missed my grandmother too much. She would not look at him or say one word; he was addressing a stranger.

253

"I was given a name at birth and I will die with it, Angelo," she said.

"We could call the baby Mike. What do you think?"

She frowned.

"Oh, Maria, your whole family wears that frown," he said on the day he finally gave in. "Such stubbornness!" he cried. "I am sure it has ruined more than one good idea."

The evening of their second day here, my grandfather registered both of them for English classes at the local school. Right from the start he was a model student, staying late, trying to improve his pronunciation, persevering.

"I leaf in New Hope, Pencil-bannia," he said hesitantly, concentrating impossibly hard on every syllable. "I live, I live, I live in New Hope, Pencil, Pencil-vay-knee-a in the United State of America." I'm sure my grandfather smiled when he got to the America part, for he could say it perfectly. He had been saying it his entire life.

"America begins and ends with the letter *A*. America. See you too-mar-rah, too-morr-row," he said to the pretty young teacher, "American redhead. Thank you very much. Good-bye."

"The accent must go," he said each night before bed. "The accent must go," he said in the morning to his small son, Michael. "An accent is no good in this new country." Maria sighed, exhausted by so much enthusiasm. He was a teacher's dream, not a wife's. She felt lonely. The village where she was born and had lived her whole life welled in her stomach; she had to eat a lot of bread to keep it down; she had to sleep under heavy blankets.

"We need new clothes for a new country, Mary," my grandfather said. She was not answering, especially to Mary. "If you'd like to come with me, I'm going into the downtown." Still she did not answer. Meticulously my grandfather observed the dress of the people on the neighboring farms before going out to get his own blue jeans and work shirts and boots. He especially noted the dress of the Negroes whom he considered the most authentic Americans. They were new and exotic like America itself. And above all they were not Europeans. Europe became "for the birds." "Oh, Mary," he would say, "Italy is for the birds. In America there is jazz music, Charlie has told me, in a place called Harem."

"Harlem," Charlie would correct him.

"Yes, Harlem," my grandfather would repeat, "where women wear flowers behind their ears and the music is hot."

"I'd like to go there," my grandfather said in his halting way, something I imagine he picked up from Charlie.

"That's cool," Charlie said.

Hot and cool, my grandfather thought. "This is some country, Mary," he said, hugging her. "Hot and cool, at the same time," he said to his small son, Michael. This wonderful place, America, beginning and ending with *A*.

∾

On the day of the Bicentennial, July 4, 1976, my grandmother got up un-usually early, about 4:00 A.M., unable to sleep. The country would be cele-brating its two-hundredth year this day in a grand way, and she had felt some of that excitement in the nursing home where preparations had been going on all week. Banners had been made. Songs had been practiced, the tenors and baritones and the multitude of sopranos getting together to re-hearse their parts. Tiny flags had been purchased to decorate wheelchairs, and red, white, and blue crepe paper, to be threaded in the wheel's spokes. The kitchen staff had made little strawberry shortcakes and had dyed the whipped cream blue. And my grandmother, the first one up, was making her own preparations, it would turn out—a different sort of independence.

In celebration, tall ships would be sailing down the Hudson later in the day. There would be elaborate fireworks displays in the evening. We asked Father if he would go to the festivities with us, and, liking water and ships of any kind, he agreed. "But we should go see your grandmother first," he said with a certain resolve. He did not like to visit her alone. God doesn't send us a cross heavier than we can bear, she had always said, but in the years since my grandfather's death she had seemed to stoop further and further into the ground with the weight of it, growing more and more bitter and resentful of everyone but particularly of my father, who was not my grandfather and never would be.

"Sure," we said, and so we went early that Fourth of July to visit Grandma, sometime near dawn.

I drove. I was just learning to drive. "Use the low beams in mist," Fletcher said from the back seat. Though Fletcher was younger than I, it was clear that he had been driving for a long time. The early morning mist was thick and I followed his instructions. Slowly we plowed through the haze to Grandma.

I was doing well: adjusting the lights, using the brakes and the blinkers, but nearing the nursing home I saw such a bizarre image, a picture of such eeriness in the fog that I had to wipe my eyes to ensure I was awake, and, lift-ing my hands from the steering wheel, the car swerved. Fletcher leaned for-ward to help.

"Look," I said, pointing. "Look." Father stared straight ahead and said nothing. Fletcher looked up.

In front of us through the early morning mist we saw what seemed to be an old, old woman, or the ghost of a woman, dressed in a strange, elaborate costume and posed on the large front lawn of the nursing home.

"That's Grandma," I said.

"No," they said, "it's not." They did not recognize her this way.

"Yes," I whispered, "that's Grandma."

"How could it be?"

She was tiptoeing about the grass now, checking her stage, testing the light, bending and stretching in preparation. She waved to us and smiled. "My family," she said. We stood at the edge of the lawn and waved back—Father, too. "My family," she smiled.

I looked closer, still not trusting my eyes. A red rosary hung around her neck. She wore a long skirt. Beads and other trinkets were sewn into it—beads from necklaces my grandfather had given her and she had never worn: crystal beads, beads of ruby-colored glass, mother of pearl. She wore a white peasant blouse, made hurriedly from a sheet, probably secretly. She had pulled the hair away from her face and made braids that she pinned up on top of her head. Attached to the braids were red and white streamers that flowed behind her when she moved. She looked like a little girl.

"Vanessa," she said, and she made a full turn for me slowly so that I might not miss anything: the intricately sewn costume, the beautiful hairdo with streamers, the red rosary. I wiped my eyes again. She turned once more and what I saw this time was the girlishness in her motion, the joy, the thrill; yes, it was joy I saw in her turned ankle! She pranced to one corner of the lawn, picked something up, and brought it back with her. It made a lovely sound. It was a tambourine she had made from tin pie plates, yarn, and bells.

"How inventive you are, Grandma! We never knew!"

She was humming something softly to herself—a beautiful, melancholy melody. I trembled, freezing suddenly on this July morning. She hummed louder and then began to sing. Her feet seemed to lift off the ground completely as she began her lilting, graceful, lighter-than-air dance. She took three steps to the right, slowly raised the tambourine and tapped it lightly, then three steps to the left, then a twirl. Instead of her regular black tie shoes she wore ballet slippers. When I saw her tiny feet in those slippers, I felt like going up and hugging her, but I did not dare disturb the dance; I was afraid that she might turn back into the old Grandma if I moved even one muscle. I held my breath.

"I never dreamt it would all come back so easily," she said, and there was a lightness in her voice, a giddiness we had never heard before.

She moved more quickly now, having been bitten, I imagined, by the tarantula of Italian folklore, the spider with a venom so potent that it had made her people crazy for centuries with the irresistible urge to dance.

"How graceful you are, Grandma!"

She smiled at us. "We used to make our own pasta," she said sweetly in her new singing voice. A weight had lifted from her. "We used to make little tortellini, ravioli. We used to make our own wine and olive oil. There were mountains there."

She was surrounded by home. It wrapped around her finally with large, comforting arms—not our home, bannered and lit with fireworks, but hers.

"Oh, Grandma," we said, "why didn't you ever make us those little tortellini? Or tell us about the mountains? Why did you keep it all from us?"

Strains of familiar songs could be heard coming from inside the nursing home—"I'm a Yankee Doodle Dandy" and "America the Beautiful." There was much excitement inside. Some were dressing to leave for the day—off to backyard celebrations. Others were getting ready for the geriatric parade of wheelchairs and walkers. Sparklers had been promised.

Grandma stopped suddenly and looked directly at us. "Your grandfather never let me speak Italian in the house," she said. "He never let me cook my own food. I missed that so much," she said in the loneliest voice I had ever heard. "He never let me sing you to sleep with the sweet songs from Italy I loved so much." My father put his face in his hands.

I thought of my grandfather as a young man in Italy straining toward some idea of America. I thought of him coming here, his dreams of being a real American—eating steaks and eggs, wearing good shoes, making a life and then another idea, some time later, something quite different, though unmistakably American, too.

A marching band could be heard somewhere in the distance.

"Oh, Angelo!" she said, looking to the sky. "I could have made an Easter torta for the children. I could have sung them the songs my mother sang. There were so many songs to sing."

"Mom," my father said. There were great tears in his eyes. "Why didn't you say something to him?"

"It was not my place," she said sadly.

"Oh, Mom," he said. He walked slowly to her. "I never knew," he whispered to her, looking into her darkened eyes.

"Mother," he said, squeezing her ancient hands in his. "We've wanted the same thing all along. Why . . ." His voice trailed off. He kissed her hands and rubbed them against his face. "Why? Why have we fought?" he asked. She shook her head, lowered it.

"My bambino, my beautiful, curly-headed bambino. You had the most beautiful curls."

My father turned to us for what seemed the first time in his life and gestured for us to come forward and enter the circle he and his mother had made with their arms. We hugged each other, all four of us. I ran my fingers through my grandmother's hair and streamers.

"My children," she whispered, "my children." I felt our arms around her. She would die in the afternoon of this embrace. She was making her peace with us and with the world at the last moment—and we with her.

"Grandma," I said, "I like your shoes."

"Oh," she said, looking at them and pointing her toe. "I've been saving these shoes for a lifetime."

"Grandma," Fletcher said, "that's a nice tambourine."

"I made it in crafts," she said. "You know, my people always loved music. My father played the mandolin like an angel."

On hearing this something rose in my father like an anthem and he began to weep uncontrollably and embraced his mother tighter.

"Michael," she said, "I'm so sorry." And he nodded. His head was pressed against her bosom, which seemed larger, more maternal somehow, softer. My father left his head on that wonderful place for a long time; when he finally looked up, her face was lined suddenly with the past.

"We used to eat these," she said, bending over and plucking a dandelion from the green lawn. "We used to like these very much. A simple weed. We cooked it with garlic and olive oil and a few flakes of red pepper. We ate weeds and we were happy."

My grandmother waved her arms above her head in some private choreography now, bending over and brushing her ankles in a wide, delicate sweep, a graceful rhythmic gesture.

She was humming the tarantella again. She separated from us and whirled and whirled, moving one hand to her eyes as if shading them from some brutal Italian sun.

"Piccolini," she said. "The piccolini—" I thought those tiny fish must be tickling her childhood ankles. "The piccolini," she smiled. To whom was she speaking? Not to us anymore—to her mother, I think. There was wonder in her voice, the wonder a daughter has for her mother when they are seeing the same thing for the first time. She pointed into the grass. "The piccolini."

Already explosions could be heard far off. Something would burst in her head as bright, as spectacular as the year's bicentennial display.

She danced now more quickly and continued to sing louder and louder as she whirled from one side of the large nursing home lawn to the other, spinning away from us, further and further away with each gesture. But then she came closer and seemed to focus for one moment, halting the dance with this last memory, arrested by it. She looked right at us. "We used to make little Christmas cakes of honey," she whispered. "We called it strufoli. It was very good." Slowly she began to dance again.

She shook her head with amazement. "I can taste it right now," she said. Her eyes were wide. She stopped. One foot was pointed into the earth, one arm raised toward the sky. "It tastes so sweet," she said, "just like I remember." She closed her eyes and smiled.

CARLTON FREDRICKS
AND MY MOTHER
Maria Mazziotti Gillan

On the counter the battered, black radio hummed with advice to the house-wife, the dieter, the car owner, the consumer, the bargain hunter, the average American. Carlton Fredricks proclaimed that vitamins could cure anything. Bernard Meltzer warned of stingy insurance companies waiting to cheat their customers. Joan Hamburg tipped single women on the best places to meet men. They alternately bellowed and soothed as their disgruntled or dissatisfied callers pleaded, fumed, and ranted, their duets complementing the clanking pots and sizzling garlic perpetually boiling and browning on my mother's stove. My mother always listened to the radio in the kitchen while she worked, her small hands, efficient and quick, cleaning the counter, washing the dishes, cutting vegetables. All day she'd listen to these in her kitchen—Carlton Fredricks and his array of vitamins meant to cure every-thing from hammertoes to cancer or Bernard Meltzer with his practical ad-vice on buying a home or saving money. The advice competed in the kitchen with the popping sounds of frying peppers and the whistling of the steam blowing out of the spout of the tin espresso pot. As she performed her daily food preparations, she was enveloped all the while in the comforting advice that for my mother had an almost olfactory presence, an elusive aroma of Americanness. It was as if Hamburg's or Fredrick's advice saturated her clothes with the essence of that intangible something that made an Ameri-can. Those voices crackling from their various A.M. frequencies comforted her, because through the democracy of radio, they treated her as American, something the rest of the world certainly never did.

Often, my mother acted as if those radio shows were lectures of a great professor and gave one oral reports on such topics as vitamin C as a cure for hair loss or avoiding scheming con artists who said they were just driving by and saw that you had a dangerous tree leaning over your house or that your house needed a new roof. She treated me to one of these mini-lectures every time I sat at the kitchen table to sip espresso or taste the meatballs before dinner. In a way, those radio shows were her university education, teaching her how to be more American or at least revealing to her the fears and foibles of a typical American. When she learned something from the radio, she seemed amazed as if something which had eluded her for many years was finally within her reach.

My mother was twenty-three when she came to America from San Mauro, a little Italian village in southern Italy where she attended school through the third grade when public education ended. Even fifty years later, she talked about her days in school as exciting, her voice taking on a lilt when she talked of it, describing the classroom, the teacher, the books. She even recited poems she'd memorized and exactly remembered things the teacher said.

My mother believed in keeping us all close to her and in a way, those radio shows provided an entrée into what she really wanted to do, gave her something to talk about she thought we'd understand and that would convince us that she, too, was learning to be an American, that this language of radio would provide her with the questions to ask that would have opened the door between us that was slowly slamming shut, even while she tried to keep us safe in her warm kitchen.

Once on one of those radio programs, she heard someone mention petting. I was about eleven years old, and she asked me, "So, what is petting?" I, who was still lost in a world of books, said "Well it's like when you touch a cat; you are petting the cat," and I made smooth motions of petting the cat's fur. My mother giggled and averted her eyes so I knew that the answer I had given her was not the one she was looking for. It was a couple of years before I realized what she wanted to know.

My mother was the hub of our lives. We all revolved around her, but as we grew older, it became harder and harder for her to give advice we didn't mock. I remember my brother teasing her. When we were in the car, he'd say, "Hey Ma, what's that little bump on your shoulders?" referring to her head. She'd sit in the front seat of the car, her head barely reaching the top of the seatback, her purse securely tucked under her arm, her hand clutching the door handle, her feet making motions as if she could stop the car. Though she'd never driven, she would direct my father, tell him, "too fast." Or "Watch out. Here comes car." My brother called her the "little general," teasing but also serious because she did, after all, want to keep her hands on our lives, kneading us into shape the way she kneaded bread in the big bowl.

Then, finally, I started college. I had dreamed of going to the University of Virginia. I can still see that picture of me I attached to the application, a picture in which I looked about as un-American as anybody could. I had rarely been out of Paterson in my life and I had no idea of what the University of Virginia would have been like. I don't know what made me think my mother would have let me go away from home anyway, and when I got a full four-year scholarship to the branch campus of a working-class university, a campus in Paterson a few blocks from the high school I had attended, the matter was settled. I would live at home, taking the bus at the corner of our street to the College.

The first day I was terrified, thought I'd never fit in, but quickly I made friends, joined everything, took as many courses as I could—twenty-one credits a semester—because my scholarship paid for as many classes as I wanted to take and I was my mother's daughter after all. I wanted to learn everything I could, hungry for the world outside the Italian neighborhood and my mother's fragrant kitchen. I threw myself into college life, made friends with other working-class students, enjoying it all, though, of course, each night I rode the bus home.

From the time she left school until she married my father when he came to Italy to find a wife, and saw her chasing the family pig up the mountain, her face rosy-cheeked, her body strong and sensual and decided then and there to marry her, she worked in the fields, cooked the family's meals, and helped her father in his grocery store.

Three months after he saw her catch that reluctant pig, my father married my mother and brought her to the Italian neighborhood in Paterson, NJ. My father went to night school to learn English, but he insisted, "Women don't need to go to school," and though she cried, he would not allow it. As a consequence my mother was illiterate in English, knew only the words we taught her or the ones that she picked up from the radio or TV.

Perhaps the voices of Meltzer, Hamburg, and Fredricks replaced the elders that my mother might have known in her village of San Mauro. Certainly, she accepted the radio hosts' advice as sage wisdom, wisdom she believed could improve my life as well. Daily she'd repeat the advice she'd heard, her mind serving up these tidbits on demand. "Oh, yes," she'd say. "Take vitamin C. Good for your hair." When we'd argue, I'd scold, "Ma, where did you hear that garbage?" She'd retreat, muttering, "Levermind, levermind," and go on believing what she chose. No matter how many times we told her the word was "nevermind," she'd continue to hear and say it that way. Her mind appeared to be a jumble of information, much of it contradictory, picked up from her favorite radio show hosts—advice on love and dating and how to raise children or where to find the perfect cashmere sweater. My mother worked in the Ferraro Coat Factory on River Street where all the women workers were Italian and they chattered all day in their own language, and at night, after dinner, we visited our aunts and uncles and my parents' friends, Italian was the only language they knew so my mother's English remained limited even after she had lived in America for fifty years, though she understood a lot more English than she could say. We'd talk to each other in a mixture of Italian and English so blended together that often I couldn't say where one language ended and the other began. My mother had trouble saying English words, the sounds too hard and clipped for her Italian tongue. She called Bernard Meltzer "Bohnarulza," and it took a while for me to figure out that she was referring to Bernard Meltzer, her favorite of all the gurus who kept her company through her days.

Once when I was in college, my father was driving us home from the farmer's market and she saw a store that said "Package Goods" in big letters across its window. "What is that?" she asked. "It says package goods, Ma," I answered. "We'll have to go there to buy material one day," she said, and I laughed. "Ma, package goods doesn't mean material. It's a liquor store!" "Oh," she said, turning her face away from mine, but not before I saw the shame that colored it.

Twenty-five years after I left home to get married, my daughter graduated from the kind of college I would have liked to have attended—ivy-covered buildings, brick paths, archways, and towers. My mother sat with my daughter's huge yearbook with its brightly colored photographs in her lap. She gazed at the pictures of the beautiful, upper class young men and women with their vitamin-enriched skin, their straight teeth, their shining hair, and she kept saying, over and over, "Look how beautiful they are! Can you believe it? Look," and I understood that to my mother these young people represented a world she could not have imagined twenty years ago, the grass and gracious buildings in the background, the sun that seemed to shine only for them, as it had never shone for her, and she was amazed that her granddaughter, only one generation removed from San Mauro, that town on top of that Italian mountain where my father first saw her chasing that pig, her granddaughter could go to a place like this one and look as though she belonged. She rubbed her small hand across the faces in the glossy pages as though she had discovered something miraculous. She kept shaking her head, and saying, "Oh, how beautiful!"

She turned to me then, said, "Ah, I was so proud of you when you graduated from college. The first one in our family and I was so proud, I thought I'd burst."

"But Ma," I said, "You never said anything. I didn't know."

"Ah," she said, "It wasn't for me to say. I'm your mother. I didn't want to bring bad luck on you."

She smoothed the yearbook one last time, and then she tied her apron tighter and automatically flipped on the radio, half listening to her second-hand information, pleased when she'd hear some tidbit she could share with us. How many hours of her life she'd listen to those radio voices, the clues they offered to her, closed off as she was from the world of America, the world her children inhabited with such ease. "Ah," she said, "I love America. There's no place like it in the world," and smiled at us, her children and grandchildren, American to the bone.

GREENWOOD LAKE
Diane di Prima

Jeanne was staying in my parents' summer house at Greenwood Lake, New Jersey, and Emma invited me and the new baby to come out too. I decided to take her up on it. I badly needed to be taken care of for a while, and then too, I felt sure that the sooner my mother got to know the baby the more she would love her, and I really wanted my folks to love Dominique. I knew that their hearts would override any prejudice or hesitancy that their heads had set up about her being partly Black, and me still not being married, and all the rest of it.

When my father drove to the Lake for the weekend with some of my cousins, I got a ride with them.

I always had mixed feelings about the "house on the lake"—in many ways, it was too crowded and chaotic for my taste, it lacked privacy, life there lost some of its middle-class veneer and became more tribal than it was in the city. Then too, it was bought with my college money. But as it turned out there were to be several times in my life when "the house on the lake" functioned as a safe house, a retreat or convalescent home for me and/or my friends.

The first time was when I had gone there after chaos broke loose with me and Roi and Hettie. I had written "What I Ate Where" for *Dinners and Nightmares* there while I waited to find out if in fact I needed an abortion.

This visit with Dominique was only the second time I used the place as a refuge, but there would be occasions in the future when I would go there when the family wasn't around to hang out and write, while John Wieners or Kirby Doyle or some other friend tried to cold-turkey from speed or heroin in the spare bedroom, and I kept a kind of watch and sometimes fed them.

When I got there this time with Mini, as we were already calling her— Freddie's nickname for her, from the middle of Do*mini*que—she was about two weeks old. The house was full, as it often was in the summer, cousins of mine in their teens and early twenties were inhabiting all available nooks and crannies. My mother and her sister Ella were there full-time, and my brothers came and went. My father came for the weekends, and spent the weeks working in New York. Jeanne of course was ensconced as a guest of honor: this had been her home away from home since her very first summer, and she lorded it over the neighborhood toddlers and her various relatives with a natural grace.

I was given a bed in one of the side rooms with my kids alongside, but during the day, since I was actually working—and work was regarded by all as sacrosanct—I had privileged use of the living room with its tables and stereo. I proceeded to set it up as my study, installing my electric typewriter.

Various girl cousins slept in the living room at night, and their habit of course was to sleep late. I was an early riser, as also was Emma, and in order to get my workspace cleared out at what I considered to be a reasonable hour, I would go quietly in amongst my sleeping cousins and put Ornette Coleman's *Free Jazz* or some other advanced and cacophonous album on the stereo. They would then arise, the poor dears, amidst groans and curses, but as Emma was morally in agreement with me for once in our lives, my cousins didn't dare complain about any of it.

We'd all together clear the bedding away, and I would get to work.

Aside from the book I was editing for Bettita (with scissors and rubber cement, as was the wont in those primitive times), I was also doing another project on which I pinned some hopes. Bettita had suggested that I do a book of translations of medieval Latin love poems for Simon & Schuster, and at the same time had proposed it to her bosses. They wanted to see a prospectus with five or six translations, and I was working on those. I'd brought along some Latin texts and dictionaries and a reference grammar, and plugged away for hours every day, often uncovering the hidden sexual meaning of a metaphor, or a place where a stanza or two had likely been cut in copying by a prudish monk.

It was perhaps some of the happiest work I've ever done, certainly the happiest job I'd had to date. I love translating, love the absorption in another time and place and mind. And it was real, legitimate work, proposed by a real publishing house, which certainly helped my status in the eyes of my family. As did the fact that I was translating poems from a distant—and therefore surely respectable—past. There was a certain sense of "be quiet, Diane's working" in the air, which contrasted oddly with the mix of nervousness and contempt with which my folks regarded my own literary productions.

In the end, of course, Simon & Schuster decided not to do my book of medieval Latin love songs, but by then I had finished and polished the handful I had been working on, and when I finally got a press of my own and began to publish books, I put them out in a chapbook called *Seven Love Poems from the Middle Latin.*

In the midst of all this activity, Mini was thriving. I nursed her whenever she wanted, in spite of dire predictions from my mother that I was making her self-willed. She had a habit of eating a little, and then going starry-eyed and dreamy at the breast, and I would put her down and in no time at all she'd want to eat some more. This, I was warned, was *giving her her own way*, but I went on doing it, as I pondered Latin syntax.

And, of course, she had completely won over Emma and all the girl cousins, and elicited the interest of Jeanne. A beautiful and happy baby, she went from one pair of arms to another, surrounded by family and summertime.

❧

I put in two or three good weeks at Greenwood Lake: everything was taken care of. I didn't have to lift a finger to cook, or take care of Jeanne and Mini. They would appear as if by a miracle, clean, clothed, shod, and fed, and I would hang out with them. Breast-feed Mini.

Wonderful meals, too, appeared miraculously in the hot, noisy kitchen, and wondrous girl-cousins with the intense unconscious beauty of early Italian movies set the table. I could translate medieval Latin to my heart's content, write new poems, play cut-and-paste with the manuscript I was editing, and if I wanted a break, a "fall" into the reality of daily life, I could come out of the living room/study and have coffee with my mother and some of her sisters, and we would talk endlessly, at the kitchen table.

I was intensely grateful, took none of this for granted. Something about the past year—the legal battle over *The Floating Bear*, the social battle: bucking public opinion to have Mini, the many struggles that came into focus around the theatre, I am not sure what it was, exactly—but something about the year just past had made me very conscious of ease, of leisure. There was a feeling of having come in out of the rain for a moment.

Though certainly my ways were enough different from the ways of this household, and in particular from the ways of Emma, that often a weird tension would fill the cottage over seemingly nothing at all.

On one such occasion, when my mother and I were sitting in silence at the kitchen table, four-year-old Jeanne came by with an open umbrella and handed it to me. "Hold this over you, Mommy," she advised me solemnly, her eyes very wide, "hold this over you, so *things* don't fall on your head." It made me laugh, but it also made me think.

What I thought was that it was time, it was probably time to go home, to go back to my apartment, and to the city. Back to my own life. And this didn't make me feel very good. In fact, it terrified me, and that was a response to my life—the personal freedom so hard-won—that I had never had before.

The idea of going back to take care of two kids on whatever I could manage to earn, however I earned it, of going back to all that *work*, that wonderful but non-paying work: *Floating Bears*, Poets Theatres, whatever—I could feel how exhausted I was, down to my bones—the notion of going back to all those dear friends and other karmic relationships: whatever Roi might be feeling by now about Mini, however Freddie and Alan's lives were coming apart at the seams, whatever might be bothering Jimmy, etc., etc. All that for the first time looked not enticing, but dangerous. More than I could handle, hence frightening.

I had no idea how to do or say anything about my fear. Had no notion even that there was a kind of sanity in it: the voice of the body, saying "Enough."

I was not trained to think in terms of alternatives, other courses of action that might be possible. I felt, myself, that I had chosen this life, chosen each part of it, each friend, involvement, commitment, bill, low-paying-but-freelance job, and that therefore there was nothing for it but to *go through with it*, somehow. Though I couldn't have really said what I was going through with.

Even as I wasn't taught to think of alternatives, so too, at that point in my life I had no way of talking about these feelings. This terror. This knowing I had "bit off more than I could chew," and that I had no sense how to navigate it.

Perhaps if I had been able to bring myself to talk to Emma, had mentioned even a part of what I was feeling—cold mist in my solar plexus, my belly—she might have come up with something, some way of helping. I am sure at this point she could see the problem, and that she find some way in. I'm sure she and Dick were as baffled as I was by my life.

Perhaps I thought it would have been admitting defeat. Afraid of the many forms of "I told you so," or the door shut in my face again, as had been when I wanted to go back to college.

In writing this chapter I have come to wonder for the first time, what would have happened if I had said right then: *I'm scared. I hurt and I'm tired. I need to figure out what to do.* Because I know now, finally—and it took me more than fifty years to find out—that there are always human alternatives, parallel pathways, though some of them require that we rely on others. Ask for help.

I am sure I gave the impression that everything was cool, that I knew exactly what I was doing when I announced that it was time to go back to the city. What internal clock I was using I have no idea, but the tension in the cottage was growing: Emma's ways of being with babies and mine were so different. And I knew that if I stayed away any longer the life I'd set in motion in the city, and which only cohered through my effort, my vision (Will), would have slipped too far out of recognizable shape, and it would take more than I had going to retrieve it.

Emma was sad—she was having a good time with the kids. The cousins were sad too, but mightily relieved as well: they'd be able to sleep in without being roused every morning by the Avant-Garde. Jeanne protested loudly, and Dominique looked curious and tranquil. As she usually did at that point.

I had anyway finished the *Seven Love Poems from the Middle Latin*, and written a prospectus for Simon & Schuster, and was hoping for a contract and advance. I had masterfully finished the freelance editing job too, and so a check would be wending its way down the pipeline sooner or later to help pay for my household. I had definitely recovered from the birth itself—but the tiredness, the exhaustion I was still feeling, went much deeper than that recent event, and I didn't seem to be recovering just yet.

And so me and the kids and a great number of our possessions: papers and books and toys and diapers and such like, were delivered to my door on East Fourth Street one Sunday night, and carried on up the stairs.

ELIZABETH

Susanne Antonetta

When the Toms River cancer cluster first made news—dying children in the headlines—it started a panic. People moved away, and houses for sale stayed for sale. Everyone drank bottled water. Local politicians got sick of the turmoil, of the story. A city councilman said, "No one is going to tell me we have more of a cancer rate than they do in Newark or Elizabeth."

Elizabeth, my other home and the first place I remember besides Holly Park, had a queen's name. Every land's an extension of the monarch's body, a great green *I Am* of the royal person, and Elizabeth's city showed she'd been gone a long time. It was gassy and bad-smelling as any dead woman. Her skin—grass, buttercups, sweetgums—had long ago been lost, closed over by a concrete embalming, which like any embalming didn't hold off decay but substituted one more acceptable kind of decay for another. It seemed prophetic that they went to the long-gone Renaissance to name this, a city that quickly became a great ungreen *I Am Not*. And I'm sure it galls that a place like Ocean County could compare to such a city and be found wanting.

Our neighborhood in Elizabeth was called Elmora. Our street, Lower Road, was a block of row houses broken into apartments. We had a first floor two-bedroom—one bedroom for my parents, one for my brother and me—with a small dining area/parlor that looked out onto the street. A huge Evergreen Cemetery bulked at us across Lower Road—a weedy, urban cemetery, without the precise sentiment of the suburbs but only plastic flowers in pickle jars and a huge, vague melancholy in the epitaphs. So loved, they said. So special. So missed.

The Evergreen seemed in permanent dialogue with the young mothers sitting on their stoops on my side of the road, painting their nails arterial red, pinning rollers in their hair, and shushing babies. A sign at the Evergreen gate that faced us inexplicably warned *No Food* and *Absolutely No Cooking*.

It's a contamination to eat with the dead, like you're trying to share with them something they can't share, or shouldn't.

Elizabeth has an air like no other air—heavy, gray, like an odor become a scarf wrapped around your face: an olfactory purdah.

The city, and Newark, which squats next to it, survives on heavy industry. They're amazing cities to see from far away: the rows of long smokestacks sticking up like goosenecks, breathing black clouds that roll together to become a lower level of the atmosphere. Sluices dripping muddy brown sludge matter-of-factly into the water. I remember how many days, especially in the summer, began with the radio declaring our air quality unacceptable. Like you had a choice about whether or not to breathe.

Most of the plants are oil refineries and paint factories. I have vivid memories of crossing the bridge to New York, watching the Little Dutch Boy smile mindlessly as fumes turned slow somersaults around his painted form. I try to identify the smell of the place: sulfur, something mustardy, something corrosive. In its heaviness, its moist almost oily presence, it reminds me of the ashes of my Italian grandfather's fourth wife. We cremated her and tried to sprinkle her ashes on the sea when a wind blew up. My grandfather had too many wives for me to get sentimental about them, but I remember the utter surprise when she blew back in our faces, mine and my family's: an ash fine as confectioner's sugar, black, greasy in its cling. We inhaled her, brushed her off our lips.

"Oh," my mother said, "Marcie," as if Marcie had formed out of the little cyclone of her dust. Maybe in Elizabeth we inhaled the body of a dead queen.

Wondering what to do with the can of ash that had been Marcie brought her closer to me than she'd ever been in life. The can—a cardboard tube—sat on my parents' mantel for a year before we could figure out what to do with it. It came packed in a stiff brown carton and arrived from the mortician's a few months before my wedding, so Bruce and I flayed it open, thinking it was a gift. Bruce held up the tube, a sticker on it printed with the word *CONTENTS:*, where someone had carefully written out "Marcelle Antonetta." We put her on the mantelpiece.

I didn't have much contact with my father's father, who had lost my father's mother to a damaged heart and his next two wives to cancer. He moved away from New York when I was seven, to a doublewide in Vero Beach, Florida. We once drove down there. His house smelled bad because he had hundreds of parakeets in cages stacked one on top of the other, plus it was loud because the parakeets never shut up. People could drive on the beach, and all day pickups pulled up to the water with paper bags of their garbage and dumped it. I was ten or eleven and hated the place. Marcie (I don't remember the other wives) always quoted supermarket tabloid stories, telling me one day that cats really had nine lives, and showing me the article. She got on my nerves, an adult and dumber than I was, dumber even than my little cousins.

My grandfather and Marcie moved back up north when I was in my twenties. In between we had very little contact with him though my father sent him money. I know my grandfather had a twenty-year feud with his youngest son, my uncle Larry, and never saw or spoke to him, and that he died without reconciling. We didn't see or speak of Larry either, I guess as a consequence. Other than my aunt Phil and her brood we didn't see much of my father's family, though they were all close by. My father blamed that on his mother's early death. She died when he was in his twenties, of a rheumatic heart. He said no family could stay together without a good woman at its head.

Elizabeth's cemetery, a vacant lot, and eventually Robert Morris Grammar School defined my life, and my brother's. We raced to school past the factions of kids waiting to beat up other factions of kids. We bought candy at Gould's on the corner. Each phone pole flapped with staplegunned flyers. The one I remember best showed a middle-aged man, a WASPy face, bland, cleanshaven, with the words *This man is a childkiller* under him.

Our everyday playground was the vacant lot, just a little larger than a driveway, weedy and full of broken glass. A speck of a cell of the larger body, but we loved it. We brought Legos and dolls and played there every day. But my brother, Chris, and I loved the cemetery most. We weren't allowed to go there—drug dealers used it—but we snuck over pretty often anyway. "I'm goin' down Gould's," Chris told my parents, then walked down Lower Road a little way, shuttling across the street to the Evergreen.

The cemetery seemed like the one thing that had been built with our needs in mind. Lots of concise, simple English; everything eye level; four- and five-foot tombs, carved with droopy angels, that looked like luxury cottages built to our scale. On the Lower Road side of the cemetery a huge grave of black marble—three-pillared, kind of a triptych—dwarfed the others; it had brass musical notes and LPs stuck all over it. *Singin' Sam,* read the plaque, *Singer, Songwriter, Peacemaker.* A muse was loose somewhere.

I felt an odd allegiance to Elizabeth the queen. I liked to read about her. She had herself played the muse for male courtiers, through an act of will much like the one that produced such a grave in a city with little use for songwriting, peacemaking, or singin'. Raleigh praised Elizabeth's "snowe and silke" beauty, though a German visitor wrote of her indifferent features and black, utterly black, teeth. Courtiers called her the Sun Queen.

I've written poems to my Elizabeth, Elizabeth the place. My father'll say to me, "Can't you take out Elizabeth and put in Fanwood?" Fanwood is the *suburby* suburb where my parents live now, in a split-level, painted loud colors inside, with various shag carpeting: orange, brown, and yellow twists in the living room, watercolors crowded on the walls.

I say no because I never lived there. They moved in during my second year away at college.

"But we live in Fanwood," my father says, continuous present.

Here is the harmony between my father's and my mother's families: rearranging. My cousin Helen, my mother's murdered aunt, her uncle Frederick, and my father's brother Larry all gone. They, along with countless cousins and aunts and uncles who appear and disappear and whom I lose track of, hauled in and out of our own private Tower of London. When I say we don't speak of them I mean literally, don't speak. I'm sure my parents have their versions of them, though, ghosts of their ghosts, or faces or voices or steps that reappear at odd hours. My revenant is a city.

Elizabeth was my grammar school home, my aboriginal home, my prepuberty home. Partway through my childhood my father bought a house in a blue-collar suburb at the edge of the city. We moved, and soon I got to middle school. My sphere of action shifted irrevocably to my own body. It produced brackish blood each month, it grew conical and fat on top, it felt alive below when I thought about other bodies. I had something called a *bust* where a chest had been, *pubes* where my legs met. I had a menses and pelvic exams where my friendly doctor began vising me apart. I felt overhauled, like a car being remodeled, parts ripped out and replaced with new parts, fattier, touchier, and the objects of obsessed attention from those around me. My friend Lisa's mom stood by her at every pelvic exam, right up at her labia, to make sure, Lisa said proudly, she didn't get "broken."

This looking, this weird scrutiny and obsessed protection, tamponaded me inside myself: there was no way out. I spent time thinking about my own face. I thought about my body, which had suddenly contracted, become painful and specific and, at the same time, weaker. In Elizabeth, Elizabeth itself had been my body, or seemed like it, physically, as it had been the queen's metaphorically: my sphere of action, my center. I treated it carelessly, as one big sharded extension of myself. I left my stuffed animals in the lot, and Barbie dolls and Barbie clothes on gravestones.

Childhood is external, adolescence and adulthood are internal. In Elizabeth smokestacks poured up thick plumes, men killed children, Singin' Sam stayed strangely quiet. I took it all in, the way I accepted my hands lifting Babe Ruths to my face. How to argue? It was all there, laid out like anatomy. It seemed to be both outside me and within my head.

The cemetery gave Chris and me a psychic as well as a physical focus. It was in a sense two cemeteries, and we kept them separate—the cemetery aboveground and the one below. The first cemetery delighted us: a marble and cement playground with lots of trees and plastic flowers, and though we loved to play dead we never did around the graves. Not to avoid being ghoulish but because we found the place cheerful, a little child-sized city waiting for its population to drift in. We never forgot the other cemetery, the resting ground of the dead my parents told us about, we just never thought about it when we were actually there. At bedtime, though, my normally sweet brother sent me off with stories of our neighbors, our departed who weren't so much departed as very close by, boxed and held with just a little frosting of dirt.

"They come out at night," he used to tell me, adding solemnly, "They'll eat you."

They wouldn't eat him, he said, because girls tasted better.

That cemetery marked me. I sleep with a sheet up over my face still, folded so a little channel of air can reach my nose—looking ridiculous, a Muslim woman entering the marketplace of dreams—as I learned to do then, in some belief that the scrap of sheet would protect me. Though I don't play in cemeteries now.

Chris and I don't talk the way we did, when "wouldn't eat him" would have come out *wudden eaddum*. We've moved on. We're professionals. We try to talk like newscasters: that accent that implies you didn't grow up anywhere, but sprang full-blown into the realm of the commercial. I love New Jersey accents, though saying so proves how far away I am.

So he says to me, he says, What? And I says to him, I says, What What!! I love the instinctive use of the present tense, the immediacy, the way dialogue is insisted on as dialogue.

My dad, who's retired, has been losing his job English and reverting to his father's English, the immigrant English of Brooklyn. It's kind of existential. Nothing gets *through* for my father anymore, it gets *true*. The New York Thruway has been exalted to the *Trueway*. His language reframes the world as a Pilgrim's Progress. Everything imperfect, even thin soup, is a *sin*. He calls me to talk about his garden.

"Everything's comin' good," he says, adding, "The *mulenyans* is comin' up good'; using a dialect form of the Italian *melanzana*, "eggplant."

My cousin Anna Marie goes the other way. She gets a secretarial job and works to upgrade her speech.

"When we got to the place where we was goin'," she begins a story. And she says all the time, "I says to myself I says, Self . . ."

I can't bring myself to lose *come by us*. It means come to us, come over: *come by us at six*, and I notice myself when I say it. It sounds so paradoxical, so deconstructionist, as if you request the opposite of what you request: for people to just miss you rather than visiting at all, to slow their cars perhaps, give you an instant of lingering attention, then go about their own business.

∾

Those posters didn't tell the whole truth about the childkiller. He didn't kill children, just little girls. He didn't molest girls or dally with them but murdered them quickly. He seemed to be a figure from one of my brother's nightly stories, an Evergreen ghoul, lingering in broad daylight and undissuaded by sheets. He was the word made flesh.

His first victim, a seven-year-old named Wendy Sue Wollen, was walking with her mother on a street in downtown Elizabeth when the mother moved a few feet off to look in a window. The childkiller must have kept a knife on him. He marched up to Wendy Sue, purposeful but not dramatic, and sank it into her stomach: then dissolved like the regular man he was, back into the regular crowd.

Wendy Sue Wollen never knew she'd been stabbed. No one else did either, not for a few minutes. She said, "That man punched me," and repeated it a few times, bent over a little and bleeding out between her fingers, thinking some guy had just walked up to her and, for no good reason, socked her one. Then she collapsed and died.

I was also seven. Soon the man stabbed another little girl on a playground. Our lives went on Childkiller Alert. My father instructed my mother to walk us kids to and from school, though after a week or so she grew plainly annoyed about it. The childkiller was never caught; the cops finally gave up and announced he must have moved on, to another city. My mother, always the pragmatist, had long since quit the escort business. To me, the man never left but joined the physical world of Elizabeth, my extended self. A jowly man, not angry looking but uncle-y, benign in that semi-abstracted adult way, like he could be selling insurance or Fuller brushes or handing you licorice. Like a wound could be just another inscrutable adult gift. When men passed me on the street my abdomen grew tender.

◈

Kikes, krauts, Polacks, wops, hunks, greaseballs. In my neighborhood we had ricks, spicks, micks, nips, jigs, chinks, ricans, hicans. And of course niggers and the much more common mooleys, another corruption of *melanzana*. Negotiating ethnic names was a precise skill and one we picked up early. We kids all used them, often of ourselves, and other than the really loaded *kike* and *nigger*, none were off limits. A mixture of tone and body language signaled whether a word was meant to be aggressive. Most of the time it wasn't, just descriptive, and would be taken that way. "You a kraut?" "You a rican?" were ordinary conversation. Add "ugly" or somesuch to it, and lots of emphasis and a friendly look—"you ugly mick!"—and the use became affectionate. When I was a kid and I first met my friend Alice's mother, she said, "Oh, you've really got that guinea nose."

I had a Greek aunt, a Puerto Rican aunt, an Irish uncle, a West Indian grandfather, Jewish cousins; I could usually find some connection to people. Down the shore my aunts and uncles sat around needling each other.

What's a seven-course meal to an Irishman? (A six-pack and a baked potato)

How did Mussolini get eight bullets in him? (Seventy-five *Italian* sharpshooters)

When Jackie K. married Ari Onassis my aunt said darkly, "It won't last. She doesn't know the Greeks."

Our part of Ocean County had a lot of immigrants and children of immigrants, especially Italians and Poles. An old Italian couple bought the lot next door to ours and set up a bait and candy shop, with a couple of pool tables and pinball and ice cream. Fat Mrs. Schipano bent over to dip out the cones, sweat rolling down from her forehead into the chocolate and strawberry and vanilla.

Ethnicity in all its forms was part of our talk, holding the place jobs hold in other American cultures, or your therapist and your feelings, or what part of town you're in. "What are you?" was a standard conversation starter, our version of "'What do you do?" We loved—love— declarative sentences about the self. Even a question about how you eat an Oreo might spin off an "I am" answer.

"I'm not the kind of person who likes cubbyholes," my dad says about a desk, and, "I'm not a person who stays up late." "I'm a people person." "I'm not a sit-arounder, I'm a doer."

When people asked me about my background I'd say, "Well, my mother's mother was English and her father was from Barbados and she met my father, who's Italian." All that distance plummeting somehow into my body. Though the person I talked to always knew someone who came from a village near some branch of my family's village, or at least pretended to know someone.

We reached for connections, we worked them out, even where they barely existed, because so many of us had a dizzying sense that there was no one else like us, not really. My grandfather was a British subject of a colonized Caribbean island who'd also been Canadian and American; his wife was an English Christian Scientist. My father's grandfather came here from a remote village and stayed to set up his shadow family, his rhyme children, in Brooklyn. His son, my grandfather, had a fourth-grade education and worked as a grave digger and mechanic, or driving truckloads of dynamite for minimum wage, when he could find work.

I played with a girl named Renee, whose parents had both been held in concentration camps in Germany. My friend Barb's Armenian grandparents fled the Turkish massacre. We talked all the time about our families, each with our own portion of family bitterness.

"Your hair is like mine," Renee said to me once.

Renee had wiry, black hair, nothing like mine. Our resemblances were fleeting and coincidental. So we accepted these metonyms of what we were—greaseballs, dagos, yids—and carried on from there.

Elizabeth was realms within realms. The lot, the cemetery, home, other places. We often went to Peterstown, the Italian section a few miles away. Once a year, in August, Peterstown erupted in a nine-day street fair honoring St. Rocco, the city's patron. Rocco appeared on posters for the feast: a sad-looking fellow lifting up his robe to show what looked like a skinned knee. The Virgin Mary seemed like more of a go-getter, paraded through the streets with her gilt crown, streamers of dollar bills covering her plaster body, along with rhinestone jewelry glittering in its colorless way, armloads of Timexes: all gifts of the faithful. Like a new incarnation of the spirit, beyond flesh and into cash. Such abundance marked St. Rocco's. Rides, music, vendors selling sandwiches of sweet and hot sausages roasted with onions and peppers, the sausage blackened and the onions and peppers caramelized in olive oil, deep fried *zeppole* dredged in sugar. Sometimes the packed crowd would bend like the muscle of a snake, and in the middle you'd see a knot of old women, short and plump, bouncing like black balloons as they danced the tarantella.

In warm weather we went to Peterstown for the Sneaker Lady, an old Italian lady in tennis shoes who mixed up lemon and orange ice in a huge wooden churn. She stood in front of an ancient storefront, a five-and-dime or something, selling ices, which tasted like fruit wearing its glorious heavenly form: itself, but intense, cool in the asphalt heat, perfectly sweetened. We went to other Italian neighborhoods: Newark, Little Italy in Manhattan. My father liked Poppalardo's in Little Italy for bread. Poppalardo's sold round loaves with crust an inch thick knobbing up all over it. The bakery also had Italian loaves six feet long, smudged with cornmeal and alive with sesame seed. Once we brought one to my aunt Philomena's house, and my father and brother carried it in across their shoulders, like pioneers.

After we moved to Roselle Park I didn't have much contact with Elizabeth, until I hit fourteen and fifteen and started going there to drink.

Roselle Park bars were pretty relaxed about the drinking age, but Elizabeth bars were even more relaxed, as well as cooler and scarier, and if they hassled you, you could zip across the Goethals Bridge to Staten Island, where the drinking age was eighteen and nobody ever got carded. We liked a bar called the Hearth, pronounced the Heart', on Westfield Avenue. Bikers hung out there, and greasers, and junkies, who liked their drinks sweet as Kool-Aid. If I went with all girls we'd have drinks in front of us practically as soon as we walked through the door.

"He likes you," my friend Bonnie would say, of whomever: "He thinks you're a little Lo-Lee-Ta."

None of us knew who Lo-Lee-Ta was.

Girls drank sloe gin fizzes or 7&7s; guys, junkies excepted, drank beer or whiskey, or beer and whiskey together in boilermakers, or tequila. Often we'd go from Elizabeth bars to Staten Island bars, weaving across the Goethals Bridge on the backs of motorcycles. Smoke stacks rose around us spewing out their fumes, that heaviest substance that could go by the name of air.

When I quit going to high school I spent even more time at the Heart,' which I forgot was really called the Hearth. I couldn't have spelled anything then. The word Elizabeth itself came out Elizabet', slur on the e, so it sounded, not inaccurately, a lot like Loseabet.

A few years ago my husband and I were heading through Elizabeth to Manhattan. On a side street a guy drove into us, very matter-of-factly, as if we'd asked him to. We got out; he got out. He had the classic Loseabet look: boiled. Eyes at half mast. He had no insurance, so we decided to clear out.

"I'm sorry man," he said like an alcoholic. "Gimme your number I'll give it to ya next check. I'm sorry man sorry man sorry man sorry man hey, sorry, man."

I'm forty now. Everyone I know is going back somewhere, digging for roots, sifting through old soil. Though I think about Holly Park and dream about it and go there, I only went back once to Elizabeth, driving to Elmora to visit my neighborhood. Nothing had changed: the cemetery, the apartments, even the weedy, scabby lot. That sameness sounds comforting but it wasn't. I stood looking at the place—the glass glitter and old brick and *Absolutely No Cooking* sign—waiting for it to tell me if I had loved it or hated it. It looked back, not seeming to care much one way or another.

I disagree with Eliot. The end of the journey is returning to the starting point and not knowing it for the second time. Letting that seep in. Absorbing its silence. Evergreen Cemetery: Plastic & scratchy dacron flowers. Drooping Marys & rhyming couplets ("Weep not for me/I wait for thee"). Singin' Sam's triptych monument covered with jaunty brass musical notes, a stone record with birth & death dates, flushed 8" x 10" photo," Singer, Songwriter, Peace Maker," a carved stone & brass electric guitar. Death the saccharine mother, the unflagging dance partner. (6/30/87, age 30)

Once in a while I still eat in Peterstown. It's also the same. Elizabeth's a low-income city, with no tax base for the kind of strip mall/office park development that would edit me out of its landscape. The city waits like a childhood room preserved by a mother crazy with nostalgia. It forces me to individuate, to cut myself free.

❧

Of course, to do that I have to define somewhere else as my place, stop, scatter the pepper off my feet.

"You're Spanish," a woman said to me last night.

People guess Mexican, Greek, Latina, Italian, other things, like Finnish and Russian. A man once got belligerent when I told him I wasn't Jewish. "You are," he said, "obviously."

"Exotic," my husband says. More to the point, children have pointed to me and said, *witch*. Once, when I gave a lecture at another school, a strange blank woman came up to me and told me my evil thoughts had no power there.

I wonder, if I had uttered some curse, if she'd be suffering with it, feeling a graveyard fly at her through the air: or expecting to die at the hands of an ordinary man in broad daylight, or calling herself a queen, a Renaissance queen. I believe I have swallowed these things, and they erupt in my face: dark heavy-lidded eyes, hooked nose, bow lips, pale skin, each dying to tell its story. My mother's West Indian family defined itself by its hatred of Catholics, then she went ahead and married one, producing two children who grew and grew, oversized, much bigger than either parent: as if all our cells could figure out was division.

I remember faces well and honestly, my own and others': Queen Elizabeth's staunch, serene, whippet-nosed, lips clamped around her teeth. The pouchy placid face of the childkiller, and the Virgin Mary's otherworldly face, floating above her dress of money. I remember eating graveyard dirt when I was a child, and inhaling my grandfather's fourth wife, and inhaling the city. We drank and ate the sediment of photos from the Denzer & Schafer plant, drank and ate the image. What does my body consist of?

I bet myself I'd never miss the place. But even my computer stores the word as *Elizabet*. Loseabet.

It's much safer where I live now. Children don't have to worry walking to school. I see them streaming off each morning, a parade of fair heads, mainly of Dutch or German descent, each no doubt with his or her own mouthful of sorrow. I miss mine. I miss the mingling. A place where everyone frictioned together in a small space, not just people of different races and ethnic groups but even the dead and the hopelessly evil, the ones so evil they lost a sense of themselves, and dressed as if evil itself were a job.

My friend Maureen and I compare our childhoods. She's vibrant and pretty with a face that fits together, and she's from Kalispell, Montana.

"I miss it," she says of Montana. "The landscape's compelling. Open space and rivers."

When I ask her about returning she says, "It's the culture . . . the racism. I can't go back."

I can't go back either, though I'm much less sure of what compels and repels me.

There's not much I'd call landscape in my part of New Jersey. Even the rivers hardly feel like rivers, running along banks of factories like big sluiceways for industrial waste. We have racism but not exactly Maureen's us-them racism: our stereotypes often come self-generated, Jews telling you they're cheap, Poles they're dumb. Partly they're internalizing the larger culture, partly grasping that an edge is near—sensing the vertiginous drop out of something, anything, and into nothing at all.

I imagine the childkiller thinking that in one swift instant he'd established himself, become a word.

CONTRIBUTORS

FLAVIA ALAYA is professor emerita of literature and cultural history at Ramapo College. She is the author of a memoir, *Under the Rose: A Confession*. Recipient of Fulbright, NEH, and Guggenheim awards, she has made notable contributions to nineteenth-century Anglo-Italian and women's studies. She has authored several Paterson, New Jersey, stories as part of an activist mission she calls "scripting the landscape."

SUSANNE ANTONETTA grew up in New Jersey and now lives in the Pacific Northwest, where she teaches half-time and writes. She is the author of *Body Toxic: An Environmental Memoir*. Her book of poems, *Bardo*, is the recipient of the Brittingham Prize. She is currently finishing a book of poems titled *The Lives of the Saints*. Her father's family emigrated from the town of Gesualdo in Campania.

JUNE AVIGNONE lives in Paterson and was the editor of *The Mill Street Forward*, the city's progressive arts and political newspaper. She currently writes a column called "The Progressive Entrepreneur" about socially responsible businesses for *Fortune Small Business*, and is working on a novel titled *The Day Jack Reed Left Town for Good and Other Stories from Synthetic City*. Her publications include *On Going Home Again, Downtown Paterson, Cianci Street: A Neighborhood in Transition*, and *A Place Like Paterson*.

MARIA BARBIERI immigrated from the Italian-Swiss Alps in 1899. She settled in West Hoboken and had a son with Sante Barbieri, an active anarchist. Together, they were members of the local anarchist Circolo di Studi Sociali: they performed in local radical plays, organized workers during labor strikes, and circulated the radical press. In 1903, their infant son was killed by a pot of boiling water, which fell on him while Maria and Sante worked in the mills. This would politicize her further to organize mothers to protest their particular oppression.

SALVATORE AMICO M. BUTTACI has lived in New Jersey since the 1950s. The son of a Sicilian father and a Sicilian American mother, he himself lived in their old village of Acquaviva Platani for a year in 1965. "Nothing makes me prouder," he claims, "than being an Italian American."

ROSETTE CAPOTORTO is a poet and writer who was born and raised in the Bronx and lives in Hoboken. Her work has been published in numerous literary journals including *Long Shot, I Am Lower East Side, VIA: Voices in Italian Americana* and in the anthologies *The Milk of Almonds: Italian American Women Writers on Food and Culture* and *Curaggia: Writing by Women of Italian Descent*. She has also published a chapbook called *Bronx Italian*. She is currently working on a novel, *Pop Beads*.

TOM DEBLASIO CARROLL grew up in Paterson. He is a folklorist and ethnographer who has done extensive work for a variety of organizations, including the Library of Congress. He lives in Pittsburgh, Pennsylvania.

GRACE CAVALIERI was born and raised in Trenton. She has authored thirteen books of poetry and eighteen produced plays. She has produced and hosted *The Poet and the Poem* on public radio since 1977. It is now broadcasted from the Library of Congress via NPR satellite. Grace has won numerous awards including the Allen Ginsberg Award for poetry, the Pen-Fiction Award, and the Silver Medal from the Corporation for Public Broadcasting.

FRANK DECARO grew up in Little Falls, New Jersey. He is the author of *A Boy Named Phyllis: A Suburban Memoir*. He covered fashion for *New York Newsday* and was the author of *Frank's Place*—the only openly gay humor column in a major newspaper. He writes for the *New York Times* and *TV Guide*. He also cohosts Comedy Central's *The Daily Show*.

DAVID DELLA FERA was raised in Kearny, New Jersey. He has written for several New Jersey newspapers. His work has appeared in *VIA: Voices in Italian Americana* and *Paterson Literary Review*. He teaches in central New Jersey.

LOUISE DESALVO was born in Jersey City, and now lives in Teaneck, New Jersey. She is Jenny Hunter Professor of Literature and Creative Writing at Hunter College. She has published fourteen books, among them, *Writing as a Way of Healing, Adultery, Virginia Woolf: The Impact of Childhood Sexual*

Abuse on Her Life and Work, and the award-winning memoir, *Vertigo*. She is co-editor with Edvige Giunta of *The Milk of Almonds: Italian American Women Writers on Food and Culture*. She is currently writing a memoir, *Crazy in the Kitchen*.

RACHEL GUIDO DEVRIES was born and raised in Paterson. She is the author of two books of poems, *Gambler's Daughter* and *How to Sing to a Dago* and a novel, *Tender Warriors*. Her recent work has appeared in *VIA: Voices in Italian Americana* and in *The Paterson Literary Review*. A graduate of St. Joseph's Hospital School of Nursing in Paterson, she teaches creative writing in the Humanistic Studies Center of Syracuse University.

PIETRO DI DONATO, a bricklayer since the age of twelve, was born in 1911 in Hoboken, New Jersey, of Abruzzese parents. He published the highly acclaimed novel *Christ in Concrete* in 1939. It became a Book-of-the-Month Club selection. He was also the author of *This Woman, Immigrant Saint: The Life of Mother Cabrini, Three Circles of Light*, among others. Pietro di Donato died in 1992.

DIANE DI PRIMA is a poet, prose writer, and activist, who has published thirty-nine books of poetry and prose. Her ties to New Jersey go back to her teen years when her family bought a summer home on Greenwood Lake. In the ensuing years she completed her early work, *Dinners and Nightmares*, and wrote *Seven Love Poems from the Middle Latin* there. Later, several members of her family, including her mother and brother, moved to New Jersey and Diane visited them frequently. She currently lives in San Francisco, where she continues to write, and teaches privately.

BILL ERVOLINO is the humor columnist for *The Record* in Bergen County, New Jersey. He has also written for the *New York Times, Entertainment Weekly, Vogue*, the *New York Daily News*, and *Parents Choice*. His column was recognized by the National Society of Newspaper Columnists as being one of the best humor columns in the United States. Ervolino is the author of *Some Kind of Wise Guy: Stories about Parents, Weddings, Modern Living, and Growing Up Italian*. He lives in Wood-Ridge, New Jersey.

FRANK FINALE is a second-generation Italian and the author of the regional best sellers *To The Shore Once More*, Volumes I & II. In 1996 he edited, with Rich Youmans, *Under a Gull's Wing*, the critically acclaimed anthology of poems and photographs about the Jersey Shore. He is currently the poetry editor for *the new renaissance* and recently retired from thirty-eight years of teaching in the Toms River Regional Schools. His latest book is *A Gull's Story*.

MARY ANN CASTRONOVO FUSCO writes the weekly *In Season* column for the Savor section of *The Star-Ledger*, New Jersey's largest daily newspaper. She has held senior positions at *Business Week Careers* and *Attenzione* magazines, and contributed to the *New York Times, New York Daily News*, and numerous consumer magazines. Born in Venezuela to Italian parents, Fusco grew up in Union City, New Jersey, and currently lives in Leonia, New Jersey.

JENNIFER GILLAN grew up in Hawthorne, New Jersey. With Maria Mazziotti Gillan, she has edited three award-winning multicultural anthologies, *Unsettling America, Identity Lessons*, and *Growing Up Ethnic in America*. An associate Professor of English at Bentley College, she has published articles in *American Literature, Cinema Journal, American Drama, African American Review*, and other journals. She is currently completing *Ivory Soap Nation*, a study of American monuments, literature, and policy.

MARIA MAZZIOTTI GILLAN, born and raised in Paterson, New Jersey, is the founder and the executive director of the Poetry Center at Passaic County Community College in Paterson. She is also the director of the Creative Writing Program at Binghamton University-SUNY. She has published eight books of poetry, including *Where I Come From, Things My Mother Told Me, The Weather of Old Seasons*, and *Italian Women in Black Dresses*. She is the editor of the *Paterson Literary Review* and co-editor with her daughter Jennifer of the anthologies *Unsettling America, Identity Lessons*, and *Growing up Ethnic in America*.

DANIELA GIOSEFFI is the author of four books of poetry, *Eggs in the Lake, Word Wounds and Water Flowers, Going On Poems 2000*, and *Symbiosis: Poems* and a novel, *The Great American Belly Dance*. She has edited two award-winning anthologies, *Women on War: International Voices*, reissued by the Feminist Press in 2002, and *On Prejudice: A Global Perspective*, and currently edits *www.PoetsUSA.com*. She founded the Bordighera Poetry Prize to promote Italian American poetry.

ARTURO GIOVANNITTI emigrated from Campobasso, Italy at the turn of the twentieth century. He was a seminarian, an IWW organizer, and an antifascist agitator. He edited radical and socialist magazines and was a perennial speaker at labor gatherings, especially among the Italian working community. He was the chief eulogist at the funeral of his friend Carlo Tresca, the Italian anarchist murdered in 1941.

EDVIGE GIUNTA is associate professor of English at New Jersey City University. She was born in Sicily and moved to the United States in 1984. Her recent publications include *Writing with an Accent: Contemporary Italian American Women Authors, Dire l'indicibile: Il memoir delle autrici italo americane,* and *The Milk of Almonds: Italian American Women Writers on Food and Culture,* co-edited with Louise DeSalvo. Her articles, reviews, memoir, and poetry have been published in many journals and anthologies. She is poetry editor of *The Women's Studies Quarterly.* She has lived in New Jersey since 1995 and currently lives in Teaneck with her husband and two children.

JENNIFER GUGLIELMO is an assistant professor of history at Smith College. Previously she taught women's studies and history at William Patterson University in Wayne, New Jersey. She is currently writing a book on Italian women's political cultures in the New York metro area, including northeastern New Jersey (1880 to 1945). She is co-editor of *Are Italians White? How Race Is Made in America.* Her work has appeared in the collections, *Women, Gender and Transnational Lives* and *The Lost World of Italian American Radicalism* as well as in the Italian feminist journal *tutteStorie.*

CARLA GUERRIERO, the daughter of southern Italian immigrants, was raised in Orange, New Jersey. Her poems, which have appeared in the *Paterson Literary Review,* often deal with issues of Italian-American identity. Guerriero is the founding editor of the *Newark Poetry Review.* She is most inspired by Diane di Prima.

WILLIAM HARRY HARDING was born in Paterson to a first-generation Italian American mother and raised in the Riverside section of the city, and later in Wayne. He authored three novels, *Young Hart, Mill Song,* and *Alvin's Famous No-Horse* (for children). As a naval flight officer, he made two combat cruises, earned twenty-one air medals, and the Naval Commendation Medal for Valor. He has been a regular contributor the *L.A. Times Book Review.*

ANNIE RACHELE LANZILLOTTO is a Bronx-born writer of Barese parentage. In this volume, she writes about a major turning-point in her life which took place in New Jersey. Past performance works include: *Confessions of a Bronx Tomboy, Uprooting Cement, a'Schapett!, How to Cook a Heart,* and *Mammamia You'll Never Get a Straight Answer Again!* She performed *A Stickball Memoir* at the Smithsonian Folklife Festival.

MARIA LAURINO, who grew up in Short Hills, New Jersey, is the author of *Were You Always an Italian? Ancestors and Other Icons of Italian America.* She is a former staff writer for *The Village Voice* and chief speechwriter for Mayor David N. Dinkins. Her articles and essays have appeared in numerous newspapers, magazines, and anthologies.

MICHELE LINFANTE was born in Paterson, New Jersey, in 1945. She moved to San Francisco in 1969 where she has worked in theater as an actress, director, and playwright. She has been awarded a National Endowment Playwriting Fellowship and her one-act play *Pizza* was first published by West Coast Plays, a project of the California Arts Council.

LORYN LIPARI received her bachelor of arts in English with a concentration in creative writing at New Jersey City University. She has received the New Jersey City University Poetry Prize and Honorable Mention for Prose. Her work is included in *The Milk of Almonds: Italian American Women Writers on Food and Culture, Delinium* and *Women on Campus* and she is freelance writer for *High-Rise Expressions.*

MARY ANN MANNINO is a visiting assistant professor of English at Temple University. She is the author of *Revisionary Identities: Strategies of Empowerment in the Writing of Italian/American Women.* She is co-editing, with Justin Vitiello, an anthology of Italian American women writers discussing the influences on their works. Mannino is also a fiction writer and poet. Her grandparents and father were born in the Campania region of Italy. She has spent all the summers of her life on the beaches of southern New Jersey.

CAROLE MASO, born in Paterson, New Jersey, has published six novels: *Ghost Dance, Ava, The American Woman in the Chinese Hat, The Art Lover, Aureole,* and *Defiance.* She also authored a collection of essays, *Break Every Rule,* as well as *The Room Lit by Roses: A Journal of Pregnancy and Birth* and *Beauty Is Convulsive: The Passion of Frida Kahlo.* The recipient of the Lannan Literary Fellowship for Fiction, Maso is a professor of English at Brown University where she was also director of the Creative Writing Program.

Contributors

ARTURO MAZZIOTTI was born in 1906 in Philadelphia, Pennsylvania and taken back to Italy by his parents when he was three years old. At sixteen, he returned from Galdo, Cilento, in southern Italy to Paterson, New Jersey, to work in the silk mills. He married Angelina Schiavo and they had three children. Mazziotti was active in the labor movement and for fifty-two years he was secretary of the Società Cilentano on Butler Street in Paterson. He died in 1998.

TOM PERROTTA grew up in an Italian American family in Garwood, NJ, and currently lives outside Boston. He is the author of four books of fiction: *Bad Haircut, The Wishbones, Election,* and *Joe College.* Perrotta helped adapt *Election* into an acclaimed feature film released by Paramount Pictures in 1999. He has taught writing at Harvard and Yale and has moonlighted as a journalist and screenwriter.

MARIA RODA, born in 1874 in Como, Italy, crossed the Atlantic at sixteen after serving three months in prison for activity during a local strike among silk workers. She settled in Paterson and became active in the local anarchist circle. She was close friends with many of prominent anarchists, including Emma Goldman, and married Pedro Esteve, a Catalan immigrant anarchist, who edited the Italian-language, Paterson-based, anarchist newspaper *La Questione Sociale.* Roda organized separate activist circles for Italian women. She raised eight children while becoming part of the community of revolutionary working-class leaders that extended beyond Paterson and across the United States.

AGNES ROSSI, born and raised in New Jersey, is the author of *The Quick: A Novella and Stories,* a *New York Times* Notable Book, and the novels *Split Skirt* and *The Houseguest.* She was the finalist for the *Granta* Best of Young Novelists Award. She lives in Montclair with her husband and four children.

ED SMITH was born in Newark and currently lives in Manasquan at the Jersey Shore. Smith lived, worked, and grew up with his Italian American friends and cousins. His maternal grandmother Espedita Forte Lotito told him stories about Italy and taught him Italian words in Lyndhurst, New Jersey. He is the director of the Manville Public Library. His book of poetry is entitled *I Am That Hero.*

JOSEPHINE STIFANO, a lifelong Paterson resident, was born in January 1903. She worked in the mills as a child through adulthood. She married Nicola

Stifano, an Italian immigrant from Salerno, and had four children. She died in 1998.

GAY TALESE was born in 1932 on the small island of Ocean City, New Jersey. He joined the reportorial staff of the *New York Times* in 1955. He contributed many articles to magazines, principally *Esquire*. He is the author of *Unto the Sons, Honor Thy Father, Thy Neighbor's Wife, The Kingdom and the Power,* and *The Bridge,* among others.

MARISA TRUBIANO is assistant professor of Italian at Montclair State University where she has coordinated an oral history project concerning the Italians of Montclair. She is a member of the Italian American Heritage Commission of New Jersey. She is presently completing a book on Ennio Flaiano.

JANET BALLOTTA ZANDY, born in Hoboken, grew up in Union City and Lyndhurst, New Jersey. A graduate of Montclair State Teachers College, she is a professor of language and literature at Rochester Institute of Technology. She is also the author of a collection of essays *Hands: Working-Class Bodies* and the editor of *Calling Home: Working-Class Women's Writings, Liberating Memory: Our Work and Our Working-Class Consciousness,* and *What We Hold in Common: An Introduction to Working-Class Studies.*